When Soldiers Rebel

Military coups are a constant threat in Africa and many former military leaders are now in control of "civilian states," yet the military remains understudied, especially over the last decade. Drawing on extensive archival research, cross-national data, and four in-depth comparative case studies, *When Soldiers Rebel* examines the causes of military coups in post-independence Africa and looks at the relationship between ethnic armies and political instability in the region. Kristen A. Harkness argues that the processes of creating and dismantling ethnically exclusionary state institutions engender organized and violent political resistance. Focusing on rebellions to protect rather than change the status quo, Harkness sheds light on a mechanism of ethnic violence that helps us understand both the motivations and timing of rebellion, and the rarity of group rebellion in the face of persistent political and economic inequalities along ethnic lines.

Kristen A. Harkness is a Lecturer in International Relations at the University of St. Andrews. Her research has been published in *Democratization, Journal of Conflict Resolution, Journal of Peace Research, Journal of Strategic Studies,* and *Parameters.* Her work on ethnicity and African militaries won the 2017 African Politics Conference Group Best Article Award and is currently being funded by the British Academy.

When Soldiers Rebel

Ethnic Armies and Political Instability in Africa

KRISTEN A. HARKNESS
University of St Andrews, Scotland

CAMBRIDGE
UNIVERSITY PRESS

CAMBRIDGE
UNIVERSITY PRESS

University Printing House, Cambridge CB2 8BS, United Kingdom

One Liberty Plaza, 20th Floor, New York, NY 10006, USA

477 Williamstown Road, Port Melbourne, VIC 3207, Australia

314–321, 3rd Floor, Plot 3, Splendor Forum, Jasola District Centre,
New Delhi – 110025, India

79 Anson Road, #06-04/06, Singapore 079906

Cambridge University Press is part of the University of Cambridge.

It furthers the University's mission by disseminating knowledge in the pursuit of
education, learning, and research at the highest international levels of excellence.

www.cambridge.org
Information on this title: www.cambridge.org/9781108422475
DOI: 10.1017/9781108500319

© Kristen A. Harkness 2018

First published 2018

Printed in the United States of America by Sheridan Books, Inc.

A catalogue record for this publication is available from the British Library.

Library of Congress Cataloging-in-Publication Data
Names: Harkness, Kristen A., author.
Title: When soldiers rebel : ethnic armies and political instability in
Africa / Kristen A. Harkness.
Description: New York : Cambridge University Press, 2018. |
Includes bibliographical references and index.
Identifiers: LCCN 2018007400 | ISBN 9781108422475 (hardback)
Subjects: LCSH: Ethnic conflict – Political aspects – Africa, Sub-Saharan. |
Political stability – Africa, Sub-Saharan. | Africa, Sub-Saharan – Armed
Forces – Political aspects. | Africa, Sub-Saharan – Ethnic
relations – Political aspects. | Africa, Sub-Saharan – Politics and
government–1960–
Classification: LCC DT30.5.H365 2018 | DDC 967.032–dc23
LC record available at https://lccn.loc.gov/2018007400

ISBN 978-1-108-42247-5 Hardback

To my family.
For all the sacrifices over all the generations
that made my dream possible.

Contents

Figures

Tables

Acknowledgments

"C'est impossible," said the head archivist at the Senegalese national archives after I described my project to him. The military files, he explained, had never been organized or catalogued. There were no guides to the holdings, just a large room with many dossiers full of mildewy paper that needed the attention of a proper conservationist. But he would help me, despite the difficulty, to track down possible duplicates in the civilian administration files. To say the least, the data necessary for this project was challenging to obtain. Beyond the normal decay of information over time, which all students of history lament, the decisions described in these pages, and the events they led to, were often controversial or clandestine. Both protagonists and observers thus had ample incentives to hide or distort information. There were many, including at times myself, who doubted that I could ever collect enough reliable data to write a compelling piece of social science. These acknowledgments are thus dedicated, first and foremost, to those who believed in this project – or, barring belief, helped me anyway.

I owe a deep debt of gratitude to the members of my dissertation committee, who nurtured this book in what I now consider its infancy. Jennifer Widner was my committee chair, my mentor, and the one who lured me into African politics to begin with. Had I taken my graduate field seminar in comparative politics from anyone else, this book would never have been written. Beyond the superb feedback and sound professional advice that she has always given me, what I have valued most about Jennifer is her unrelenting faith in me – that I belong in this community of intellectuals and that my research will contribute in important ways to how we understand our world. Bob Keohane reached out to me early in my graduate school career, offering to read my work and assist in any way he could. He has unfailingly followed through on that promise. His critiques pushed this book to levels of excellence I doubt would have been achieved in his absence. When my project took a strong turn towards analyzing the dynamics of ethnic politics, Evan Lieberman did me a great service by agreeing to come on board. He has encouraged me to think more deeply about the complexity of identity and taught me to better frame my arguments, present source material, and discuss methodology.

I am also grateful for the support and encouragement of the broader Princeton intellectual community. Many colleagues read pieces of this project and provided me with valuable feedback, including the participants of the Comparative Politics Research Seminar and the Pizza and Politics graduate student working group. I benefited, in particular, from the insights of Mark Beissinger, Sarah Bush, Stephen Chaudoin, Rex Douglass, David Hsu, Sarah Hummel, Mike Hunzeker, Amaney Jamal, Dan Kliman, Alex Lanoszka, Oriana Mastro, Mike Miller, and Tom Scherer. I would particularly like to thank the members of my dissertation writing group: Jing Chen, Mike McKoy, Mike Woldemariam, and Alden Young. Our regular discussions over the course of two years were a priceless source of intellectual growth and shaped this book in ways beyond measure.

As I transformed my dissertation into a proper book, I had the good fortune to be nurtured by two other extraordinary intellectual communities and a great number of other colleagues. I spent my postdoctoral fellowship year at the Kroc Institute for International Peace Studies at the University of Notre Dame, where I had engaging and thought provoking conversations with colleagues across disciplinary boundaries, including Jaime Bleck, Laura Heideman, Jennifer Keister, George Lopez, and Kristin Michelitch. I then joined the faculty at the University of St. Andrews where I have been encouraged and nurtured by both senior and junior colleagues alike, especially Marc DeVore, Caron Gentry, Richard English, Jaremey Mcullin, and Nicholas Rengger.

I received invaluable feedback from a book workshop I held in October 2016. Jonathan Caverley, Erica De Bruin, Jonathan Powell, and Ches Thurber read the entire manuscript, provided detailed written comments, and engaged in hours of intense discussion with me. Even though they could not attend in person, Phil Roessler and Thomas Flores also volunteered to read the manuscript. I thank all of them for their deep engagement with my work and I hope that this final book reflects their advice. I also thank Glenn Palmer and the Peace Science Society for institutionally supporting my workshop and providing tasty treats.

I am deeply thankful for all the support I received throughout the publication process itself. Caron Gentry shared all of her materials on book publishing with me and helped me to write a successful book proposal. Thomas Flores opened a door for me at Cambridge by introducing me to his editor. Two peer reviewers, including Hein Goemans, provided immensely supportive and yet still deeply thoughtful critiques of my work. I am further indebted to Rex Douglass and Tom Scherer for teaching me how to work with maps in R, which prevented a last minute catastrophe with one of my figures. And, of course, I must thank Cambridge University Press and my editor, Sara Doskow, for their enthusiastic support of this project.

I would also like to thank the countless others who assisted this project in myriad ways, both small and large. I presented selections or chapters of this book to the Comparative Politics Research Seminar at Princeton University; the Program on Democracy, Citizenship, and Constitutionalism at the University of Pennsylvania; the Buffett Center Working Group on Security Studies at Northwestern University; the Global Security and International Relations program at the University of Glasgow; the School of Government and Public Policy at the University of Strathclyde; as well as at the annual meetings of the American Political Science Association, the Midwest Political Science Association, and the Peace Science Society. Many discussants, fellow panelists, and audience members thought deeply about my work and shared their insights.

My many archival research trips were supported with funding from the Bobst Center for Peace and Justice, the Princeton Institute for International and Regional Studies, and St. Andrews University. Nicki List and Paul Ocobock provided crucial help with logistics and navigating the archives in, respectively, Senegal and Kenya. Lastly, but perhaps most importantly, I would like to thank the many dedicated and underpaid archivists and their assistants in Dakar, Nairobi, London, Paris, Aix-en-Provence, and Washington, D.C. They provide an invaluable service, not just to researchers like myself, but to all of us: they preserve our record of the past.

Parts of this book draw from work that has been previously published. Selections of the statistical analysis and excepts from the Cameroon and Senegal case studies appear in my 2016 article, "The Ethnic Army and the State," in the *Journal of Conflict Resolution*. Some of the empirical narrative of Senegalese democratization overlaps with discussions in my 2017 *Democratization* article, "Military Loyalty and the Failure of Democratization in Africa." Finally, I first developed my ideas concerning the role that the international community could play in helping democratizing African states to reform their militaries, discussed in the conclusion, for a piece I wrote in 2015 for *Parameters*, "US Security Assistance in Africa." I am grateful to the editors of these journals for allowing me to build on this prior work and bring some of my core insights into this book.

Finally, this book is dedicated to my family, and especially my parents Robert and Carla Harkness. I would not have been able to complete it without their love and support. They were even graciously willing to read and copy-edit chapters on short notice. Thank you.

Introduction

> It has been the involvement of the military in politics that has generally paved the way for the militarization of ethnic conflict.
>
> – Pradeep P. Barua[1]

Ethnicity has profoundly shaped African military institutions and, through the involvement of the military in politics, the instability of the postcolonial state. Learned from colonial practices, African leaders have often built security institutions on ethnic foundations: conflating loyalty with coethnicity. Constructing such systems of ethnic privilege within the military has led to repeated, violent, and ethnically-based resistance from soldiers facing imminent exclusion. Their coups and mutinies have perennially destabilized the region. Even if successfully built, ethnic armies feed into other dynamics of instability and violence. Removed from one of the most important and powerful state institutions, excluded groups may rebel through other tactics, such as insurgencies or terrorism. Dictators supported by ethnically loyal institutions may discount potential challenges to their rule, untying their hands to pursue increasingly repressive practices. Nor do ethnic armies embrace recent trends toward liberalization, processes that threaten their continued dominance of the security sector, making them an obstacle to further democratization. Understanding the intersection between practices of ethnic politics and civil-military relations thus reveals fundamental tensions in the African state that have resulted in enduring instability.

The unraveling of Ugandan democracy following independence aptly illustrates these dynamics. In 1966, Prime Minister Milton Obote used

[1] Barua 1992, 134.

I

the military to dissolve his own government after a vote of no-confidence in Parliament. This autogolpe rapidly assumed an ethnic dimension as Bagandan leaders, whose ethnically-based political party had controlled the Presidency and were constitutionally guaranteed reserved seats in Parliament, protested. In response, Obote purged the army of Baganda soldiers, filling their places with fellow northerners, and then deployed the military to the Buganda Kingdom. He also constructed a paramilitary General Services Unit with recruits from his home district of Akororo.[2] After two assassination attempts in 1969 and 1970, and with growing suspicion of his protégé Idi Amin who had been recruiting his own following of coethnics, Obote decided to further narrow the ethnic basis of the officer corps to fellow Langi and the allied Acholi.[3] Facing perceived imminent exclusion, Amin struck first. He claimed that, just prior to his coup, a secret meeting was held between Obote and senior police and military officers in which it was decided that Acholi and Langi troops, who already constituted roughly 75% of the army, would be used to disarm and purge all other officers and enlisted men.[4] In the following months and years, Amin then massacred Acholi and Langi troops and ethnically stacked the military with fellow Kakua as well as Nubians and southern Sudanese rebels.[5] Idi Amin's resulting dictatorship was one of the most brutal and unstable in Africa's history: suffering at least seven separate coup attempts and multiple ethnic rebellions, eventually being overthrown by neighboring Tanzania.

Even in far more stable countries, the construction of military institutions on ethnic grounds has created the conditions for sporadic violence. Kenya, for example, has a long history of ethnically stacking both security and civil service institutions. Kenya's first president, Jomo Kenyatta, created a new air force and paramilitary units recruited from coethnic Kikuyus to act as counterweights to the regular army. He then reconstructed the army's officer corps, recruiting its ranks almost entirely from the Kikuyu community, while also ethnically stacking the powerful provincial administration.[6] After their successions to power, subsequent Presidents Daniel arap Moi and Mwai Kibaki, have dislodged their predecessors' appointments from the police, military, and provincial

---

[2] Byrnes 1990; Horowitz 1985, 466; Minorities at Risk 2009.
[3] Horowitz 1985, 455; Minorities at Risk 2009.
[4] *Keesings* 1971.
[5] Keegan 1983, 598–600; Minorities at Risk 2009.
[6] Hassan 2015, 594; N'Diaye 2001, 123–126.

administration, replacing them with coethnic Kalenjins and then Kikuyus, respectively.[7]

These practices have contributed substantially to ethnic violence in Kenya. It was during the transition from Kenyatta to Moi that Kenya experienced its only coup attempt: as Moi attempted to dismantle his predecessor's ethnically stacked military institutions, initially purging the high command, Luo and Kikuyu junior officers rose up and seized Nairobi airport, the Voice of Kenya radio station, and other public buildings. Although the coup was put down by loyal units of the army within a matter of hours, the event deepened the historically tense cleavage between the Kikuyu and Kalenjin.[8] Following the coup, Moi continued his restacking of the Kenyan state apparatus with coethnics, who were later used to influence election results during liberalization and the opening of politics to multiparty competition. Kalenjin internal security officers were specifically deployed to swing districts and ethnically unaligned areas and used to intimidate and obstruct the opposition, stuff ballot boxes, and coordinate local ethnic violence.[9] The construction of ethnic security institutions in Kenya thus directly facilitated ethnic violence and contributed to political instability during regime transitions.

Rarely have the fields of civil-military relations and ethnic conflict been brought together to understand the African state and its seemingly endemic political instability. This is thus, first and foremost, a book about the military as a fundamental state institution in Africa – as tantamount to the state in many contexts – and the intertwined problems of ethnic violence and military intervention in politics. Ethnic conflict, and pervasive ideas of ethnic loyalty, have shaped the very development of African militaries while soldiers have played a central role in the competition over state institutions. Throughout much of Africa, the military is not a homogenous or neutral agent, but rather an institution complicit in and riven by ethnic conflict. I argue that building and dismantling systems of ethnic privilege within the military has led soldiers facing exclusion or the loss of their historic advantages to rebel. This has, in turn, further militarized ethnic politics. For while coups are the soldiers' first tactical choice of resistance, as they leverage their remaining access to state resources to halt their deteriorating circumstances, successful exclusion from important state institutions instigates further social violence.

---

[7] Decalo 1998, 229–230; Hassan 2015, 594; Hornsby 2013, 712–713.
[8] *Keesings* 2001; N'Diaye 2001, 132.
[9] Hassan 2015, 594; Hassan 2017.

CURRENT UNDERSTANDINGS OF ETHNIC VIOLENCE

The broadest contribution of this book is to the ethnic conflict literature. Organized political resistance along identifiable ethnic cleavages has come to characterize most civil conflict in the contemporary world, whether in the form of separatist insurgencies, civil wars, terrorist campaigns, or military coups.[10] The devastation of this violence is staggering. In the most extreme cases, ethnic tensions have culminated in ethnic cleansing, genocide, and other forms of mass killing, claiming hundreds of thousands of lives across all regions of the globe.[11] Insurgencies, including those with quite low fatality counts, increase government authoritarianism, regardless of initial levels of democracy or of the ultimate success or failure of the rebel movement.[12] And ethnically-based military coups displace civilian governments, often leading to years of military governance and the repression which sustains it: suspending the constitution, significantly undermining civil liberties, and banning political parties and associations. Ethnicity overwhelmingly conditions the struggle for state power with often deadly consequences.

The prevalence and consequences of ethnic violence have led many scholars to question, why do ethnic groups rebel? Three schools of thought have emerged advocating different causal mechanisms that link ethnicity to organized political violence: institutionalization of ethnic cleavages, horizontal inequalities, and ethnic political exclusion. In all three, how the state categorizes and treats ethnic groups is central to explaining the "propensity for political identities to become violent."[13]

Lieberman and Singh argue that the mere institutionalization of ethnic categories, boundary drawing between groups by the state, generates

---

[10] Since the end of the Cold War, ethnic wars have comprised over 75% of all civil wars (Gleditsch et al. 2002; Harbom & Wallenstein 2010; Fearon & Laitin 2011, 199; Wimmer, Cederman, & Min 2009, 316). Using a lower fatality threshold, Fearon and Laitin also find that sons of the soil movements, that defend ethnic homelands from the incursions of outsider migrants, constitute 31% of all civil conflicts (2011, 199). Ethnically orchestrated coups have also been commonplace throughout sub-Saharan Africa, the Middle East, and Southeast Asia (Horowitz 1985, 480–492; Quinlivan 1999, 139–141; Roessler 2011, 307).

[11] Our best estimates indicate 500,000 Tutsi civilians were killed in the 1994 Rwanda geno-cide, 200,000 non-combatants by the Sudanese government in Darfur, 100,000–200,000 indigenous Mayans in the Guatemalan civil war, 85,000–265,000 Kurds in Iraq, and 25,000–155,000 Bosnian Muslims between 1990–1995. Casualty figures were drawn from the following sources: for Rwanda, see Kuperman 2001, 19–21; for Sudan, see Downes 2008, 2; for Bosnia, Guatemala, and Iraq see Valentino 2004, 77–83.

[12] Chenoweth & Stephan 2011, 212–216.

[13] Daley 2006, 663.

emotional dynamics that lead to an increased risk of violent conflict. They contend that the state draws and reifies group boundaries when it explicitly bases law and policy on identity categories. Such institutionalization can take on many forms, including the use of ethnic categories on the census, the adoption of affirmative action policies in education and employment, the delegation of autonomy to particular groups, and the legalization of differentiated voting and citizenship rights, among others.[14] Highly institutionalized ethnic categories, drawn repeatedly across policy domains, make identities increasingly visible and thereby both susceptible to prejudice and easier to mobilize.[15] Additionally, institutionalization "signals that a dividing line exists between 'us' and 'them,' priming relational status concerns and shaping how subsequent facts are likely to be interpreted within a political context."[16] They find that ethnic enumeration on state censuses correlates both with an increase in the politicization of ethnic identity and with ethnic violence.[17] The deep institutionalization of ethnic categories thus increases the risk of conflict by raising the probability that prejudice and discrimination will be practiced and perceived while simultaneously making ethnic mobilization easier.

A second school of thought builds on Gurr's concept of relative deprivation, arguing that large social or economic disparities between ethnic groups, or horizontal inequalities, generate grievances that motivate the relatively deprived to rebel.[18] According to Gurr, relative deprivation is the gap between what men expect and what they have the capability to achieve. The greater this gap, the greater the grievances and the higher the risk of rebellion as frustration driven aggression mounts.[19] Inequality that falls along group cleavages additionally violates important social norms of justice and equality, aggravating emotions of anger and resentment amongst members of the deprived group.[20] Visible socioeconomic disparities between groups also increase the salience of ethnic identity as well as

---

[14] Lieberman & Singh 2012a, 209.

[15] Lieberman & Singh 2012b, 5.

[16] Ibid., 2.

[17] Lieberman & Singh 2017.

[18] The concept of horizontal inequalities also builds on Horowitz's concepts of horizontal and vertical ethnic differentiation. The former occurs when ethnic groups parallel each other in socioeconomic stratification, each stretching across the domain of possible positions. The latter transpires when ethnic groups are hierarchically ordered with one socioeconomically subordinate to another, like a caste-based system (1971, 232).

[19] Gurr 1970, 22–58.

[20] Cederman, Weidmann, & Gleditsch 2011, 481.

enhance group cohesion and loyalty. These, in turn, provide groups with mobilizational resources for overcoming the collective action dilemma and thus further contribute to the potential for violence.[21] For example, participation in rectifying group-based deprivation or discrimination confers values of dignity and self-respect on individuals, furnishing them with positive incentives to contribute to collective goods even if that participation entails high costs and personal sacrifice.[22] Findings suggest that group-based inequalities in education, wealth, and life expectancy significantly predict political violence, including insurgency, terrorism, coups, and democratic breakdown.[23]

A third school of thought argues that the exclusion of ethnic groups from political power constitutes a grave risk for organized rebellion. Political exclusion entails both symbolic and material sacrifices. Groups standing outside the halls of power tend to lack equal access to state employment, patronage, and public services as well as the ability to ensure for themselves protection from state discrimination, disadvantageous policies, and unfair treatment under the law. As norms of democracy and inclusion spread, overt political exclusion, particularly of large demographic groups, also runs increasingly counter to the foundations of state legitimacy. This generates mounting feelings of injustice toward exclusionary states, thereby facilitating recruitment into resistance movements.[24] Robust findings across studies indicate that ethnic exclusion from political power greatly increases the probability of violent conflict, especially when the excluded groups are large and located far from the capital.[25]

[21] Houle 2015, 475; Østby 2008, 144; Østby, Nordås, & Rød 2009, 304.

[22] Varshney 2003.

[23] See Barrows 1976; Buhaug, Cederman, & Gleditsch 2013; Cederman, Gleditsch, & Buhaug 2013; Cederman, Weidmann, & Gleditsch 2011; Gubler & Selway 2012; Han, O'Mahoney, & Paik 2014; Houle 2015; Houle & Bodea 2017; Kuhn & Weidmann 2015; Murshed & Gates 2005; Østby 2008; Østby, Nordås, & Rød 2009; Piazza 2011.

[24] Cederman, Gleditsch, & Buhaug 2013, 47; Wimmer, Cederman, & Min 2009, 321.

[25] See Asal et al. 2016; Azam 2001; Bodea, Elbadawi, & Houle 2017; Buhaug, Cederman, & Gleditsch 2013; Buhaug, Cederman, & Rød 2008; Cederman, Buhaug, & Rød 2009; Cederman, Gleditsch, & Buhaug 2013; Cederman & Girardin 2007; Cederman, Wimmer, & Min 2010; Cederman, Weidmann, & Gleditsch 2011; Chiba & Gleditsch 2017; Kuhn & Weidmann 2015; Miodownik & Bhavnani 2011; Ray 2016; Roessler 2011; Rustad et al. 2011; Wimmer, Cederman, & Min 2009; Wig 2016; and Wucherpfennig et al. 2011. Similar results hold for the effect of political exclusion and state discrimination on non-violent protest (Jazayeri 2016) and terrorism (Boylan 2016). Relatedly, studies have found that ethnic accommodation, declining discrimination, and the inclusion of ethnic groups in cabinet representation, as well as local-level inclusion and power-sharing, has decreased coup, civil war, and inter-religious violence

Relatedly, Roessler argues that ethnopolitical exclusion results from a strategic choice made by leaders to substitute civil war risk for coup risk. Fearing the "enemy within," that ethnic rivals will leverage their access to state institutions in order to fully seize power, leaders have expelled them from the inner halls of authority – only to find those same groups organizing resistance from the outside. Not only does such exclusion foment grievances, it also severely limits the state's ability to gather intelligence and conduct "cooperative counterinsurgency." Weak states lack strong institutions and bureaucracies; rather, they govern through managing rival networks of violence specialists and the populations they control, usually territorially-based ethnic groups. When an ethnic network is excluded, the government curtails its penetration of that community and sacrifices its means to cooperate with local leaders to ensure broader social peace. Roessler thus adds strategic and institutional opportunity mechanisms to existing grievance explanations of civil war.[26]

All three explanations make important contributions to how we understand why ethnic groups rebel against the state. Ethnic institutionalization primes individuals to understand and interpret their world in ethnic terms, making legible group grievances such as political exclusion and socioeconomic disadvantage – grievances which inspire organized, and often violent, political resistance. Yet, these explanations suffer from two main faults. First, they tend to highlight fairly static and slow moving variables which do a poor job of explaining the rarity and timing of resistance.[27] Ethnic institutionalization is rampant and yet organized

---

risk (Arriola 2009; Bunte & Vinson 2016; Cederman, Gleditsch, & Wucherpfennig 2017). Lacina also makes a non-monotonic argument for the relationship between the political importance of ethnic and linguistic groups (the flip side of exclusion) and their propensity for organized violence. The state accommodates highly important groups without the need for conflict while extremely disadvantaged groups do not revolt as they anticipate their own defeat. The groups in the middle – those moderately important but somewhat excluded – can tip the scales through violence and coerce the state into granting their demands (2014; 2015). As an exception, Basedau et al. find that state discrimination against religious practices does not predict conflict outbreak, although they do not directly test religious exclusion from government (2017). Lewis also critiques the EPR studies for selection bias and, based on fine-grained data from Uganda on failed rebel groups, argues that ethnic exclusion and discrimination do not shape the early formation of rebel groups but rather which ones survive to pose a significant threat to the state (2017).

[26] Roessler 2011; Roessler 2016, 11–13 & 56–57.

[27] Less than 1% of group-years have witnessed the onset of violent conflict, both during and after the Cold War (Asal et al. 2016, 11; Cederman, Weidmann, & Gleditsch 2011, 487). And measures of social inequality, in particular, are, "notoriously persistent" over time (Houle 2015, 500).

ethnic violence is rare. Many relatively deprived or excluded ethnic groups fail to resist and those that do often choose timing that remains opaque. The strategic trade-off between coups and civil wars is perennial, especially in ethnically politicized regions such as Africa, and yet both types of instability remain rare events.[28]

Second, existing ethnic-based theories of political violence tend to assume that it is the relatively deprived, politically excluded, or discriminated against who rebel.[29] This misses much of the ethnic violence we witness where it is the powerful and advantaged groups that initiate hostilities.[30] For example, the relatively privileged white members of the Ku Klux Klan perpetrated organized violence against southern Blacks after the American Civil War; extremist Hutu's already in control of the Rwandan state and military orchestrated the genocide against Tutsi's after ousting and killing moderate Hutu's; and the M'Boshi dominated armed forces of Congo-Brazzaville, from a position of inclusion, overthrew a newly elected democratic government, led by an ethnic rival, launching the country into civil war.

Of course, the strategic trade-off posited by Roessler indicates that included groups do rebel, in the form of military coups. His framework, however, has yet to develop causal mechanisms explaining when and why the included seize power, focusing instead on civil war dynamics and why leaders choose ethno-political exclusion despite its clear risk of social violence (to avoid coups). His model also neglects the possibility that exclusion may simultaneously increase both coup risk and civil war risk, as groups leverage whatever tactics and resources they have to fight against their declining status. Indeed, Sudduth finds that leaders facing a high-risk of military overthrow often decline to coup-proof due to the very likelihood that purges would provoke the very coup they seek to

---

[28] This is a classic critique of the grievance-based literature on civil war outbreak, leading many to turn towards resource and opportunity based explanations for violence (see Collier & Hoeffler 2004; Fearon & Laitin 2003). Nonetheless, recent studies develop compelling theory and find robust statistical evidence, even controlling for opportunity factors such as foreign financing and natural resource endowments, that grievances are crucial to understanding political violence. My argument thus refines and builds on the grievance perspective.

[29] As a notable exception, building on ideas first espoused by Horowitz 1985 (249–250), Cederman, Weidmann, & Gleditsch 2011 argue that regionally concentrated, economically advantaged groups may resent state redistributive policies that detract from their net prosperity. Such groups might rebel to capture the benefits of greater economic autonomy or independence.

[30] Horowitz 2001, 41.

prevent.[31] Given this more complicated picture of risk trade-offs, better understanding when included groups seize power will also shed further light on when leaders may risk both coups and civil wars in the short-term to better consolidate their rule over the long run.

THE ARGUMENT: REACTIONARY VIOLENCE AGAINST BUILDING AND DISMANTLING SYSTEMS OF ETHNIC PRIVILEGE

This book argues that, in addition to these other mechanisms, the processes of creating and dismantling ethnically exclusionary state institutions engenders organized and violent political resistance. Where practices of clientelism and patronage combine with ethnic privilege, excluded groups face high political, economic, social, and emotional costs that generate deep-seated grievances. Exclusion, however, also reduces the available means for resistance. In contrast, the included can leverage their access to state resources and existing patronage networks to better organize and fund rebellion. Ethnic groups currently included but facing future exclusion thus possess both the strongest motives to rebel and the greatest capabilities to do so. It is the very processes of creating or destroying systems of ethnic privilege that produce the greatest risk of violence.

Ethnic groups often rebel, in other words, to preserve the status quo. This helps us understand both the timing and relative rarity of group rebellion: while exclusionary institutions and group grievances may persist over many years, it is in relatively brief and rare intervals that entire systems of ethnic privilege and disadvantage are created or destroyed. These moments of change provoke violence from losing groups, regardless of their relative political or socioeconomic position.

This argument builds on an important and notable exception to the aforementioned trend of existing ethnic explanations for violence to focus on the relatively deprived and aggrieved. Work by Cederman et al. finds that the most likely groups to engage in civil war are actually those that have recently lost power. Ethnic groups with a history of advantage sometimes witness quick reversals in their political fortunes. It is argued that such "recently downgraded" groups are especially likely to rebel as the "shock of demotion is likely to trigger strong emotional reactions."[32] Downgraded groups thus react violently to restore their previously

---

[31] Sudduth 2017a; 2017b.
[32] Cederman, Gleditsch, & Buhaug 2013, 62; See also Cederman, Wimmer, & Min 2010.

advantaged political position. My theory places this finding in context and further develops the causal mechanisms of why the loss of political advantage, and the loss of privilege and patronage it entails, provokes particular kinds of reactionary violence. The downgraded argument is thus subsumed within a broader understanding of how systems of ethnic privilege function within the state and how both their construction and dismantling lead to violence.

Focusing on the narrow empirical context of African militaries and when soldiers rebel against the state on ethnic grounds, I argue that when leaders attempt to build ethnic armies, or dismantle those created by their predecessors, they provoke violent resistance from military officers. The first process, when leaders attempt to construct ethnically-based security institutions, creates grievances amongst soldiers who now face exclusion from an important source of state power and patronage – closely following the ethnic exclusion argument but concentrating on the original process of generating that exclusion as a time of grave risk. I analyze this part of the argument in the context of African decolonization, a similar political shock experienced across the continent that allows for a relatively clean test of the theory prior to later endogenous ethnic dynamics within military institutions. Colonial military recruitment practices in Africa relied extensively on race and ethnicity as foundations for military loyalty. While officers were imported from Europe to command, rank-and-file soldiers were drawn from tribes deemed both politically loyal and "naturally martial." Facing a deteriorating regional security environment and pressing domestic threats, many independence era African leaders turned to this model when building new national armies, binding soldiers to the state through coethnicity. Where leaders had inherited a diverse officer corps from departing colonialists, such ethnic restructuring provoked violent resistance from soldiers now facing exclusion. Initial mutinies and coup attempts then sparked further violence as ethnic factions within the military vied for control over the state.

The second process, when new leaders attempt to dismantle ethnic armies, creates reactionary violence by those whose existing privileged position in the political system is threatened. Whether they subscribe to myths of their own deserved superiority or merely fear revenge and exclusion at the hands of those they have dominated, historically privileged groups will defend their monopoly over power and patronage. Here, I analyze the later period of democratization. The third wave of democracy that followed the end of the Cold War provides another exogenous political shock experienced simultaneously across many African countries, interrupting endogenous processes within civil-military institutions and allowing for radical changes. Again, this provides a relatively clean test of the theory. Democratization has posed a fundamental threat to Africa's legacy of ethnic armies. In highly diverse societies, which characterize most of sub-Saharan Africa, elections bring to power leaders who no longer share the identity of inherited ethnic armies. Leaders in this position face strong motivations to restructure the military, either diversifying the officer corps to better represent their societies or, perhaps, purging the ranks and building their own coethnic security institutions. In either case, the very context of liberalization threatens the existing ethnic army, eliciting violent resistance and undermining the democratic experiment.

FURTHER CONTRIBUTIONS TO THE MILITARY COUP AND DEMOCRATIZATION LITERATURES

Beyond its contribution to the ethnic conflict literature, this book also furthers our theoretical understanding of the causes and dynamics of military coups by bringing back the recently neglected centrality of ethnic politics to African civil-military relations. Case studies and ethnographies have long suggested that ethnic dynamics are central to understanding when African militaries seize power.[33] These insights, however, have been hard to generalize. The wave of military coups across recently decolonized countries in the 1960s and 1970s inspired a large statistical literature concerned with the structural risk factors underlying coup propensity. These works analyzed a wide range of variables, many derived from classical theories of civil-military relations,[34] including the underdevelopment of political institutions, strength of civil society, degree of military professionalization, number of soldiers and their relative pay, economic development and growth rates, commodity dependency, and past coup history, among others. Many of these studies were also deeply concerned with ethnic dynamics and included measures of ethnic diversity and dominance in their regressions. Yet, they produced no systematic or compelling evidence that ethnicity mattered to the occurrence of military coups. Indeed, these early quantitative studies generated only two consistently statistically significant findings: that coups beget more

---

33 See, for example, Hutchful 1985 on Ghana; Luckham 1971 on Nigeria; Cox 1976 on Sierra Leone; and Decalo 1990, Decalo 1998, and Horowitz 1985 for multi-case comparisons.

34 See, for example, Huntington 1957 on military professionalism; Huntington 1968, 192–205, on political institutions; and Finer 1976 on political culture.

coups and that they tend to occur more frequently in poor countries.[35] This inability to compellingly link ethnic politics to military behavior has led recent statistical and formal work on coups and coup-proofing to almost entirely neglect ethnic dynamics, at most including ethnic fractionalization as a control variable.[36] This is a serious oversight and diminishes our theoretical understanding of African coups.

Two important exceptions resist this general neglect of ethnic politics in the quantitative coup literature. Roessler argues that ethnic inclusion in the security forces permits antagonistic ethnic groups a foothold within the government from which to launch coups.[37] Houle and Bodea further demonstrate that horizontal inequalities between ethnic groups increase the likelihood of coup attempts as well as insurgencies.[38] I contribute to this renewed focus on analyzing the role of ethnic politics on coup attempts by examining the variance in ethnic recruitment practices and patronage building within military institutions. The construction and dismantling of ethnic armies is central to understanding African coups. Moreover, I test this argument cross-nationally, through the original and sophisticated conceptualization and measurement of ethnic dynamics, demonstrating its generalizability across contexts and thereby transcending the limitations of past case study research.

Finally, my work furthers our understanding of how militaries influence processes of democratization and democratic consolidation. In their seminal work, Bratton and van de Walle argue that military organizations crucially determine the ultimate success or failure of liberalization. Where soldiers have stepped in to support democratization, democracy prevailed; where militaries moved against liberalization, autocracy was restored.[39] Some have thus advocated for coups against repressive dictators as the only realistic avenue for their removal,[40] sparking a debate

---

35 Jackman 1978; Jackman et al. 1986; Jenkins & Kposowa 1990; Jenkins & Kposowa 1992; Johnson et al. 1984; Kposowa & Jenkins 1993; Londregan & Poole 1990; Lunde 1991; McGowan & Johnson 1984; O'Kane 1981; Przeworski et al. 1996; more recently, see Bazzi & Blattman 2014; Belkin & Shofer 2003; Collier & Hoeffler 2005; Galetovic & Sanhueza 2000; McGowan 2005.
36 See Arbatli & Arbatli 2016; Aksoy, Carter, & Wright 2015; Bell & Sudduth 2017; Besley & Robinson 2010; Biddle & Zirkle 1996; Casper & Tyson 2014; Girod 2014; Kim 2016; Lindberg & Clark 2008; Little 2017; Marcum & Brown 2016; Pilster & Böhmelt 2011; Piplani & Talmadge 2016; Powell 2012b; Powell & Lasley 2012; Savage & Caverley 2017; Sutter 2000; Svolik 2012; Wig & Rød 2016.
37 Roessler 2011.
38 Houle & Bodea 2017.
39 Bratton & van de Walle 1997, 211.
40 See, for example, Collier 2008.

over whether coups can indeed serve to further democratization. Marinov and Goemans find that, at least since the end of the Cold War, coups have increasingly led directly to elections, particularly where Western governments give high amounts of aid and can thus exert pressure for democratic reform.[41] Relatedly, Chacha and Powell demonstrate that strong international economic ties motivate post-coup governments to democratize[42] and Thyne and Powell argue that coups are most likely to promote democratization in highly authoritarian contexts with long-standing rulers who are least likely to liberalize via other paths. Their results indicate that such coup-based democracies are no more likely to collapse than democracies established through other means.[43] On the other hand, Derpanopoulos et al. find that, even post-Cold War, successful coups have not systematically led to democratization and are more likely to replace one type of dictatorship with another while also increasing repression levels.[44] Similarly, Acemoglu et al. contend that strong militaries created under authoritarian rule threaten new democracies who cannot credibly commit to not reform security institutions when given the opportunity.[45] And Tusalem finds that the higher the degree of military politicization and past coup interventionism, the more deleterious the effect on democratic consolidation. In contrast, my work suggests that not all militaries behave the same in the face of liberalizing pressures.[46] Ethnically stacked armies may be far more recalcitrant to further democratization because their privileges and access to patronage depend on an inherently undemocratic and non-inclusive vision of the state.

RESEARCH DESIGN AND SCOPE

I employ a multi-methods research design, combining statistical analysis with structured case study comparisons. Regression analysis tests my central theoretical claims against the historical experiences of all African countries, controlling for relevant alternative explanations. The effects of constructing systems of ethnic privilege within security institutions are analyzed in the decolonization period, using count models of subsequent coup attempts. The effects of dismantling these ethnic armies are then

---

41 Marinov & Goemans 2014.
42 Chacha & Powell 2017.
43 Thyne & Powell 2016.
44 Derpanopoulos et al. 2016.
45 Acemoglu, Ticchi, & Vindigni 2010.
46 Tusalem 2014.

analyzed in the later democratization period, employing logit models of whether the armed forces attempted to overthrow the newly elected regime.

These two contexts were chosen because they provide the cleanest test of each part of the theory, with the fewest endogenous threats to inference. While internal political movements were certainly important in shaping the particular experiences of both decolonization and democratization, they arose because of dynamics external to any given country. These shocks then created broad opportunities for ethnically restructuring the armed forces. This is not to claim that practices and pathways endogenous to civil-military relations cannot also create opportunities for the radical ethnic restructuring of military institutions, which in turn provoke the dynamics of resistance theorized here. Indeed, as the case studies will show, they often do.

Structured, case study comparisons enrich the statistical analysis, allowing for more depth and contextual nuance. Two paired comparisons were selected to examine the causal mechanisms linking the construction of ethnic armies during decolonization processes to soldier rebellion: Sierra Leone/Cameroon and Ghana/Senegal. The first pair compares countries whose initial leaders both chose to construct new national security institutions on ethnic grounds. They differ as to the officer corps they inherited: while Cameroon had no officer corps at the time of independence, Sierra Leone had a growing and ethnically diverse office corps. This paired comparison thus allows me to trace the impact of ethnic diversity in the late colonial officer corps on attempts to construct ethnic armies.

The second paired comparison involves two countries, Ghana and Senegal, that initially based military loyalty on ethnically inclusive recruitment and promotion policies, thereby creating diverse armies. Kwame Nkrumah of Ghana, however, abandoned inclusivity in the mid-1960s and began ethnically manipulating the security forces to counter internal threats to his rule. This within case variation allows me to trace once again how ethnic factions within a diverse military react to the construction of systems of ethnic privilege. Senegal, whose leaders have maintained diverse security institutions to the present day, serves as a contrast of inclusive stability to both Ghana and the other cases.

The two paired comparisons were carefully chosen to control for potential confounding variables (see Table 0.1). All four countries achieved independence around the same time, between 1957 and 1961, corresponding to when most African countries decolonized. Each pairing shares similar economic development levels at independence, weak but

TABLE O.I. *Decolonization Case Studies: Values on Key Alternative Variables*

Country	Loyalty Choice	Colonial Power	GDPk at Independence	Avg Growth in first 5 years	Ethnic Heterogeneity (ELF)	Largest Ethnic Group	Coup Attempts (first 20 years)
Cameroon	Ethnic	French	$829	1.6%	High (0.89)	Bamiléké (25%)	1 (0)
Sierra Leone	Ethnic	British	$858	2.8%	High (0.77)	Mende (30%)	13 (4)
Ghana	Inclusive then Ethnic	British	$1241	2.8%	High (0.71)	Akan (45%)	10 (3)
Senegal	Inclusive	French	$1445	0.8%	High (0.72)	Wolof (44%)	0 (0)

positive growth rates in the initial five years following decolonization, and high ethnic heterogeneity with no single group constituting a majority. While the two countries with a British colonial legacy are the most unstable, elsewhere it is shown that British colonialism neither conditioned the choice to build ethnic armies nor the frequency of later coup attempts.

A structured comparison of three cases is then employed to analyze the mechanisms leading an existing ethnic army to resist democratization: Nigeria, Benin, and Senegal. All three countries embarked upon democratization around the same time, in the late 1980s and early 1990s, while facing severe economic crisis, domestic protests, and pressure from international donors. All three also held elections whose results brought, or threatened to bring, to power new leaders who did not share the ethnic identity of the prior regime. Yet, each military reacted differently to this shared context: in Nigeria, senior northern Hausa-Fulani officers annulled the election results and eventually seized power; in Benin, rogue northern officers resisted democratization but could not gain traction across the military as a whole; while in Senegal, the military embraced democracy and has become a staunch defender of the constitution. The shared context of the cases allows me to isolate the role of the military and its legacy of ethnic recruitment practices in explaining the divergent outcomes.

Three notes on the scope of the empirical analysis are necessary. First, why coups? A narrower focus on military institutions and coups, as opposed to all violent conflict, allows for a more tractable test of the theory and its causal mechanisms. High-quality cross-national data could be collected not only on military coups, but also on the processes of creating and dismantling ethnically exclusionary armies. Collecting similar cross-national data on the construction and disassemblement of ethnic patronage networks in ministries, civil services, congresses, regional governments, and other important state institutions would require prodigious time and resources.

Such a narrow empirical context, however, raises issues as to the generalizability of the causal mechanisms, especially to other forms of violence. While distinct, the various tactics of ethnic rebellion, such as coups and insurgencies, are integrally linked and often substitutable. As Roessler has argued, coups and insurgencies are "alternative antiregime technologies" both used in the struggle over centralized state power.[47] Indeed, scholars have treated coups, civil wars, insurgencies, and even riots as related manifestations of the same underlying concept of political

---

[47] Roessler 2011, 303; Roessler 2016, 37.

instability, [48] with Bodea, Elbadawi, and Houle finding that they share important structural determinants such as ethnic exclusion and partial democratization.[49] Compelling evidence also exists that coups sometimes directly ignite insurgencies. In West Africa, McGowan links coups in Côte d'Ivoire, Guinea-Bissau, Liberia, Nigeria, and Sierra Leone to the subsequent outbreak of civil wars.[50] Fearon and Singh similarly both argue that military coups weaken the central government, and particularly the security sector, opening up opportunities for rebellion[51] while, statistically, Sambanis establishes a positive and significant correlation between political instability and civil war onset.[52] Coups and insurgencies are thus simultaneously interconnected and substitutable, part of a tactical repertoire that can be mobilized by elite ethnic entrepreneurs struggling for control over the state. There is thus good reason to believe that the causal mechanisms proposed here, over what motivates ethnic rebellion, will generalize across resistance tactics.

Of course, distinct contextual circumstances may drive tactical choice and we should be cautious in generalizing any theoretical framework across heterogeneous processes of violence.[53] For example, coups and insurgencies arise from substantially different organizational bases. Partial access to the state means that coup plotters need not devote themselves to large-scale social mobilization as insurgents must.[54] We might thus expect dissidents to attempt a coup before other tactics of resistance and for coups to occur closer in proximity to instigating events than insurgencies. Coups also require a foothold in state institutions. Groups already completely excluded thus cannot mount a coup attempt and must rebel through other means.

Second, the empirics are limited to the African context. The type of fine-grained, cross-national data on ethnic politics and military recruitment strategies needed to convincingly test the theory required intensive data collection. A global approach, while desirable, must wait for future research. Considering the severely unstable history of civil-military relations that African states have faced – and the threat that African armies continue to pose to democratization and stability today – a regional focus

---

[48] Arriola 2009, 11–12; Houle 2016, 694.
[49] Bodea, Elbadawi & Houle 2017.
[50] McGowan 2006, 247.
[51] Fearon 2004; Singh 2011.
[52] Sambanis 2004, 843.
[53] Brubaker & Laitin 1998, 447; Houle 2016, 20.
[54] Roessler 2016, 37; Thyne 2017, 3.

on Africa ensures that my findings and policy recommendations will have the most relevance where they are most needed.

Military coups have posed a serious and persistent threat to political stability in Africa. Since independence, over 225 coup attempts have been made across the continent including very recent coups against the governments of Burkina Faso, Burundi, Egypt, Guinea, Guinea-Bissau, Lesotho, Madagascar, Mali, Mauritania, and Niger. Nearly half of these coup attempts have been successful, many undermining recent democratization efforts. Between the end of the Cold War and 2012, Africa experienced 68 electoral transfers of executive power, where an incumbent leader peacefully stepped down after losing at the polls or not contesting the election. Fully 26.5% of these new regimes were overthrown by the military.[55] Understanding why may help African countries to overcome their legacy of military intervention and deepen nascent democratic practices.

Although the empirical context is constrained to Africa, nothing inherent to the argument limits its applicability to a single region. Wherever ethnicity constitutes an important frame for understanding and interpreting political and social realities, the act of delegating control over state institutions to privileged ethnic patronage networks, or undoing that control, should provoke the same dynamics of conflict. Colonialism ensured that throughout most of the world, ethnicity became the focal point of politics. Almost everywhere they went, European colonizers saw the societies they came into contact with through simplified lenses of ethnic identity – categorizing and counting populations via ethnic-racial classifications[56] and establishing institutions of rule that heightened the meaning of those identities through discrimination. Systems of indirect rule invested intermediary political power in the traditional authorities of a small subset of pre-colonial groups.[57] Missionary education gave differential early advantages to those groups whom they chose to "civilize," which often translated into dominance of the colonial civil service and pre-independence politics by those same groups.[58] And martial race doctrine – the idea that some identity groups made for better soldiers than others – pervaded colonial military recruitment practices across the globe, originating in India and then spreading to the Middle

---

55 For data on military coups, see Chapter 2 and Appendix B.
56 Anderson 1983, 164–170.
57 Young 1994, 76.
58 Baldwin 2011.

East and Africa.[59] The dynamics that this book identifies and tests in the African context should thus have broad applicability elsewhere in the postcolonial world.

Finally, I only consider ethnic group identities, albeit through a broad conceptualization of ethnicity inclusive of ethnoregional, religious, clan, and other ascriptive and kinship groups.[60] I exclude corporate, political, and other non-ascriptive identities from the analysis. Ethnicity is widely regarded as central to the organization of political competition and violence in Africa and thus focusing on such identities makes a certain intuitive sense.[61] Moreover, the ascriptive nature of ethnicity differentiates it from other types of groups in important ways, including the difficulties individuals encounter in hiding or switching their ethnic identity in the face of discrimination. Nonetheless, any group whose recruitment, retention, and promotion within the military is conditioned by their identity could react violently to potential exclusion or to the dismantling of their existing privilege. The dynamics theorized here could thus apply to a much broader range of identities. I leave these applications to future research.

OVERVIEW OF CHAPTERS

Chapter 1 further develops the central argument of the book: that the construction and dismantling of ethnic patronage networks within African security institutions has led soldiers to rebel against the state. The effects of constructing ethnic patronage networks are theorized in the context of African decolonization, when independence era leaders made important decisions regarding how to structure military loyalty. Where leaders chose to build ethnically homogeneous armies, despite existing diversity in the officer corps, they sparked coup attempts which then led to deepening political instability. Inclusive military recruitment was far less likely to cause soldier rebellion, although the leaders of deeply ethnically politicized societies often abandoned their initial commitments to inclusivity. When they began to ethnically manipulate the military, soldiers rebelled. The effects of dismantling these historic ethnic patronage networks are then theorized in the context of African democratization. Due to Africa's remarkable ethnic diversity, the opening of political competition entails a high likelihood that elections will bring to power

---

[59] Wilkinson 2015; Young 1994, 105–106.

[60] Following Chandra 2012.

[61] See, for example, Bayart 2009; Bratton & van de Walle 1997; Cederman, Gleditsch, & Buhaug 2013; Roessler 2016; Young 1994.

leaders from different ethnic groups. These leaders have strong incentives to dismantle the ethnic armies of their predecessors. Fearing a decline in their power and privilege via military reform, existing ethnic armies may then block democratization or violently reverse the outcome of elections.

Chapter 2 tests the argument against original cross-national data on African military history and ethnic manipulations within security institutions. The data was compiled from extensive archival research in Africa, Europe, and the United States as well as from a broad array of secondary and tertiary sources. I find that building ethnic armies against the background of a diverse officer corps, in the postcolonial context, led countries to experience nearly four times as many coup attempts as others. I also find that dismantling ethnic armies in the later period of democratization destabilized governments. When elections brought to power leaders no longer sharing the identity of the ethnic armies they inherited, coup propensity increased dramatically, from under 25% to 66%.

Chapters 3 and 4 examine the mechanisms linking the construction of ethnic armies to soldier rebellion through the comparison of four case studies. Chapter 3 analyzes a paired comparison of countries that chose to structure their militaries along ethnic lines, but experienced divergent outcomes in terms of stability: Sierra Leone and Cameroon. The critical difference between them lay in the colonial army they inherited: while newly independent Sierra Leone tried to restructure an already diverse officer corps along ethnic lines, Cameroon's leadership was able to build an ethnic army from the ground up under the protection of the French. Faced with resistance from losing officers, Sierra Leone devolved into instability while Cameroon remained highly stable. Chapter 4 compares Ghana and Senegal, both of whose initial leaders attempted to create inclusive military institutions. Yet, Ghana quickly succumbed to a series of coups and counter-coups while Senegal remained politically stable. Early ethnic politicization is critical to understanding their different trajectories: in Ghana, pre-independence political party mobilization along ethnic lines created deep ethnic politicization that undermined Kwame Nkrumah's early attempts to build nationally representative institutions. When he began ethnically manipulating security institutions in the mid-1960s, disadvantaged soldiers soon rebelled. In Senegal, on the other hand, early political parties were built along an urban–rural divide, with the dominant party mobilizing support through linkages with the Islamic brotherhoods who controlled rural votes. With ethnicity exerting a negligible influence on politics, Léopold Senghor was able to consistently recruit inclusively into the military without encountering resistance.

Chapter 5 analyzes the mechanisms linking the dismantling of ethnic armies to reactionary violence. The democratization experiments of the late 1980s and early 1990s in Benin, Nigeria, and Senegal are compared. Despite facing similar contexts of economic crisis, domestic unrest, and international pressure for liberalization, their militaries reacted differently to democratization. It is shown that these outcomes varied in accordance with each country's history of building ethnic privilege into its security institutions. In Nigeria, northern Hausa-Fulani officers had long dominated the officer corps, privately enriching themselves and building robust clientelist networks within the military from the state's vast oil rents. When elections resulted in the victory of a southern Yoruba, the northern officer clique annulled Nigeria's democratic experiment and quickly resumed full military governance. Senegal, in contrast, maintained inclusive and diverse security institutions since independence with no evidence of ethnic discrimination or privilege within the ranks. Senegal's professional and apolitical military has not only tolerated increasing liberalization but become its defender. Benin represents a middle course. At the time of democratization, Benin possessed an ethnically diverse military with regional quotas ensuring inclusion at all ranks. However, the government also practiced discrimination in promotion practices at the highest ranks, privileging northern officers. Some of these northern officers engaged in small-scale protest and violence, but were unable to garner enough support across the military as a whole to seriously challenge democratization.

Finally, the conclusion summarizes the book's argument and then develops the scholarly and policy implications of its findings. My work adds an important causal mechanism to the ethnic conflict literature, linking the creation and dismantling of ethnic patronage networks to violence. My work also suggests that civil-military relations should be central to the study of democratization and democratic consolidation. The tendency of African leaders to ensure stability in the past, by tying soldiers to the state through shared identity and ethnically-based patronage, can lead to military intervention when elections grant power to new ethnic groups. My findings also have important ramifications for peace-building efforts in the aftermath of ethnic conflict. My work emphasizes just how difficult it is to build nationally representative security institutions in ethnically tense and politicized contexts. Finally, I build a case for merit-based military institutions as both normatively desirable and necessary for long-term peace and stability and suggest ways in which the international community can assist in military reform.

I

Ethnicity, Military Patronage, and Soldier Rebellion

The military is both a resource and an object of ethnic conflict. It is a resource in conflict because ... the military can become a hotbed for ethnic resentment and an instrument for the advancement of ethnic claims to power. Like the civil service, it is an object of ethnic conflict, because military positions, with substantial salaries and perquisites, are coveted, because skewed ethnic composition means these advantages are unevenly distributed, and because control of the military is a significant symbol of ethnic domination.

– Donald L. Horowitz, *Ethnic Groups in Conflict*[1]

The construction and dismantling of systems of ethnic privilege within state institutions provoke reactionary violence by losing groups, which helps us to better understand both the timing of ethnic violence and which aggrieved groups actually rebel. Postcolonial African politics have been deeply shaped by widespread informal practices of patronage, which funnel state resources, employment, and investment to select groups and constituencies in return for political support. The combination of this entrenched clientelism with systemic ethnic privilege burdens excluded ethnic groups with high economic, political, and emotional costs. Even the fear of ethnic exclusion can generate sharp grievances. Yet, violent resistance is not equally likely across time nor across aggrieved groups. Ethnic groups currently included in the institutions of the state, but facing exclusion, possess both greater motivation to resist and more abundant resources with which to do so. Impending loss of privilege, and the fear of marginalization it engenders, evoke strong emotional reactions

[1] Horowitz 1985, 443.

22

that encourage resistance. Impending exclusion also creates a window of opportunity for resistance in which groups can still mobilize their established patron–client networks and leverage their current institutional access to organize and fund rebellion. Combined, these mechanisms suggest that ethnic groups are most likely to rebel when facing a negative change to their inclusion within state institutions. Both the construction and dismantling of systems of ethnic privilege forge these conditions. The construction of ethnic privilege naturally entails the exclusion of other groups; where such groups possess an institutional foothold, they will resist. The dismantling of historic systems of ethnic privilege, on the other hand, threaten currently dominant groups with a reversal of fate and marginalization at the hands of those they have systematically excluded. Privileged groups will thus fight to retain their dominance.

This argument is then applied to the military as a critical state institution and to the causes of soldier rebellion. Two contexts were chosen to provide the cleanest and most exogenous articulation of the theory and later empirical tests: decolonization for the construction of ethnic armies and democratization for their dismantling. Without denying the importance of internal political movements and actors, these transformative moments arose largely because of global dynamics external to any given African country. These external shocks then created important opportunities for ethnically restructuring the armed forces.

First, the retrenchment of empires in the aftermath of World War II led to widespread decolonization and the construction of new national armies, over which independence era African leaders had wide discretion. Prior ethnic and racially-based colonial military recruitment practices, combined with the acute security threats of the decolonization period, led many of these leaders to bind soldiers to the state through shared ethnicity. The construction of these ethnic armies threatened to permanently exclude non-favored groups from the security institutions of the state, with profound implications for their ability to access state patronage, ensure fair treatment, and protect themselves from state violence. Those groups with the resources to resist – those already represented in the officer corps – turned to violence to halt their exclusion. Attempting to seize power through coups, they often set off reactionary chains of violence as ethnic factions vied for dominance over the military.

Africa was then left with a legacy of ethnic armies who were profoundly threatened by democratization. The end of the Cold War brought with it the spread of democracy as Western powers, no longer fearing communist takeovers, pressured African states to liberalize. Free and fair elections then brought to power leaders who often no longer shared the identity of the ethnic armies they inherited. Such leaders had both incentive and opportunity to restructure these armies, undoing historic patterns of ethnic privilege. They sought to create diverse armies more compatible with democracy or to reassign patronage opportunities to their coethnics. Either way, restructuring deeply threatened the existing ethnic army, who resisted its own dismantling with reactionary violence.

While these two exogenously determined shocks created widespread, comparative moments where leaders could and did transform security institutions – highlighting, respectively, the effects of building and dismantling ethnic armies – endogenous dynamics can also create opportunities for the wholesale ethnic restructuring of military institutions. For example, the repeated purging of the officer corps until it practically ceases to exist allows leaders to radically change ethnic recruitment and promotion practices without facing resistance. Similarly, defeat in civil war may bring to power an entirely new group with the ability to create and shape its own institutions. My theoretical mechanisms should apply equally well within these endogenous transformations, explaining when and why ethnic resistance to change emerges.

UNDERSTANDING ETHNICITY

The argument developed in the rest of this chapter is primarily concerned with activated ethnic identities – those to which individuals claim membership, or to which the broader community assigns them membership, in a given context[2] – at the intersection of institutionalized (militaries and bureaucracies) and non-institutionalized (patronage) politics and the ethnic practices they produce. I follow Kanchan Chandra's minimal constructivist definition of ethnicity that focuses on the shared ascriptive nature of ethnic identities and how their visibility and stickiness constrain ethnic fluidity and change over the short-term. Chandra argues that ethnicity comprises the set of identity categories for which descent-based attributes are necessary for membership.[3] Attributes are sets of characteristics that individuals possess that may take on a range of values, such as skin color, place of birth, parents' place of birth, or language. Descent-based means that the associated traits are either inherited,

---

[2] Chandra 2012, 58.
[3] Ibid., 51.

genetically or by virtue of family membership, or endowed with a culturally ascribed myth of inheritance.[4] This focus on ascription follows long-held comparativist understandings of ethnicity. As Horowitz argued, "some notion of ascription, however diluted, and affinity deriving from it are inseparable from the concept of ethnicity."[5]

This minimal definition leaves the content of ethnicity blank. An ethnic group's sense of shared belonging could be based on cultural, linguistic, religious, racial, caste, regional, or tribal markings, among other possibilities. The particular attributes that grow to define groups likely emerge endogenously from processes of continual construction between self and other with neighboring groups – changing over time and across contexts.[6] Shared cultural practices may distinguish ethnic groups in one context while linguistic differences separate groups in another. Religious difference may equate with ethnic difference in some places, where conversion is taboo or exceedingly difficult and thus religion is governed by descent, but not others.

Furthermore, Chandra argues that membership in some ethnic categories may require, in addition to the necessary descent-based attributes, adherence to other, non-descent-based rules of membership. For instance, participation in community life is required of those claiming Native American identity in the United States along with indigenous ancestry. These non-descent-based rules of membership are idiosyncratic, contextually generated, and fail to differentiate ethnicity as a type of social identity from other identities that rely on achievements and practices that can, theoretically, be acquired by anyone – such as professional and political identities.[7] Trying to precisely define which types of attributes signal ethnicity, apart from their shared ascriptive character, would thus be a misleading way to think about ethnicity.

Placing ascription at the center of how we understand ethnicity underscores two distinctive characteristics of ethnic identity, visibility and stickiness, that constrain the choices of individuals in their ethnic identification practices. Descent-based attributes, especially physical attributes such as skin color, are more difficult to change and thus more sticky than acquired attributes, such as educational level. Alteration may also generate inconsistencies that betray the original trait. Lightened or

4 Ibid., 59.
5 Horowitz 1985, 52.
6 Ibid., 59–60.
7 Chandra 2012, 60.

darkened skin may no longer match hair color, eye color, and facial bone construction. Even successful alteration is perpetually vulnerable to discovery. Once revealed, the inherited trait rather than the modified trait is likely to define the individual's ethnic identity in the eyes of the community because of the centrality of inheritance, or at least a mythology of inheritance, to ethnicity. In the same vein, descent-based attributes are more likely to be visible and thus difficult to hide.[8]

These properties restrict people in important ways. While individuals may wish to emphasize different ethnic identities according to circumstances, they are constrained to doing so within the narrow range of identities into which they were born.[9] Moreover, because ethnic identities are extremely difficult for individuals to alter, the mechanisms of ethnic change across the population as a whole tend to operate over the long-term rather than the short-term. While new ethnic categories may come into existence or old ones disappear, and while the sets of attributes that define particular ethnicities and the values of those attributes necessary to attain membership may change, they do so slowly. This grants most ethnic categories stability in the short-term.[10]

Two implications of this understanding of ethnic identity are integral to the argument to come. First, ethnic categories are broadly stable and individuals and communities cannot simply reinvent themselves, recognizing that context conditions which categories are salient and whether individuals and communities activate those identities. Nonetheless, at least in the short-term, most individuals cannot simply redefine themselves into a more privileged or less threatened group. Second, the visibility and stickiness of ethnic identity markers allow others to activate identities that individuals might prefer to hide or change, imposing material, emotional, and psychological circumstances onto individuals not of their choosing.

ETHNIC PRIVILEGE AND PATRONAGE WITHIN STATE INSTITUTIONS

Neopatrimonialism and the systems of patronage and clientelism that sustain it have long characterized African states. Alternately referred to as prebendalism or the "politics of the belly," neopatrimonialism is a core feature of African politics, begun under colonial systems of rule that

---

[8] Ibid., 117–123.
[9] Posner 2004b; Posner 2005.
[10] Chandra 2012, 21.

granted salaries and tax collection rights to local chiefs in exchange for loyalty, routinized by the first generation of post-independence leaders with their newfound access to sources of accumulation, and persisting thereafter as well-established behavioral norms and political practices.[11] Neopatrimonialism builds on Weber's concepts of patrimonial authority and rational-legal authority. In the former, personal relationships and the direct exchange of resources and benefits for political support structure the politics of small societies. The latter, on the other hand, describes the separation of authority from personal rule through the creation of laws, the construction of modern bureaucracies, and the explicit separation of the public and private spheres.[12] Neopatrimonialism lies at the intersection of these ideal types of political authority, describing "hybrid political systems in which the customs and patterns of patrimonialism co-exist with, and suffuse, rational-legal institutions."[13] Here, systematic clientelism, or the routinized exchange of patronage in return not just for personal loyalty but also for the political mobilization of communities and nested patron–client networks, infuses the bureaucratic institutions of the modern state.

Neopatrimonialism thus entails the widespread transfer of state resources, in the form of patronage, to local elites. Such local elites independently exert influence over networks of followers due to their social, religious, familial, or cultural positions of authority as well as from their control over important local matters such as customary justice, trade and transport, and land allocation. In return for access to the state's largesse, local elites then facilitate the support and incorporation of their followers into governing institutions.[14]

Patronage assumes a variety of forms and opportunities to build clientelist networks exist across a broad array of state institutions and programs. Elite office holders control ministerial portfolios, policy tools, and sometimes vast amounts of resources that can be used to build political followings. President Félix Houphouët-Boigny of Côte d'Ivoire, for example, siphoned millions in cocoa export revenues to his personal

---

[11] Bayart 2009, 51–74; Bratton & van de Walle 1997, 63; Lemarchand 1972, 69; Lynch & Crawford 2011, 285–288.

[12] Bratton & van de Walle 1997, 61–62; Theobald 1982, 552; Weber 1978, 952–954 & 1006–1007.

[13] Bratton & van de Walle 1997, 62.

[14] Riedl 2014, 104–105. It has also been shown that, in democracies, electoral appeals to party patronage increase coethnic voting (Wantchekon 2003) and patron endorsement increases candidate support amongst the patron's coethnics (Baldwin 2013).

bank accounts for redistribution to his political clients.[15] Presidents also often control appointments to positions in the armed forces, police, and administrative bureaucracy. Indeed, all of Kenya's presidents have distributed patronage by stacking positions in the extensive provincial administration with coethnics.[16]

The depth and pervasiveness of patronage politics transcends public employment and crude cash transfers, encompassing a broad array of methods. Agricultural subsidies, loans, and credits, access to import and export licenses, and lowered effective tax rates can all be distributed on a preferential basis. In post-independence Ghana, only members of the "farmer's wing" of the ruling party were granted loans in the cocoa industry and, in Senegal, powerful rural brokers supportive of the government were given privileged access to important agricultural subsidies such as fertilizer, land, and equipment.[17] Similar perks can be granted to business and industry clients. Patronage can also be distributed in the form of employment in the state and parastatal sectors, including in the civil service, police, military, state-run enterprises, and in development projects. President Daniel arap Moi, for example, appointed politically loyal followers to high-level positions in Kenya's state corporations as did President Mobutu of Zaire.[18] Many of these jobs, beyond their base salary and fringe benefits (cars, housing, travel allowances, etc.), also entail rent-seeking opportunities and vital access to credit.[19]

Public investment and development projects, due to their spatial dimension, also provide opportunities to distribute patronage. Roads, schools, clinics, airports, and other infrastructure must be placed somewhere and they can be strategically located to help key supporters reward their constituencies.[20] Provision for their later maintenance also ensures local employment. President Ahmadou Ahidjo of Cameroon built extensive road networks in the north of the country, where his political base was located, while neglecting infrastructure development elsewhere. No paved road connected the country's two largest cities, Yaoundé and Douala, until the mid-1980s.[21] Having a coethnic president or minister

---

[15] van de Walle 1994, 132.
[16] Hassan 2015, 594.
[17] Bates 1981, 110–111.
[18] Ibid., 105.
[19] Bayart 2009, 75–76.
[20] On the spatial dimension of public investment and infrastructure, see Bates 1983; Fearon 1999. Using nighttime satellite data, Hodler & Raschky 2014 find that leaders preferentially divert resources to the regions in which they were born.
[21] van de Walle 1994, 141.

of education has been shown to increase educational achievement, with teaching jobs, scholarships, and school buildings preferentially allocated to coethnics.[22] Patronage can also include privileged access to valued state services such as university and school admissions, legal titling to land, and favorable court rulings. Administrators in the Nigerian Ministry of Education, for example, were known to grant admission to prestigious federal secondary schools to their ethnic and kinship networks in return for small bribes.[23]

Neopatrimonialism does not necessarily entail a politics of ethnic privilege and exclusion. Principles of shared ethnicity need not structure clientelist relations; they can also be organized around personal, oligarchical, class, or geographic allegiances.[24] Even where patronage networks are built on shared ethnicity, such networks can inclusively exist within particular state institutions or across the state as a whole. Many African cabinets expanded rapidly in the post-independence period as new ethnic groups were incorporated into the state and granted a portion of available resources, with senior ministerial positions often distributed proportionally across ethnic groups.[25] In Cameroon, President Ahidjo coopted the country's major ethnic groups by appointing tribal and ethnic leaders as ministers and legislators who could, in turn, grant state funds and projects to their clients and ethnic homelands.[26] In Indonesia, political leaders build alliances across ethnic divisions, thereby broadening their electoral support bases, by running on cross-ethnic tickets and granting material incentives to the patron–client networks of non-coethnic constituencies.[27] Leaders may sometimes even disadvantage their coethnics, such as in Mali, charging them higher taxes or granting fewer patronage benefits, leaving more resources available to coopt other groups.[28] Ethnic patronage and inclusion can exist side by side.

Yet, neopatrimonialism can, and often does, combine with ethnic privilege to produce systematic ethnic exclusion. A system of ethnic privilege exists when an ethnic group, or small alliance of groups, dominate the opportunities for patronage across the state as a whole or within a particular state institution – such as the executive, legislature,

---

[22] Franck & Rainer 2012; Kramon & Posner 2016.
[23] Kendhammer 2015, 149.
[24] As has occurred in countries such as the United States and Brazil (Theobald 1982, 551).
[25] Bratton & van de Walle 1997, 66 & 75; Francois, Rainer, & Trebbi 2015.
[26] DeLancey 1987, 15–16.
[27] Côté & Mitchell 2016, 665–666.
[28] Kramon & Posner 2013, 467–468; see, also, Kasara 2007 on the propensity of African leaders to more heavily tax coethnic farmers of key export crops.

judiciary, military, or police, etc. The political and financial benefits of dominating patronage opportunities then produce strong incentives to block the inclusion of other clientelist ethnic networks, institutionalizing the existing privilege. This results in the systematic exclusion of non-privileged ethnic groups and of all individuals who do not possess the requisite descent-based attributes to claim membership in the privileged group. Ethnic privilege and exclusion thus go hand in hand. If we assume that those who can activate identities in their available repertoire to integrate themselves into available patronage networks will do so, then a further consequence becomes apparent: the construction of ethnic privilege within state institutions will influence which identities gain political relevance and social salience. For example, both the preferential land grants offered to Kikuyu under Jomo Kenyatta and the Kikuyu's domination of the armed forces raised the political salience of tribe over other potential identity categories within Kenya, such as race or religion.

This intersection of ethnic privilege and neopatrimonialism also makes exclusion particularly costly. Ethnic exclusion is economically costly because members of excluded groups must forego the financial resources and opportunities provided by state employment, rent-seeking, investment, subsidies, development projects, and other investments and cash transfers. Mostly, these costs are born by ethnic elites, but ordinary farmers and workers without the requisite membership ties to included groups may also lose important economic opportunities as they fail to benefit from preferential taxes, crop pricing, or public investment in their area. Ethnic exclusion is also politically costly. By denying ethnic group elites the state resources to build and maintain clientelist networks, exclusion reinforces itself, leaving members of the excluded group with little prospect of recapturing access to state institutions in the future. Finally, when experienced as unjust discrimination, ethnic exclusion is emotionally costly. Discrimination violates important principles of justice and the equitable distribution of resources that are shared across many African cultures,[29] hurting group members and undermining their dignity and self-esteem.[30] Ethnic exclusion also violates principles of nationalism and self-determination, especially when the central institutions of the

---

[29] For example, Habyarimana et al. find that, while playing the dictator game, their subjects in Kampala, Uganda, who hailed from a variety of ethnic groups, adhered to a strong norm of equal distribution (2009, 76).

[30] Varshney 2003, 92–93.

state are involved, leaving members of excluded groups feeling as if they are under alien rule.[31]

VIOLENCE AS RESISTANCE TO THE CONSTRUCTION AND DISMANTLING OF ETHNIC PRIVILEGE

This intersection of ethnic exclusion and neopatrimonialism lends itself to violence. Systems of ethnic privilege within state institutions, and the exclusion they entail, generate both material and non-material grievances that lead to frustration, resentment, and resistance.[32] Insurgency by excluded ethnic groups is already well documented.[33] Additional work also links political exclusion to ethnically-based terrorism and non-violent protest.[34] However, these works struggle to explain who amongst the excluded will rebel and when. Many, if not most, excluded ethnic groups never resist and those that do often choose timing that remains opaque. Existing work on political exclusion also, naturally, focuses on the aggrieved. This misses much of the ethnic rebellion we witness where it is the relatively advantaged and included groups that initiate hostilities.

To address these gaps in current understanding, I argue that we need to focus on the processes of constructing and dismantling systems of ethnic privilege and exclusion within and across state institutions. These periods are especially prone to violence as those facing future exclusion, or the loss of their current privileged inclusion, resist change. In other words, ethnic rebellion is often reactionary – a fight to maintain the status quo. Understanding who faces a degradation of their current position,

---

31 Cederman, Gleditsch, & Buhaug 2013, 59.
32 This argument is naturally restricted to countries with some meaningful degree of ethnic heterogeneity. While rare in Africa, ethnically homogeneous countries do exist, where the vast majority of the population share an ethnic identity and no important sub-group cleavages divide the population – such as the small kingdoms of Swaziland and Lesotho. Within such states, "ethnic" patronage does not entail exclusion and thus the violent dynamics theorized below will not apply.
33 See Asal et al. 2016; Buhaug, Cederman, & Gleditsch 2013; Buhaug, Cederman, & Rød 2008; Cederman, Buhaug, & Rød 2009; Cederman, Gleditsch, & Buhaug 2013; Cederman & Girardin 2007; Cederman, Wimmer, & Min 2010; Cederman, Weidmann, & Gleditsch 2011; Kuhn & Weidmann 2015; Miodownik & Bhavnani 2011; Roessler 2011; Rustad et al. 2011; Wimmer, Cederman, & Min 2009; Wucherpfennig et al. 2011. Conversely, political inclusion of ethnic elites in state patronage networks lowers their propensity to rebel (Arriola 2009).
34 See, respectively, Boylan 2016; Jazayeri 2016.

and when they are threatened with such change, enhances our ability to predict which groups will rebel and when.

Two primary mechanisms explain why the processes of building or dismantling systems of ethnic privilege will be particularly likely to provoke resistance by losing groups. First, those who are currently included in the institutions and patronage systems of the state, and facing exclusion, generally possess greater resources to resist. They can both mobilize established ethnically-based clientelist networks and leverage their positions within state institutions to acquire materiel, funding, and other resources necessary to rebellion. All of which eases the collective action dilemma through facilitating communication, enabling organization, and providing material rewards (selective incentives) to participants.[35]

Second, loss or threatened loss of position evokes strong emotional reactions and fears that motivate resistance. In describing why recently downgraded groups rebel, Cederman, Gleditsch, and Buhaug argue that "the shock of demotion is likely to trigger strong emotional reactions that spill over into violence in order to 'reverse a reversal.' "[36] To expand on this initial insight, we can draw on prospect theory which suggests that individuals consider that which they already own more valuable than hypothetical gains and that they are more willing to take risks to recoup losses than to garner currently unpossesed advantages.[37] Losing inclusion or privilege is thus more likely to engender action than never having possessed it in the first place. Moreover, fear of marginalization and exclusion may be greater motivators of action than their reality. Lynch and Crawford argue that ethnically-based political party support in Africa is driven less by patronage already received than the fear of marginalization if other ethnic parties win at the polls.[38] In particular, this may help to explain why currently dominant groups react violently

35 The collective action dilemma rests on assumptions of individual rationality and argues that it is very difficult to organize large numbers of individuals to provide collective goods. Collective goods are non-excludable in the sense that all individuals benefit regardless of their contribution to attaining the good, such as security, clean air, or in this case ethnic rebellion. Because individuals can free-ride, relying on others to pay the costs of contributing while still ultimately enjoying the outcome, no one has an incentive to participate in collective action and hence the good goes unprovided. Overcoming the collective action dilemma requires either applying negative sanctions to non-contributors or granting positive selective incentives to contributors (Olson 1974; Olson 1982, 17–35).

36 Cederman, Gleditsch, & Buhaug 2013, 62.

37 Kahneman & Tversky 1979.

38 Lynch & Crawford 2011, 289.

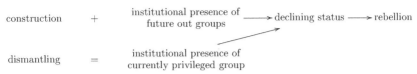

FIGURE 1.1. Causal Mechanisms: Building and Dismantling Systems of Ethnic Privilege and Rebellion

to the dismantling of their systems of privilege. Rather than trust in a more egalitarian inclusion of all groups, they fear that the previously excluded will turn the tables of privilege.

Ethnic groups are thus most likely to rebel when facing a negative change in their incorporation into state institutions and associated patronage resources. Figure 1.1 summarizes these mechanisms: the construction of systems of ethnic privilege necessitates the exclusion of other groups, who will leverage what current inclusion they have to resist. The dismantling of systems of ethnic privilege also entails demotion and a negative change in ethnic identity-based advantages. The historically privileged will thus also rebel when threatened with the loss of their dominance. Even when the proposed changes merely rectify existing grievances and create more inclusive institutions, fear of marginalization may still drive resistance.

BRINGING THE ARGUMENT TO THE MILITARY

The argument thus far developed applies broadly to the construction and dismantling of ethnic privilege in and across state institutions and the various technologies of resistance it engenders. The rest of this book, however, will focus on ethnic privilege and exclusion within the military and the preferred form of resistance by military officers, the coup d'état. This narrowing of focus allows for empirical traction while testing a more broadly applicable set of mechanisms. Honing in on one type of institution and one technology of rebellion made data collection and empirical testing feasible.

The military was chosen because it is a critical state institution that has, as Horowitz argued, been both a resource and an object of ethnic competition and conflict.[39] The military is an important source of employment and patronage and has often, but certainly not always, been dominated by particular ethnic groups in Africa. Indeed, military

---

[39] Horowitz 1985, 443.

loyalty has been structured around even quite small ethnic groups, such as the Tutsi in Rwanda and Burundi, making these dynamics relevant to all but the most ethnically homogeneous countries. Control over the military is also fundamental to maintaining ethnic domination over other state institutions and stabilizing the political control of the government. Understanding when soldiers rebel thus has important substantive implications.

While rank-and-file positions may also be distributed on a preferential ethnic basis, I focus more narrowly on the officer corps. Rank-and-file soldiers have neither the power nor the types of elite benefits and perks of military officers. They are thus less central to clientelism and ethnic control over the military than officers. Moreover, rank-and-file soldiers do not command others and cannot proffer legitimate reasons to be in routine contact with other units, especially those geographically dispersed from their own, decreasing their ability to coordinate. Enlisted personnel cannot organize much more than a local mutiny, which rarely threatens the regime. Military officers topple governments.[40]

Coups are the preferred technology of rebellion for military officers. Coups are attempts by a faction of regime insiders to oust the current government and take control over the state. They typically last for only a few hours, or perhaps days, and are often bloodless. Military officers logically prefer coups because they are easier to organize than other forms of resistance, such as protests or insurgencies. A small core of plotters can organize a coup, minimizing both the risk of early detection and the need to recruit and coordinate large numbers of participating individuals. Nigeria's first coup in 1966, for example, was led by merely 30 officers in an army of over 500 officers and 10,000 men.[41]

---

[40] Jong-A-Pin & Yu 2010 code the rank of coup leaders for 358 coup attempts drawn from Powell & Thyne's 2011 global dataset on coups. They find that 166 such attempts were conducted by senior officers (Flag or Generals), 140 by mid-rank or field-grade officers (Majors to Colonels), 44 by junior or company grade officers (Second Lieutenants to Captains), and 8 by NCOs. None were led by ordinary rank-and-file enlisted soldiers. Similarly, Singh (2014) was able to code the rank of coup leaders for 75% of the coup attempts in his dataset. Using the same categorization system, he finds that 174 attempts were conducted by senior officers, 122 by the middle ranks, and 57 by junior officers. NCOs are capable of staging coups, such as Sergeant Doe's coup in Liberia, but usually only in exceptionally small militaries or those whose officer corps has already been decimated by coups and purges. In such circumstances, NCOs have de facto acquired the privileges and authority usually reserved for commissioned officers.
[41] Luckham 1971, 33.

Indeed, coups almost entirely obviate the collective action dilemma. Small numbers of participants increase the salience of social ties, ensure that individuals impact the outcome of collective efforts, and facilitate the application of selective incentives (usually the post-seizure division of spoils).[42]

Military officers can also leverage their position in the command hierarchy to increase their likelihood of successfully unseating the regime. Senior officers have the power to control information, manipulating the beliefs of their subordinates. Since most military officers prefer to avoid fratricidal bloodshed by coordinating around the winning side, expectations concerning the behavior of others become critical. Generals can thus make a coup "a fact" by holding meetings and disseminating information that portray widespread support and the inevitability of success.[43] Middle-ranking and junior officers, on the other hand, can access armaments and issue largely uncontestable orders, moving troops and even engaging in combat without revealing their antigovernment intentions to their subordinates. During the 1971 Moroccan coup, for example, 1400 cadets from the NCO training academy were mobilized to attack the Royal Palace, where the key leaders of the country had gathered for the King's birthday celebration. The cadets were led to believe that they were saving the regime rather than toppling it.[44] Organizing resistance outside the resources of the military hierarchy would sacrifice these advantages.

For these reasons, the remainder of this chapter discusses how the construction and dismantling of systems of ethnic privilege and exclusion within African military institutions provokes violent resistance from military officers, in the form of the coup d'état. First, the exogenous shock of decolonization is analyzed to understand how the construction of ethnic armies provokes violent resistance from excluded groups. Then, the later shock of democratization is theorized to show how the dismantling of previously constructed ethnic armies also motivates violence.

COLONIAL MILITARY PRACTICES AND THE RISE OF THE ETHNIC ARMY

Decolonization was both a moment of great transformation for African security institutions and a time when loyalty concerns became paramount. The capacity to reshape institutions combined with the pressing need for

[42] Houle 2009, 597–598.
[43] Singh 2014, 36–37.
[44] *Keesings* 1971 v.17 (September).

a stable and loyal military led many African governments to construct systems of ethnic privilege and patronage within their armies. Within such "ethnic armies," recruitment, promotion, and retention depended on shared ethnicity with the regime leadership, resulting in the routinized exclusion of other ethnic groups from security institutions.

For the vast majority of African countries, decolonization was a time of great institutional flux. Even the most far-sighted of the colonial powers, Britain, withdrew with only a decade of preparation. The Belgians left like thieves in the night. Yet, even a decade provided insufficient time to build adequate national security institutions. Instead, African leaders tended to inherit small colonial armies that needed to be rapidly transformed along three important dimensions: the territorial basis of command, the scale of recruitment, and the composition of the officer corps.

First, most colonial forces had been organized on a regional basis, with integrated command structures across colonial administrative units. Under British rule in East Africa, the King's African Rifles (KAR) incorporated battalions drawn from Nyasaland (Malawi), Kenya, Tanzania, and Uganda. Similarly, in British West Africa, the Royal West African Frontier Force (RWAFF) included units of varying sizes from the Gambia, the Gold Coast (Ghana), Nigeria, and Sierra Leone. Under the French, the Tirailleurs Sénégalais recruited from across Côte d'Ivoire, Dahomey (Benin), Guinea, Mauritania, Niger, Senegal, Soudan (Mali), and the Upper Volta (Burkina Faso); while French Equatorial Africa had its own forces pooled from Chad, Gabon, the Middle Congo (Congo-Brazzaville), and Oubangui-Chari (Central African Republic). Devolution of military power to smaller territorial units thus involved sweeping organizational changes including the transformation of the upper command structure.

Second, the scale of colonial military recruitment was inadequate to support new national armies. Colonial armies had been designed to enforce internal pacification, overlapping significantly with police duties, and to serve as a reserve force for metropolitan armies in case of widespread conflict, such as during both World Wars. They were not intended for national border defense, or to defend against direct external aggression, and were consequently extremely small in size.[45] Indeed, the most densely populated country in Africa, Nigeria, inherited a mere

---

45 Cole 2013a, 2.

five battalions comprised of 800–1000 soldiers each.[46] Many African countries inherited no more than a single understaffed battalion, including Uganda.[47] Thus, independence often brought with it the need for rapid military expansion.

Finally, even after World War II, African colonial militaries collectively contained only a handful of low-ranking African officers. Europeans historically staffed and continued to staff throughout the 1950s and early 1960s, the vast majority of officer positions at all ranks. Africanization of the officer corps thus presented a difficult hurdle to the successful transition of colonial militaries to new national armies. Even the British, who perceived the issue first and began remedial measures the earliest, had made limited headway by independence. In 1960, the Nigerian army had appointed only 82 indigenous officers and continued to rely on 243 seconded British officers to fill its ranks.[48] On independence, the Ghanaian army possessed 28 native officers out of a total of 212.[49] The situation elsewhere was more dire. The Belgian Congo had no African officers upon independence – not a single one in an army of 25,000 men.[50] In the best of circumstances, then, new African leaders had to plan for the training and recruitment of no less than three-quarters of their officer corps.

Nationalizing African militaries were thus being simultaneously transformed along three important dimensions: the territorial scope of command, the extent of society inducted into service, and the basis of identity for officer corps membership (from European to African). Countries emerging from insurgencies, such as the former Portuguese colonies, faced additional challenges. They had to either integrate rebel forces with the native troops that had defended colonialism, or manage large-scale demobilization and its associated risks. In all cases, security institutions were in a state of deep flux and leaders faced important decisions, with lasting effects, over many details of military organization and recruitment. This was a moment where agency mattered and it mattered a great deal: independence era leaders could and did construct new rationales for military service and new principles of inclusion and exclusion for the officer corps.

---

[46] See regimental note cards in The National Archives of the UK (TNA), War Office (WO) 379/94, "Royal West African Frontier Force: Gambia Regiment, Cold Coast Regiment, Nigeria Regiment, Sierra Leone Regiment," 1950–1955.

[47] Byrnes 1990.

[48] Clayton 1989, 160.

[49] Ibid., 218.

[50] Adekson 1979, 161; Meditz & Merrill 1993.

At the same time, as African decolonization progressed, troubling events in the region made concerns over military loyalty, and especially military loyalty in the event of ethnic conflict, acutely urgent. Almost immediately after Sudanese independence in 1956, civil war broke out as black Christian and animist southerners resisted incorporation into a discriminatory Arab north who had already disbanded southern army units.[51] Similar tensions along racial, ethnic, and religious fault lines divided most Sahelian states – divisions created during the fourteenth-century Arab conquest and longstanding trans-Saharan slave trade and reinforced by colonial policies that granted political autonomy to northern Arab regions while disproportionately developing infrastructure, education, and economic opportunities in southern districts. In 1959, with the tacit consent of Belgian officials, the "Rwandan Revolution" overthrew the Tutsi monarchy. The political upheaval was accompanied by pogroms in which several thousand Tutsis were massacred, highlighting the vulnerability of ethnic minorities in new states.[52] In August 1960, the Congolese government disintegrated after rank-and-file soldiers revolted against continued Belgian officership, spreading fears of state failure across the continent.[53] New African states thus faced the real potential for ethnic violence, civil war, and state disintegration.

Given these threats, African leaders were hard pressed to find an effective means to tie soldiers to the state. Against both foreign and domestic threats, governments rely on their militaries for security. A disloyal military affords no protection: it may watch from a distance as revolution unfolds, stand to the side as foreign armies invade, or decide to seize power themselves. The military can be a regime's greatest ally or its worst enemy. Of primary importance is the loyalty of the officer corps. The rank-and-file can be drafted and coerced to fight, but officers must lead and enforce discipline. As previously noted, neither can rank-and-file soldiers easily organize large-scale resistance themselves, unlike officers who can topple governments.

Colonial military practices provided a ready model of ensuring loyalty through racial and ethnic manipulations.[54] While native soldiers comprised their rank-and-file, colonial armies were officered almost

---

[51] Metz 1982.
[52] Newbury 1998, 13.
[53] Meditz & Merrill 1993.
[54] Practices of racial and ethnic manipulations were not exclusive to colonial militaries. For example, the US military excluded African-Americans from officer rank prior to World War II and the British home army excluded Irish-Catholics from service from the seventeenth century until the 1780s (Enloe 1980, 46).

exclusively by white Europeans. Africans were not trusted to command conquering armies. Despite high death rates due to disease, colonial governors relied upon white European officers to first expand their territories and then to internally pacify them.[55] Minor exceptions did exist. The French commissioned a small number of African officers under the ancien régime. The mid-nineteenth-century commander of the Tirailleurs Sénégalais, General Faidherbe, believed wholeheartedly in assimilation and in the revolutionary Jacobin ideology of a democratic army. He successfully expanded the base of low-ranking native officers in the Tirailleurs, mostly recruiting from Senegal.[56] On the other hand, the first two Africans to receive officer rank from Britain were commissioned in 1942 and 1945, both from the Gold Coast Regiment.[57] The Belgians failed to commission a single native officer, in any of their African colonies, by the time of independence.[58] Throughout colonial Africa, race generally defined who could be trusted to command. This remained the case on the eve of independence and, in many countries, even after the formal transfer of sovereignty.

Conceptions of ethnic loyalty also shaped rank-and-file recruitment practices. British martial race doctrine, developed first in India after the disastrous 1857 Sepoy mutiny and uprising, stipulated that some ethnic groups were naturally more politically reliable and suited to combat and military discipline than others. Once groups were classified as martial, they were preferentially recruited into the British colonial forces. Groups considered too educated, too political, too rebellious, and even too effeminate were all barred from military service.[59] Frederick Lugard, the High Commissioner (1900–1906) and then Governor-General (1912–1919) of Nigeria, further developed this doctrine in Africa. He proscribed that one ethnic group should dominate the colonial army, provided that that group was both politically reliable and unable to dominate civilian political life (i.e., the local civil service). Where all three conditions were not simultaneously possible, he advocated instead for a conscientious mixing of ethnic groups within the colonial military to approximate this ethnic divide between the military and political spheres. It was a policy of "making the politically strong militarily weak and the politically weak militarily strong."[60] In Nigeria, where education and civil service

---

55 For settler mortality rates, see Acemoglu, Johnson & Robinson 2001, 1398.
56 Echenberg 1991, 19.
57 Clayton 1989, 160.
58 Lefévre & Lefévre 2006, 11; Meditz & Merrill 1993.
59 Ray 2012, 561; Wilkinson 2015, 42–52; Young 1994, 105–106.
60 Adekson 1979, 154.

appointments had favored the more educated Ibo and Yoruba in the South, military recruitment primarily targeted the Hausa, Tiv, and Kanuri tribes living in the North of the country.[61]

Lugard's model was widely emulated elsewhere in Africa, especially throughout the British colonies.[62] By such logic, the Kamba and Kalenjiin came to dominate the Kenyan battalions of the King's African Rifles, while the politically powerful Kikuyu were purposely excluded.[63] In Uganda, northerners, and especially the northwestern Acholi and Teso ethnic groups, were singled out for military recruitment.[64] Beyond the British, Belgian colonial administrators also established ethnic recruitment quotas based on racialized perceptions of martial prowess.[65]

Even the French, who initially avoided deterministic group-based evaluations of military fitness, were drawn to such practices over time. In French West Africa, military recruiters attempted to draw evenly across ethnic groups according to population density. Each administrative unit, or cercle, was assigned a quota calculated from its population figures. Mobile draft boards would then visit the cercle each year, inspect the called-up batch of eligible young men, usually the 19-year-olds, and fill the quota.[66] One consequence of this brand of equity, however, was that large ethnic communities came to dominate the army through weight of numbers, including the Bambara of Mali and the Mossi of Upper Volta (later Burkina Faso).[67] Over time, the French began to view many of these larger ethnic groups as more martial, due to their past service, and hence more desirable as future army recruits. Likewise, tribes from the sparsely populated linguistic communities of the forest zones were eventually seen as undesirable soldiers because they lacked a strong martial tradition. The forest peoples of the lower regions of Côte d'Ivoire were even declared "too feeble and unwarlike" to serve.[68] Thus, through an evolving lens of racial bias, the French reinforced their own early recruitment patterns.

Moreover, exceptions abounded to the official quota system. The draft boards were ill-suited to coping with highly mobile populations, allowing the nomadic peoples of the Sahara and Sahel to largely escape their grasp,

---

[61] Barua 1992, 126; Echenberg 1991, 64.
[62] Ray 2012, 563; Ray 2016, 804.
[63] Keegan 1983, 336–337; Parsons 1999, 58.
[64] Keegan 1983, 598–600.
[65] Adekson 1979, 160–161.
[66] For a rich history of military conscription in French West Africa, see Echenberg 1991, 47–69.
[67] Ibid., 63.
[68] Ibid.

including the Moors, Tuareg, and Fulbe peoples.[69] The French likewise struggled to fill quotas along imperial borders where young men could easily slip across to British territory when the draft board arrived.[70] French officials also occasionally bypassed recruitment regulations and specifically sought out more "martial" groups for colonial military duty.[71] In these ways, a system seemingly far less dependent on ethnic stereotypes still managed to create ethnically-based traditions of military service and non-service.

These colonial practices normalized the idea that race and ethnicity were linked to military loyalty and service. Colonial empires relied on their own nationals to officer far-flung armies, despite the cost and high mortality rates. Lugard's model of ethnic recruitment further embraced the notion that state security institutions were best left in the hands of loyal ethnic groups. When it came time for independence era leaders to transform their militaries and Africanize their officer corps, while facing threats of ethnic conflict and state failure, many turned to this established model of ethnically-based loyalty. Relying on mechanisms of ethnic patronage and ethnic affinity to ensure political reliability, they conditioned military recruitment and promotion on shared ethnicity.[72]

THE CONSTRUCTION OF ETHNIC ARMIES AND
SOLDIER REBELLION

Choosing ethnicity as the foundation for military loyalty was, counter-intuitively, dangerous for political stability – despite its very purpose of ensuring such stability.[73] Constructing a privileged coethnic army often required not just discriminatory recruitment, but the dismissal or marginalization of non-coethnic officers. Leaders employed two primary tactics to build such coethnic security institutions: first, restructuring the officer corps of the existing army along coethnic lines or, second, constructing coethnic parallel military institutions, such as presidential guards and militias, and then disarming or otherwise enervating the regular army. Both present a similar threat to existing out-group officers,

---

[69] Ibid., 48.
[70] Ibid., 63.
[71] Adekson 1979, 159–160.
[72] For an overview of the widespread use of ethnic recruitment practices and the "ethnic matching" of security institutions to regime leadership throughout Africa, see Decalo 1989; Decalo 1998; Enloe 1980; Goldsworthy 1981.
[73] Ethnic stacking is often cited as a successful strategy of civilian control over the military that brings long-term stability (see, for example, Decalo 1991, 72).

motivating many initial coup attempts and leading to cycles of violence wherein ethnic factions within the officer corps attempted to seize power and purge one another from the ranks.

Attempting to place a monopoly over the legitimate means of violence in the hands of a sole identity group inherently disadvantages and threatens excluded groups. Exclusion from security institutions entails discrimination, barred access to patronage resources, and declining relative power. Recent research in ethnic politics also suggests that conditioning access to a key state institution on ethnic identity heightens the salience of ethnic divides. By institutionalizing ethnicity and endowing it with imposed importance, governments prime individuals to interpret facts and events in terms of ethnicity. Indeed, the more identity shapes one's life chances and access to resources, the more useful it becomes as a cognitive device for reducing uncertainty. Questionable actions and isolated incidents of violence, that may not be motivated by ethnic differences, are then more likely to be interpreted through an ethnic lens. This, in turn, escalates communal hostilities.[74] We thus expect soldiers facing ethnic discrimination to feel threatened, primed to interpret events in ethnic terms, and faced with a shrinking window of opportunity in which to reverse their fortunes.

In these moments of change, violent resistance is likely. An initial attempt to restructure the military along ethnic lines, or perhaps even the anticipation of such restructuring, would prompt non-favored groups in the officer corps to protect themselves while they still have access to the material and organizational resources of the military hierarchy. Whether they succeed or fail, an ethnically motivated coup attempt – even if inspired by a defensive logic – then aggravates and threatens officers of other groups, who may subsequently attempt coups of their own. And, as officers are arrested, purged, and killed in the aftermath of each coup, the dynamics of fear and mistrust deepen. A cycle of tightly linked reactionary and counter reactionary violence is thus triggered within the military – an ethnic coup trap.[75]

---

74 Hale 2008, 33–40; Lieberman & Singh 2012b, 2–6.
75 This argument builds on the concept of "attritional coups" developed by Horowitz. He theorizes two types of coup traps emerging from dynamics of ethnic factionalism, what he terms the "see-saw" and "attritional" coups. "See-saw" coups occur where elections operate as an ethnic census and grant executive power to a dominant group. Non-dominant ethnic groups with a foothold in the military will then use their access to arms to reverse their electoral fates. This then sparks a series of counter-coups that replace elections as the primary means of transferring power between competing ethnic

Resistance to the construction of an ethnic army, however, could only take place where the colonial state had previously built diversity into the officer corps. Or where, as through much of Africa, martial race practices had resulted in "a debilitating legacy of split ethnic domination of military and political institutions."[76] Resistance to change requires soldiers facing exclusion to already possess a foothold in security institutions – otherwise they lack the resources to mount a coup. Yet, not all transitioning colonial armies were diverse or ethnically mismatched with the civilian government. Departing colonial powers sometimes colluded with incoming governments to construct an ethnically homogenous army, matching ethnic dominance of the military to the ethnicity of the nascent civilian leadership. This was the case, for example, in Mauritania and Rwanda where the Maure and Hutu, respectively, were granted control over both the chief executive and the military prior to decolonization.[77] Here, officers already benefited from a system of ethnic privilege within the military and were unlikely to protest its continuation.

Once established, however, an ethnically-based military loyal to a coethnic leader remains a stable institutional arrangement. Both Samuel Decalo and Boubacar N'Diaye, in their studies of long-standing civilian regimes, argue that by "ethnically matching"[78] the military to the civilian regime, leaders ensure loyalty through the dual mechanisms of ethnic affinity and ethnically conditioned patronage.[79] Visible favoritism also ties coethnic officers to the fate of their leader, since society will often hold them accountable for the behavior of the regime. This creates a self-fulfilling cycle of loyalty expectations wherein the leader relies on coethnic soldiers to implement coercion while these same soldiers rely on the leader to protect them from dismissal and retribution.[80] This triple bind then secures the regime against military coups and strengthens its hold on power. We thus only expect coups and political instability to result when civilian leaders attempt to reform the military from a diverse or ethnically mismatched institution into a coethnic one.

---

groups. According to Horowitz, this type of coup then morphs into the "attritional" coup, wherein ethnic factions in the officer corps attempt to purge one another in a progressive narrowing of the ethnic basis of the state and military, provoking more coups until one group achieves hegemony (1985, 480–496). See also Thompson 1976, 257.

[76] Ray 2012, 561.

[77] On Mauritania, see Hanloff 1990; Keegan 1983, 389–392. On Rwanda, see The National Archives of the UK (TNA), Colonial Office (CO) 822/2064 11, "Uganda Monthly Intelligence Report," November 30, 1960; Lefèvre & Lefèvre 2006, 11–12.

[78] A term coined by Cynthia Enloe 1975.

[79] See Decalo 1991, 72; Decalo 1998; N'Diaye 2001.

[80] Hassan 2017, 388.

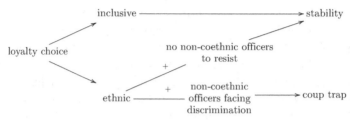

FIGURE 1.2. Causal Mechanisms: Decolonization and the Construction of Ethnic Armies

Figure 1.2 summarizes the causal mechanisms of the decolonization argument. With regard to constructing systems of ethnic privilege within the military during the context of decolonization, we thus have the following hypothesis:

Hypothesis 1: Countries whose independence era leaders chose to build ethnic armies despite inheriting a diverse (or unmatched) officer corps will develop coup traps.

ENDOGENOUS CHOICE?

Several endogeneity concerns complicate evaluating the effect of building ethnic armies on later coups. First, perhaps the loyalty choices of independence leaders and later ethnic violence were both strongly conditioned by the British colonial experience. As previously discussed, the British were the first to develop martial race doctrine and they arguably implemented it to a greater extent than other colonizers. We might then expect independence leaders in former British colonies to be more likely to continue their colonial traditions and build ethnically loyal armies.

At the same time, the British may also have practiced more rigid versions of indirect rule. According to Mamdani, the defining features of indirect rule were the organization of local communities into ethnically delineated territories, subject to the despotic rule of a native authority, charged with implementing customary tribal law and controlling land access.[81] This establishment of neocustomary land tenure systems tied land rights to ethnic identity and placed tribal leaders as intermediaries between the state and the people, with arbitration powers over land

[81] Mamdani 1996, 33, 51, 137, & 140.

TABLE 1.1. *Former Colonizer and Military Loyalty*

		Loyalty Choice	
		inclusive	ethnic
Colonizer	British	10	7
	French	8	10

Note: Bivariate correlation between ethnic loyalty and British Colonizer = −0.026; χ^2 = 0.2625 (p > 0.6084). Missing Cases: Central African Republic and Comoros. Also, Gambia did not have a post-independence military.

disputes. This, in turn, led to heightened ethnic salience and politicization as people were forced to frame their land claims in terms of identity.[82]

While acknowledging that such institutions were widespread throughout colonial Africa,[83] and that they varied within colonial empires as well as between them, Wucherpfennig, Hunziker, and Cederman assert that the British and French differed systematically in their implementation of indirect rule. While the British retained or constructed autonomous customary institutions with great power delegated to tribal chiefs, the French practiced policies of centralization and assimilation that treated their local agents as mere implementers rather than decision-makers. These differing practices resulted in former British colonies containing more consolidated and politically salient rural ethnic constituencies, established under autonomous rural despots.[84] While allowing for greater inclusion of peripheral ethnic communities into newfound states, British rule may have also heightened the salience of ethnic identity and defined political competition on ethnic lines. The propensity to build ethnic armies and later trajectories of ethnic violence stemming from ethnically-based political competition, including coups, could thus be jointly determined by British colonialism.

Table 1.1 compares British and French colonial legacies to the choices of independence era leaders to construct systems of ethnic privilege and dominance within their security institutions. Loyalty is coded as ethnic if the initial postcolonial leader purposefully recruited officers

---

[82] Boone 2014, 27–33; Boone & Nyeme 2015.

[83] As well as the British, the Belgians, Portuguese, Italians, Americo-Liberians, and South Africans all adopted indirect rule institutions (Mamdani 1996, 86).

[84] Wucherpfennig, Hunziker, & Cederman 2016, 885–886.

or created a presidential guard from their own ethnic group.[85] The correlation between British colonialism and ethnic armies is −0.026 and statistically insignificant, indicating that former British colonies were equally likely to construct ethnic versus inclusive armies. Surprisingly, former French colonies were more likely to construct systems of ethnic privilege within security institutions than their British counterparts. With a statistically insignificant χ^2 of 0.26 (p > 0.61), however, we cannot reject the null hypothesis that colonial legacy is irrelevant. Nonetheless, later tests will control for French colonialism to ameliorate this potential confounding factor.

Relatedly, ethnic armies could have been built precisely because of existing ethnic politicization, tensions, and conflict. Those leaders already facing divisive group cleavages may have recruited coethnics into the military to ensure the loyalty of soldiers in the event of anticipated ethnic violence. If this were true, then preexisting ethnic conflict would drive both loyalty choice and subsequent political instability: military loyalty would be endogenous to existing cycles of ethnic violence.

Anecdotal evidence suggests that prior ethnic conflict, at a minimum, was not deterministic in shaping the choices of post-independence leaders with regard to how they recruited military officers. Many leaders who had witnessed ethnic violence in their societies as independence approached consciously chose to pursue an inclusive and diverse security sector. Kwame Nkrumah, for example, was initially highly committed to a nationalistic vision for Ghana. He considered ethnicity "the canker-worm which, unless removed, may destroy the solidity of the body politic, the stability of the government, the efficiency of the bureaucracy and judiciary, and the effectiveness of the army and police."[86] Similarly, Nelson Mandela and the African National Congress were committed to a pluralistic vision of South African society and worked hard to assuage the fears of whites and other minority groups as they took power.[87] Both faced tense ethnic cleavages and recent violence between ethnic groups. In Ghana, pre-independence elections had led to violence between the Ashante political party, the National Liberation Movement, and any opposition that attempted to campaign in their region.[88] In South Africa, the Zulu-based Inkatha Freedom Party, with the assistance of the

[85] See Chapter 2 for a more detailed discussion of coding practices and Appendix C for the data.
[86] As quoted in Adekson 1976, 256.
[87] Cawthra 2003, 32.
[88] Mazrui & Tidy 1984, 59 & 88.

white dominated South African Defense Forces, had armed thousands against the Xhosa dominated African National Congress and initiated an ethnic insurgency.[89] Nonetheless, both Nkrumah and Mandela chose to broadly recruit across ethnic groups and to include ethnic rivals who had participated in violence into their national security institutions.

To further address this concern, I collected data on both ethnic violence and the politicization of ethnicity in the immediate pre-independence period. First, with regard to ethnic violence, I compiled data from newspapers supplemented with secondary sources, on ethnic riots and violence conducted by ethnic political parties against other identity groups. For each African country, the variable is coded 1 if there was any reported incident, of either type, between the end of World War II and the year of independence, and 0 otherwise (data is contained in Appendix A and full narratives in the Online Supplementary Materials).[90] This is a crude measure and does not capture the relative severity of ethnic violence across colonial territories. I believe this is the best measure, however, given the known biases in journalistic reporting: the media only report a small fraction of total conflict events[91] and reported events are skewed towards internationally important countries, urban areas, and locations with existing wire-services.[92] A more nuanced measure would be plagued by severe, non-randomly missing data.

Table 1.2 presents the results of comparing prior ethnic violence to whether independence leaders initially tried to build ethnic armies. The correlation between pre-independence acts of ethnic violence and the choice to build military loyalty on ethnic grounds is -0.22 with a χ^2 of 1.46, which is statistically insignificant ($p > 0.23$). Indeed, of the countries that had already experienced ethnic violence by decolonization, more chose inclusive security institutions than not.

Short of violence, and following the previous arguments on the potential effects of colonial indirect rule, antecedent ethnic politicization could have made it more difficult for leaders to choose and sustain practices of inclusion. If ethnicity already held great salience and politics

---

[89] Cawthra 2003, 35.

[90] Riots or violence directed by or against European settlers or colonial administrators was collected but not included in the final codings. Europeans generally left Africa following independence or remained in insubstantial numbers. Thus, violence between them and other groups was less likely to influence post-independence politics and its inclusion might obfuscate the effect of violence between indigenous groups on later outcomes.

[91] Earl et al. 2004, 70; Weidmann 2016, 211.

[92] Davenport & Ball 2002, 443; Woolley 2000, 158.

TABLE 1.2. *Pre-Independence Ethnic Violence and Military Loyalty*

| | | Loyalty Choice | |
		inclusive	ethnic
Prior Ethnic Violence	yes	11	4
	no	17	17

Note: Bivariate correlation between prior ethnic violence and ethnic loyalty = −0.22; χ^2 = 1.4592 (p > 0.2271). Missing Cases: Burkina Faso, Central African Republic, and Comoros. Also, Gambia did not have a post-independence military.

were already a manifestation of ethnic competition, then leaders may have felt compelled to building security institutions on an ethnic basis regardless of whether violence had yet to occur.[93] Both loyalty choice and later instability could thus be a joint result of early ethnic politicization.

To explore this relationship, I compiled data on the existence of ethnic political parties in the immediate pre-independence elections and how much of the total vote share they captured (data is contained in Appendix A and full narratives in the Online Supplementary Materials). Voting behavior is deemed a good proxy for ethnic politicization because it captures the actual relevance of ethnicity to voters themselves, beyond the ethnic appeals and motivations of political parties and elites.[94] For every country, each political party competing in the last national election prior to decolonization was categorized as ethnic, non-ethnic, or multi-ethnic following Kanchan Chandra's criteria: ethnic parties draw their support from specific ethnic groups while intentionally excluding others; multi-ethnic parties attract the support of particular ethnic constituencies but do not intentionally exclude; and non-ethnic parties draw diverse support across all groups.[95] The first variable coded from this data, *Ethnic political party* is a crude measure that captures whether there was at least one ethnic political party competing in the final

---

93 Indeed, Basedau et al. find that previous ethnic violence fails to explain variations in ethnic politicization, at least within their small sample of eight African countries (2011, 470).
94 Huber & Suryanarayan 2016, 153.
95 Chandra 2011, 162–164.

TABLE 1.3. *Pre-Independence Ethnic Politicization and Military Loyalty*

		Loyalty Choice	
		inclusive	ethnic
At Least One Ethnic Political Party	yes	13	16
	no	15	5

Note: Bivariate correlation between ethnic political party and ethnic loyalty $= -0.14$; $\chi^2 = 3.2543$ (p > 0.07123). Missing Cases: Central African Republic, Comoros, and Egypt. Also, Gambia did not have a post-independence military.

pre-independence election. The second variable measures the *Vote share* captured by all ethnic political parties in that election.

Table 1.3 compares whether leaders who witnessed at least one ethnic political party competing in pre-independence elections chose to build their militaries on ethnic grounds. The correlation is -0.14 with a χ^2 of 3.25 (p > 0.07), which is just barely statistically insignificant at conventional levels. Furthermore, regressing the choice to build coethnic security institutions on the vote share captured by ethnic political parties produces a coefficient of 0.02, which also falls just under conventional levels of statistical significance (p ≤ 0.1). This suggests that ethnic politicization may indeed have shaped the decisions of leaders, if only weakly. Where ethnicity had not come to define political party competition in the late colonial period, leaders more often chose inclusive security institutions. Nonetheless, as the table reveals, many leaders facing contexts of ethnic politicization nevertheless chose inclusion as well.

Endogeneity, at least in terms of colonizer and prior ethnic violence, thus seems of little concern. In the transformative moment of decolonization, independence leaders faced a critical juncture, in the parlance of path dependency theory, in which institutions could be broadly reshaped and human agency mattered a great deal. Choices were available over military recruitment and loyalty practices and leaders had wider latitude than under ordinary circumstances to alter them. Prior ethnic politicization, however, may still have imposed constraints. Understanding the difficulty of promoting inclusion under such circumstances, leaders may have more readily chosen exclusion. And those that promoted diversity, despite the adverse political environment, may have found such practices far more difficult to sustain. The statistical analysis and case study chapters will thus continue to explore the impact of ethnic politicization on leadership choices and their consequences.

DEMOCRATIZATION, THE DISMANTLING OF ETHNIC ARMIES, AND SOLDIER REBELLION

The ethnic coup traps that developed from decolonization processes could not sustain themselves indefinitely. Some ended when rebels overthrew a military paralyzed by factional infighting. Uganda, for example, experienced a remarkable nine coup attempts during the Idi Amin and second Obote regimes, many of which resisted ethnic manipulations by those leaders.[96] The coups ceased when rebel forces under Yoweri Museveni took over the state. Some victorious rebel groups, such as the Tutsi-based Rwandan Patriotic Front, were drawn from particular ethnic constituencies, leading to new ethnic armies when they gained power. Other coup traps came to an end through pyrrhic victory: as in Sierra Leone, when one ethnic faction finally managed to purge all others from the officer corps.[97] Thus more countries joined the ranks of those who had, with colonial collaboration, built ethnically loyal militaries from the beginning. Much of Africa was thus left with a legacy of ethnic armies.[98]

This historic tendency to base military loyalty on ethnic foundations is critical to understanding contemporary struggles over African democratization. Democracy and democratization are heavily contested concepts, endowed with a wide range of meanings and expectations across both societies and scholarly works. Yet, as Bratton and van de Walle contend, in the late 1980s and early 1990s, African countries took an "indispensable first step" on the path of democratization by adopting competitive elections to install new leaders.[99] It is in this sense that I use the term democratization, as a critical juncture in African political development denoting the transition away from authoritarian practices toward greater respect for political, civil, and human freedoms. There is nothing teleological in such transitions. They may lead to democratic consolidation, autocratic entrenchment, mixed institutional frameworks, or confusion and conflict.[100]

Democratization motivates soldier rebellion where prior leaders had built ethnic armies. In Africa, most states are highly diverse with no single ethnic group constituting a majority. The opening of political competition

---

[96] Horowitz 1985, 486–492.
[97] Minorities at Risk Project 2009.
[98] See also Enloe 1975; Enloe 1980; N'Diaye 2001.
[99] Bratton & van de Walle 1997, 10.
[100] O'Donnell & Schmitter 1986, 3.

and establishment of electoral processes – regardless of the extent or depth of other democratic reforms – thus increases the likelihood that executive power will change hands between leaders from different ethnic backgrounds. This otherwise normatively desirable state of affairs poses a danger to political stability where past leaders had entrenched systems of coethnic privilege and patronage within the military. Under a new leader, who no longer shares their identity, these military officers will fear a restructuring of the army and the dismantling of their privileged position and the material and security benefits it affords.

Like decolonization, democratization constitutes another transformative moment where leaders have wide latitude to reshape institutions, including the military. The new leader may wish to emulate their predecessor and create their own ethnic army, purging the existing one and recruiting coethnics in their place. Or the new leader could be committed to non-ethnic, inclusive state institutions and military diversification. Either set of policies requires dismantling the inherited ethnic army. Such restructuring threatens existing officers, who now face strong incentives to defend their positions of privilege. They may do so by blocking democratization or by violently reversing the outcome of elections, deposing new leaders, and restoring their coethnics to power. Such reactionary violence aims to preserve the pre-election status quo and does not usually lead to a coup trap or downward spiral of violence. Success restores the stable arrangement of an ethnic army matched to a coethnic leader. Failure, on the other hand, leads to the elimination or arrest of the plotters and opens a window of opportunity for the surviving democratic leader to enact reforms.

Figure 1.3 summarizes the causal mechanisms of the argument within the context of democratization. With regard to dismantling systems of ethnic privilege within the military, or the threat thereof engendered by elections, we thus have the following hypothesis:

Hypothesis 2: Where elections or other constitutional transfers of executive power undermine the "ethnic matching" between civil and military authorities, we should witness an increased probability of a coup attempt.

BARGAINING FAILURE

As with other conflict situations, violence is always ex post costly.[101] What prevents military officers and the government from negotiating

---

[101] For an overview of bargaining models of war see Fearon 1995; Powell 2002; Powell 2006.

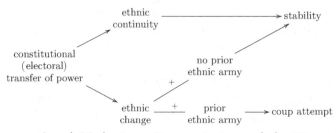

FIGURE 1.3. Causal Mechanisms: Democratization and the Dismantling of Ethnic Armies

an arrangement that would allow both to avoid fighting? The potential extreme costs for both failed coup instigators and deposed regimes – imprisonment, exile, or death[102] – should open a significant bargaining space. Surely it would make sense for the sitting government to identify threatening military factions and pay them off in order to forestall a deadly and destabilizing attack.

Yet, there are several reasons why we would expect bargaining to fail in this context. First, coupists rely on stealth. The exposure necessary for coup plotters to partake openly in negotiations would undermine their chances of operational success. Negotiating would inform not only the government of their plans but also, and perhaps more importantly, their subordinates – upon whose unquestioning obedience they depend. The only real bargaining option is thus a unilateral government concession. But to whom would they target this payoff? Bribing the whole officer corps would fail to resolve the ethnic recruitment issues that, in the theoretical story outlined here, underlie the motivations of the plotters. Everyone within the military might be receiving a higher salary, but those targeted for dismissal because of their ethnic identity would find little solace in that fact.

Alternatively, the government could direct pay-offs to the group being purged: accept a generous retirement package in return for leaving peacefully. Credible commitment issues undermine this intuitively sensible option. Officers of particular ethnic groups are being asked to surrender a key source of power within military institutions to a state that is openly discriminating against them. To accept declining relative power in return for material benefits, soldiers must believe that the government will refrain from using its increased power to renege on those concessions

---

[102] In West Africa, overthrown dictators were killed 19.2%, exiled 23.3%, and arrested 28.8% of the time (McGowan 2005, 14).

in the future. Why should they believe that a discriminatory state would not use its increased powers to discriminate further? Rather, we would expect ethnic factions to protect their power within security institutions and not to gamble their futures on unenforceable promises.

CONCLUSION

This chapter has argued that the neopatrimonial African state is characterized by widespread practices of clientelism and patronage. Where neopatrimonialism combines with ethnic favoritism, excluded groups face steep economic, political, and emotional costs that create deep grievances. The groups with the greatest resources and the strongest motivations to rebel, however, are those that currently possess a foothold of inclusion in state institutions. They can leverage their existing clientelist networks and access to materiel, supplies, and other institutional resources to organize and fund resistance. Thus we are most likely to witness ethnic group rebellion when currently included groups face future exclusion: during the processes of constructing or dismantling systems of ethnic privilege.

This argument was then applied to the military as a vital state institution and to two relatively exogenous moments of transformation: decolonization and democratization. Colonial practices normalized the idea that race and ethnicity were proper foundations for military loyalty. Faced with urgent security threats during and immediately after decolonization, many African leaders attempted to use coethnicity to bind soldiers to the state. Where they had inherited a diverse officer corps, such restructuring provoked violent resistance from soldiers now facing exclusion. Initial coup attempts often sparked further coups as ethnic factions vied for control of the state until one faction emerged victorious. This, combined with collusive departing colonizers who built ethnic privilege into security institutions prior to independence, left Africa with a legacy of ethnic armies. Later democratization then deeply threatened these historic ethnic armies. Elections in highly ethnically diverse societies bring to power new leaders who no longer share the ethnic identity of their inherited security institutions. They possess strong incentives to restructure the military, either to diversify the officer corps to better represent a multiethnic democracy or to replace it with their own loyal coethnics. Both types of restructuring threaten to dismantle the privileges of the existing ethnic army and, potentially, to marginalize them from the military altogether – provoking violent resistance.

While these dynamics have been theorized in the context of relatively exogenous moments of institutional transformation, they should also apply to the much more messy contexts of endogenous change. Whenever leaders attempt to construct or dismantle ethnic armies, and groups facing exclusion or declining privilege currently possess an institutional foothold within the military, we should expect them to use that foothold to resist.

2

Statistical Tests: Ethnic Armies
and the Coup d'Etat

Whether and how soldiers stepped in during regime transitions largely
determined whether such transitions ultimately culminated in democratic
outcomes.

– Michael Bratton and Nicolas van de Walle, *Democratic
Experiments in Africa*[1]

Using original data on ethnic practices within African militaries, this
chapter tests the argument that the construction and dismantling of
systems of ethnic privilege has provoked soldier rebellion, in the form of
military coups. Focusing on the context of decolonization, it is shown that
building ethnic armies led to deepening political instability. Independence
leaders made important decisions regarding how to tie soldiers to the state
and ensure military loyalty. Where leaders chose to create ethnic armies,
despite existing diversity in the officer corps, they sparked frequent coup
attempts: a fourfold increase over their contemporaries.

Dismantling ethnic armies also proves destabilizing. Indeed, the
historical tendency to build military loyalty along ethnic lines is critical
to understanding why African militaries have frequently deposed elected
leaders during democratization. In Africa, where most states are highly
diverse and where no single ethnic group constitutes a majority, the
opening of political competition increases the likelihood that executive
power will rotate between individuals of different identities. Where past
leaders had built ethnic armies, new leaders have strong incentives to
restructure the military: to dismantle existing systems of ethnic privilege
and either diversify security institutions to align with democratic values
of inclusivity or to build ethnic armies of their own. In either case,
the existing ethnic army will defend its position of privilege, leading
to reactionary violence. Where elections brought to power new leaders

---

[1] Bratton & van de Walle 1997, 211.

ethnically distinct from a previously constructed ethnic army, coup risk increased dramatically: from under 25% to 66%.

GENERATING NEW DATA ON ETHNICITY AND THE MILITARY

Although it has long been suggested that ethnic competition and conflict within African militaries have destabilized regimes,[2] existing cross-national data on ethnic practices within the military and ethnic relations between civil and military authorities is practically non-existent.[3] To evaluate whether the historical experiences of African countries support the theoretical framework developed here, I thus had to compile original data on a range of independent variables capturing how leaders recruited ethnic groups into the military and the legacies of ethnic practices they inherited. For the decolonization period, *Loyalty choice* captures whether independence leaders initially built ethnic armies or recruited more inclusively; *Diversity of late colonial officer corps* measures whether the existing officer corps at independence ethnically matched the new civilian leadership; and pre-independence *Ethnic violence* and *Ethnic politicization* capture whether ethnic cleavages had already generated violence or been used as the basis of political party mobilization by the time of decolonization. For the democratization analysis, *Ethnic change* in leadership denotes whether elections or other constitutional transfers of power involved a change in the ethnic identity of the head of state; and *Prior ethnic army* measures whether that newly elected leader inherited an ethnic army from their predecessor.

This original data on ethnic practices within the military and between civil and military authorities was culled from a wide variety of sources including archival documents,[4] newspaper articles,[5] reference books and

---

[2] See, for example, Cox 1976; Decalo 1990; Decalo 1998; Horowitz 1985; Hutchful 1985; Luckham 1971.

[3] Two important data collection efforts in progress should be noted: Wilkinson has begun developing a measure of "ethnic balance" in postcolonial military institutions, comparing the diversity of the military to the diversity of society (Chandra & Wilkinson 2008, 537–545). Johnson & Thurber 2017 have developed categorical variables for the ethnic composition of state militaries in the Middle East, including representation in both the rank-and-file and officer corps, and plan to expand this framework globally.

[4] From the National Archives of the UK (Kew), the French Colonial Archives (Aix-en-Provence), the French Military Archives (Vincennes), the US National Archives II (College Park), the National Archives of Senegal (Dakar), and the Kenya National Archives (Nairobi). Dakar and Nairobi were the administrative seats of colonial power in, respectively, French West Africa and British East Africa and thus contain documents pertaining to a large number of former colonies.

[5] Principally from *Keesings World News Archive*, Lexus-Nexus Academic, Proquest Historical Newspapers, and the BBC.

tertiary qualitative datasets,[6] and scholarly accounts including histori-
ographies, ethnographies, and sociological studies of African militaries.
Qualitative narratives were compiled from these source materials for
each country and then categorical quantitative variables constructed
according to the coding rules discussed below. The data is provided in
Appendices A and C and full documentation, including narratives and
sources, is contained in the Online Supplementary Materials.

Loyalty choice at decolonization: There are several potential bases
upon which African leaders could have chosen to build military loyalty. In
addition to the model of ethnic loyalty discussed in depth in the previous
chapter, armies had also historically tied soldiers to the state through
feudal, class, and civic-national structures (leaving aside mercenary
arrangements). In the middle ages, European armies were rooted in
reciprocal feudal ties. In exchange for land rights and the ability to
extract surplus production from peasants, feudal lords were responsible
for levying and supplying military units. The King commanded all and,
in turn, was ultimately responsible for defense. The highest ranks of the
nobility, who received the largest land grants and parceled smaller estates
to the lower nobility, were responsible for mustering those lower nobles
and ensuring their presence on the battlefield. The lowest lords brought a
small company of serfs with them to fight, the rank-and-file of their day.
Social and command hierarchies were thus one and the same and were,
moreover, tied into economic production.[7] As late as World War II, some
non-European armies were still operating primarily on the basis of feudal
obligations, including the army of Ethiopia.[8]

In the aftermath of the Thirty Years War, after a period of reliance on
mercenaries, the royal houses of Europe transitioned into a class-based
model of military recruitment and loyalty. In both France and Prussia,
the officer corps were legally closed to anyone not of aristocratic
birth, except for the engineering and artillery branches that relied on
scientific education and remained open to the middle classes. Indeed,
France's officer corps, due to its generous salaries, resembled an extensive
pension system for semi-impoverished nobles. England, on the other hand,
maintained a purchase system – both commissions and promotions had
to be bought – that, combined with low salaries, de facto restricted the

---

6 Of particular importance were John Keegan's *World Armies*, the Minorities at Risk
  Project, the World Directory of Minorities and Indigenous People, the Library of Congress
  country studies, and the *Encyclopedia of 20th Century African History*.
7 Spruyt 1996, 34–57.
8 Keegan 1983, 175–180.

officer corps of both the army and navy to members of the aristocracy who possessed sufficiently large hereditary estates to support their position.[9] These systems aligned class interests between the civilian regime and the military, "secur[ing] the loyalty of the army to the state by insuring that the former would be controlled by the same property interests which dominated the latter."[10] This was particularly true in England where many active-duty officers held hereditary seats in the House of Lords, commanding armies or ships while at the same time serving as legislators, and thereby creating a certain indistinguishableness between parliamentary and military interests.[11] Class continued to form the basis of officer recruitment, in countries such as Egypt, until the twentieth century. At the time of decolonization, command and staff positions in the Egyptian army were held exclusively by officers graduating from the Egyptian Military Academy, whose admissions rules restricted entrance to sons of the aristocracy. Reforms did not open the officer corps to the middle classes until 1936.[12]

Later professionalization created a civic-national model of loyalty, where officer recruitment and promotion became based on education, seniority, and merit. In the aftermath of the French revolution, ideological commitments swept aristocratic privilege aside within France's military. Combined with the mass emigration of noble officers during 1789–1792, this prompted the rapid promotion of enlisted men.[13] The Prussians quickly followed suit after their spectacular defeat to Napoleon at Jena. Deprived of a military genius on the order of Bonaparte, the Prussians invested in the systematic and superior training of ordinary men. In 1806, a series of major reforms formally abolished all class preferences within the military.[14] The British clung to the purchase system far longer, perhaps haunted by the ghost of Cromwell and a deep-seated fear of professionalizing the military.[15] After the Franco-Prussian War of 1870, however, facing a militarily dominant and threatening Prussian state, the British began merit-based reforms as well. Thus, by the beginning

---

[9] Huntington 1957, 20–25.

[10] Ibid., 47.

[11] Ibid., 24.

[12] Keegan 1983, 162–173.

[13] Ibid., 42; Scott 1971; Skocpol 1979, 190.

[14] Huntington 1957, 30–31.

[15] Oliver Cromwell led the parliamentary military forces that overthrew and executed King Charles I. He was a dominant personality in the short-lived Commonwealth of England, including serving as Lord Protector from 1653 to 1658. Following his death, the monarchy was restored and his corpse exhumed, chained, and beheaded.

of the twentieth century, the major European powers had abandoned aristocratic privilege as the foundation of military leadership. Instead, they established military academies and based recruitment and promotion on a combination of seniority and selection through merit.[16] Combined with the adoption of universal conscription that began with the French Revolution, these armies thus moved ever closer to being civic-national institutions, open equally to all citizens of the state.[17]

Despite this range of historical models, independence era African leaders tended to choose only one of two mutually exclusive possibilities: to tie military officers to the state through either a narrow sense of ethnic loyalty or through a broad sense of civic-national belonging. The fundamental difference between these two visions of loyalty is their degree of inclusiveness. Ethnic loyalty necessarily entails focused recruitment of particular ethnic groups and the exclusion of others, while civic-national loyalty is based on inclusiveness, non-discrimination, and merit-centric recruitment and promotion policies. Thus, if the initial postcolonial leadership purposefully recruited officers and/or created a presidential guard or personal militia from members of his own ethnic group – and, in some cases, their known allies – then loyalty choice was coded as *Ethnic*. The creation of a coethnic presidential guard, in particular, indicates that the leader is basing military loyalty on ethnic foundations since this tactic later enables the ethnic restructuring or disarmament of the regular army. On the other hand, if the first leader recruited officers from a diverse cross-section of society, loyalty choice was considered inclusive.

Coding identity presents a number of challenges. Individuals can activate different identities in distinct contexts and emphasize aspects of their identities in strategic and flexible ways.[18] Leaders can also marry outside of their own ethnic group and utilize the identity of their spouses to foster political loyalty.[19] Nonetheless, leaders usually self-identified, and were identified by their contemporaries, as having a single ethnic identity or a small set of layered identities. And while spousal affiliations could play a role in the political game writ large, those who built coethnic armies chose their own group and usually exclusively so (with some exceptions, as previously discussed, for traditional ethnic allies or

[16] Ibid., 38–55.
[17] The term "civic-nationalism" is used instead of "nationalism" to emphasize that nationalisms based on narrow identity constructions, especially ethnicity, are being excluded from this category.
[18] Posner 2004b; Posner 2005.
[19] Londregan et al. 1995, 6.

neutrals). Where mixed or layered identity did occur, then if any group dominated the officer corps and that group matched any component of the leader's identity, the loyalty variable was coded as ethnic.[20]

Another important concern is that the normal recruitment of demographically large ethnic groups may look like ethnic stacking but merely reflects their share in the population. The dynamic I seek to capture is one of purposeful ethic stacking beyond what population numbers alone would produce. Thus, where a group would naturally form a majority of the officer corps if recruitment were unbiased, then evidence of purposeful exclusion or discrimination against other groups is necessary to code the loyalty choice as ethnic.

A few examples may better illustrate the coding procedure. After Algeria gained independence from France, then Minister of Defense Colonel Houari Boumediene retained the largely Arab officer corps of the French colonial military and integrated it with the Arab leadership of the "external" revolutionary army. At the same time, Boumediene purged the vast majority of Berber officers and rank-and-file soldiers, who had fought in the "internal" guerrilla revolutionary army.[21] Algeria is thus coded as choosing ethnic loyalty since there was a conscious effort to make the military Arab. On the other hand, after Zambia achieved independence, military recruitment was conducted on the basis of voluntary enlistment, with no known exclusionary practices. The result was that no particular ethnic group predominated.[22] Therefore, Zambia is coded as choosing inclusive loyalty.

A small minority of cases, such as Malawi, were harder to code due to their complex ethnic practices. Hastings Banda, an ethnic Chewa, became President of Malawi upon independence. He inherited a military almost entirely comprised of southerners, many of whom were coethnics.[23] Banda then continued to selectively recruit men from the central and southern regions, particularly Chewa and Lomwe. At the same time, he discouraged Yao and other northerners from joining the military and prevented those that did from attaining high rank.[24] Yet, Banda placed

[20] This variable was generally not coded on the basis of region, even though regional identities are often politically important in Africa. Coethnic recruitment usually coincides with regional stacking practices. Indeed, for the cases that could be coded on the basis of region, the overlap was almost perfect: only one case out of 42 would have switched categories from ethnic to inclusive loyalty or vice versa.

[21] Metz 1993.

[22] Keegan 1983, 679–680.

[23] Parsons 1999, 60–61 & 91.

[24] Decalo 1998, 79 & 88.

Lomwe soldiers, rather than Chewa, in key senior positions of the armed forces because they were perceived as ethnic "neutrals" due to their "immigrant" status (despite generations of residence in the territory). President Banda's strategy of selective ethnic recruitment thus deviated in a meaningful way from other countries, with an emphasis on regional identity and the employment of ethnic neutrals. Yet, his was still a narrow and exclusionary vision of loyalty centered around his region, his coethnics, and their traditional allies. Thus Malawi is still coded as choosing ethnic loyalty.

Diversity of the late colonial officer corps: This variable builds on codings of both the ethnic heterogeneity of the late colonial officer corps and the ethnic identity of the independence era leader. If an ethnic group dominated the officer corps, and the immediate post-independence leader shared that identity, then this variable is coded as *Ethnically matched*.[25] If there was no pre-existing officer corps, then no officers could rebel against its restructuring along ethnic lines. Since this situation entails the same theoretical prediction, no rebellion, it is also coded as matched. In all other cases the variable is coded as *Ethnically unmatched*. This could reflect either diversity within the late colonial officer corps or a mismatch between the group that dominates the military and the ethnic identity of the civilian leadership.

Defining when a particular ethnic group dominates the officer corps is also difficult. Dominance should imply such a majority that no other group has a realistic chance of successfully seizing power. There is no clear numerical line, however, above which all cases would meet the qualitative standard. Dominance, as defined above, depends on many factors, including how many identity groups have representation in the military and how they are distributed across the branches of military service. I have thus stayed with more qualitative understandings: did credible observers at the time think that the officer corps was dominated by a particular group?

Bias in source materials then becomes an important concern. Perhaps observers had a vested interest in portraying colonial military recruitment practices in a certain light – as discriminating against their group or,

---

[25] Again, this variable was not coded on the basis of regional identity. Attempting to do so created too much missing data and the added value was negligible, due to the significant correlation between ethnic homelands and administrative regions. Of 43 cases that could be coded on the basis of regional identity, only two would have changed final categorization.

conversely, in down-playing their group's representation. Such tendencies could introduce significant distortion into the data. Careful attention to sources and their potential biases can alleviate some of this concern. Many countries were coded based on official military intelligence reports from the French and British archives. When such documents were unavailable, I turned to the accounts of sociologists and historians writing about these militaries in close temporal proximity to decolonization or to contemporary journalistic accounts.

Ethnic change in leadership: To begin, the ethnicity of each leader, before and after the constitutional or electoral transfer of power, was coded, usually at the highest level of ethnic aggregation, but taking into consideration other relevant identifications such as ethnic subgroups and clans.[26] If the ethnic identity of the leader prior to the transition was different from that of the leader assuming power, the power transfer was coded as an *Ethnic change*. If any part of their respective identity sets matched, however, the transition was considered one of ethnic continuity.

Transitional regimes constitute a special subset of observations and were treated slightly differently. At times, interim leaders or committees are appointed during peace processes or after military coups while elections or other constitutional procedures are arranged to determine the next head of state. In such cases, the coding is based on the ethnicity of the last head of state preceding the temporary transitional arrangements. Short-term transitional governments lack the time and capacity to reform security institutions and are highly unlikely to have altered the ethnic balance and practices of the military in their charge. It is thus the potential change of identity vis-à-vis the pre-transition leader that matters. Where the violent removal of a leader led directly to a transitional government that then quickly held elections, within one or two years, the ethnicity of the deposed leader and the ethnicity of the newly elected leader are used to determine whether an ethnic change in leadership took place.

In no case was regional identity used as the basis of coding for this variable, even though region plays an important role in the politics of many African countries, particularly in Sahelian states such as Benin, Nigeria, and the Sudan where north–south divides are arguably more important than ethnic differences in shaping the struggle for power. While such contextual awareness in coding is desirable, and an analysis of regional dynamics would be beneficial, there was far too much

---

[26] Clan identity is particularly salient in Somalia and Equatorial Guinea while the Asante form a politically relevant subgroup of the Akan in Ghana, for example.

missing data to do so (only 51 of 102 transitions could be coded). Such missingness was, moreover, likely biased. Regional identity was not systematically noted by the underlying source material and it was most often mentioned where it is most salient. That being said, recoding on the basis of regional identities would likely make a negligible difference. Of the 51 cases that could be coded, only three would have shifted final categorizations from ethnic change to continuity or vice versa. This is likely due to the strong overlap between ethnic homelands and important regional and administrative divides: a legacy of colonialism where indirect rule encapsulated communities in ethnically defined territories subject to "their" native authority.[27]

Prior Ethnic Army: This variable is coded 1 if the leader prior to the constitutional transfer of power had stacked the military officer corps or the presidential guard with their coethnics, and 0 otherwise. Similar concerns over coding identity, understanding stacking in the context of large majority ethnic groups, and identifying source material bias arose as with the *Loyalty choice* and *Ethnic change* variables and were handled in the same manner.

EMPIRICAL ANALYSIS: SYSTEMS OF ETHNIC PRIVILEGE AND THE SEIZURE OF POWER

Building and dismantling systems of ethnic privilege provokes reactionary violence from military officers who would lose out under the new recruitment regime. While these dynamics manifest whenever leaders attempt to alter the fundamental ethnic basis of security institutions, the endogenous processes that often change civil-military practices are difficult to parse out and test. I thus primarily developed the application of my theory in two relatively exogenous contexts: decolonization and

---

[27] Mamdani 1996, 33, 57, 137, & 140. Moreover, excluding regional considerations likely biases the results against the proposed theory, due to the fact that the ethnic homelands of powerful groups do not tend to cross important administrative regional divides. Recoding by regional identity not only rarely altered a categorization, but we would generally only expect to see codings of ethnic change switch to regional continuity. Regional change would invariably also entail ethnic change. We do not expect to observe coup attempts in such cases where regional identity is highly salient and power transfers between leaders from the same region. Thus, coding by region would eliminate several "false negatives" as cases originally incorrectly predicted to have coups would instead be successfully predicted as stable. Therefore, the more stringent coding rule, which excludes regional identity, biases the results in a downward direction, increasing our confidence in positive findings.

democratization. These transformative periods arose largely because of global conditions external to any particular African state, creating important opportunities for ethnically restructuring the armed forces. Indeed, even when arising endogenously, democratization can create unique opportunities for institutional change. In the decolonization context, I have argued that choosing ethnic loyalty despite a diverse officer corps should result in great instability and the development of ethnic coup traps as groups struggle to retain their foothold in the military and push others out. Later, during a democratic transfer of power, if there is an ethnic change in leadership and the previous leader had stacked the military with coethnics, then we expect the military to rebel.

The empirical tests that follow reflect this decision to analyze the construction of ethnic armies in the decolonization period and their dismantling during democratization. I thus developed two different datasets: the first covering the immediate post-decolonization period for all African countries and the second inclusive of all constitutional transfers of executive power following independence to the present. While a cleaner test, based purely on considerations of exogeneity, would concentrate only on the post-Cold War third wave of democratization, it would create an extremely low power dataset without much leverage to consider alternative explanations. I thus capture every constitutional transfer of power first and then later run robustness checks on more homogenous subsets of the data.

For the democratization tests, it is important to differentiate between elections and electoral transfers of power. Autocratic regimes routinely hold elections that restrict and otherwise control competition to ensure their hold on power.[28] Indeed out of around 320 elections for executive power in Africa, only 77 have led to a leadership transition.[29] In order not to confuse autocratic elections with at least partially democratic ones, I thus limit the universe of cases to elections that produced a turnover in executive power as well as other constitutional transfers of power.[30]

---

[28] See Morse 2012.

[29] Data on the total number of African elections was drawn from the NELDA 4.0 database (Hyde & Marinov 2012). Legislative elections in monarchies and presidential systems were removed as well as first round elections where a second round was held. Elections in pre-majority rule South Africa and Zimbabwe were also excluded.

[30] Hereditary monarchies are also excluded, including Morocco, Swaziland, and Ethiopia until Haile Selassie was overthrown. In such countries, there is no possibility of an ethnic change in leadership, violating the possibility principle. The possibility principle holds that irrelevant cases muddy the analytical waters, obscuring relationships. Thus

The democratization data is further divided into two distinct versions: the first covering all constitutional transfers of executive power and the second restricted to electoral transitions. There are a fair number of leadership transitions that occur constitutionally but not electorally (see Table 2.3). For example, after the natural death of a leader in office or after their resignation or impeachment. Such transitions take place with some regularity in democracies and democratizing countries and thus should not be summarily excluded. Yet, they also happen in autocratic contexts and their inclusion may not be appropriate when attempting to draw inferences about the challenges that militaries pose to democratization. Instead of attempting to classify the regime type of each state during the power transition – which would involve questionable coding practices given the transitional, muddy, and non-teleological nature of liberalization in the African context – I conduct the analysis both including and excluding these non-electoral power transfers.

To construct the dependent variables – the coup count in the years following decolonization and whether a coup attempt occurs following a constitutional transfer of power – I cross-referenced three large datasets on coups and irregular transfers of power: McGowan's database of sub-Saharan African military coup attempts (1956–2001),[31] the Archigos dataset of political leaders and irregular entry and exit from office (1875–2004),[32] and Powell and Thyne's global data on successful and failed coup attempts (1950–2013).[33] This process produced a large number of discrepancies, with some coups included in one or more datasets while being excluded from others. There were also disparities over the timing of coup attempts and whether they succeeded. Moreover, not all of these sources distinguished between military coups and coups conducted by other insider political factions. These disagreements were resolved by examining existing dataset narratives and by consulting newspaper and secondary sources.[34] McGowan's coding procedures for military coups were followed: a faction of the current government's military forces had to be involved in an attempt to overthrow the

---

irrelevant cases – wherein the outcome of interest cannot possibly occur – should be excluded (Goertz & Mahoney 2006, 178–179).

[31] McGowan 2003.

[32] Goemans et al. 2009.

[33] Powell & Thyne 2011 (July 2016 version of the dataset).

[34] Only the world news sections of reputable foreign papers were consulted to guard against false positives and exclude coup plots invented by dictators to arrest opposition leaders and other political opponents.

national government; evidence must exist of actual military force being used, whether in the form of violence or the occupation of important government buildings or transportation or communication centers; and, to count as a success, the coup leaders (or their appointed head-of-state) had to hold power for at least one week. A complete list of African military coup attempts is provided in Appendix B and full documentation of the discrepancy resolution process, including narratives, is contained in the Online Supplementary Materials.

Descriptive Evidence

Building and constructing ethnic armies has indeed provoked political instability in Africa. Even simple descriptive comparisons reveal clear patterns. Following decolonization, leaders who attempted to build ethnic armies despite existing diversity in the late colonial officer corps set their states on paths of instability, facing nearly three times as many coup attempts as others. The historical construction of ethnic armies also destabilized later power transfers. When elections or other constitutional processes brought to power leaders who no longer shared the ethnic identity of an ethnically stacked military, those soldiers rebelled a remarkable 66.7–72.2% of the time.

Table 2.1 presents the post-independence frequency of coup attempts broken down by loyalty choice and the diversity of the officer corps created under colonial rule. For each cell, I calculated the average number of coup attempts, across countries, in the 15 years following independence.[35] This standardizes the time frame of analysis. The results are compelling: countries with an unmatched officer corps, whose leaders chose to build ethnic armies, experienced on average nearly three times as many coup attempts as other countries.

---

[35] Some minor exceptions should be noted: first, for countries that lacked military institutions at independence (only Botswana and the Gambia), I calculated the 15 year observation window from the establishment of their first military unit. Second, Zimbabwe and South Africa enter the dataset not at independence but at the end of apartheid and the transition to majority rule, respectively. Finally, Liberia and Ethiopia require special consideration. Ethiopia enters the dataset in 1941, the year that Italian occupation forces were expelled during World War II and Haile Selassie was restored to the throne. Selassie's resumption of power marked a period of great military reform and professionalization, away from Ethiopia's feudal military obligation system and toward modern training academies. It was more difficult to determine a starting point for Liberia because of its unique history. I chose 1960, when a great number of West African countries were decolonized and the threat of colonization was permanently removed.

TABLE 2.1. *Building Ethnic Armies and Post-Independence Coup Attempts*

		Loyalty Choice	
		inclusive	ethnic
Officer Corps	ethnically matched	0.47 (n = 15)	1.25 (n = 12)
	ethnically unmatched	1.64 (n = 14)	3.11 (n = 9)

Cells contain the average number of coup attempts per country in the 15 years following independence. Missing Observations: Central African Republic, Comoros, and the Gambia. Bivariate negative binomial (coup count ~ unmatched x ethnic cell) = 1.04189 ($p \leq 0.05$). Ordinary least squares (OLS) = 0.01198 ($p \leq 0.05$). T-test (ethnic & unmatched v. all other groups) = 1.797 ($p = 0.1057$).

Interestingly, but unsurprisingly as all institutional legacies tend to fade, this effect diminishes over time. By 20 years after independence, the inclusive loyalty & ethnically unmatched and the ethnic loyalty & ethnically matched groups have begun to catch up.[36] And if we analyze the entire post-independence period, all three groups begin to look similarly unstable.[37] Only the inclusive loyalty & ethnically matched group remains consistently distinct. No matter what the time period examined, these countries experienced very few coup attempts: from 0.5 on average in the 15 years following independence to 0.8 over 20 years, to 1.8 over their entire post-independence history. Since most of these states had few if any African officers prior to independence (as many as 10 out of 15 lacked any native officer corps), it appears that the ability to construct a military command system from the ground up, combined with the choice of inclusive recruitment practices, greatly facilitated post-independence civil-military stability.

Turning to the context of democratization, from 1950 to 2012, there were 102 cases of power changing hands from one African leader to another by constitutional means. The majority of these transitions, 77, were the result of electoral processes, usually routine elections within a minimally democratic context or as part of a planned democratization.

---

36 With an average of 2.0 and 2.1 coup attempts, respectively, to 3.4 for the ethnic loyalty & ethnically unmatched group.

37 Ranging between 4.9 and 5.6 average coup attempts.

TABLE 2.2. *Reasons for Constitutional Changes of Leadership, 1950–2012*

Elections (n = 77)	
Planned democratization or regularly scheduled	50
By transitional government after coup	17
After retirement, resignation, impeachment, or death of leader	8
By transitional government after peace agreement	2
Non-Electoral Successions (n = 25)	
After death in office (natural) of leader	15
After resignation (non-militarily coerced) of leader	5
After retirement (non-coerced) of leader	4
By terms of peace agreement	1

The 25 non-electoral transitions stemmed from a variety of circumstances, mainly after the natural death, resignation, or retirement of the previous leader. Table 2.2 summarizes the reasons for African transfers of executive power by constitutional means.

Many of these power transfers were followed closely by violent military reactions: 27% experienced a coup attempt within four years. If we examine only electoral transitions, the record worsens: 34% witnessed a coup attempt within four years. Although one might expect military officers to react immediately to perceived threats to their corporate interests, in some contexts it makes more sense to wait. Coups are highly risky endeavors. The punishment for treason often involves death, imprisonment, or exile. In the absence of actual restructuring, the relative power of ethnic military factions does not decline. Officers motivated by self-preservation may thus exhaust other alternatives before attempting a coup. Four years, one year fewer than the length of a typical African election cycle (five years), was thus chosen as a reasonable observation window.

Periodizing the data by decade reveals an important temporal pattern: as the third wave of democratization swept across Africa in the 1990s, the number of constitutional and electoral leadership transitions skyrocketed, from eight in the 1980s to 30 in the 1990s. The number of coup attempts undermining those transitions grew in tandem: from two or 25% in the 1980s to nine or 30% in the 1990s. Limiting the analysis to elections fails to improve Africa's track record. While an astounding 67% of electoral transfers of power in the 1980s were closely followed by coup attempts, there were only three such transitions. In the 1990s,

TABLE 2.3. *Periodization of Constitutional and Electoral Changes of Leadership*

	Constitutional			Electoral		
	leadership changes	coup attempts	percent	leadership changes	coup attempts	percent
1950–1959	0	0	–	0	0	–
1960–1969	6	4	67	4	4	100
1970–1979	7	3	43	2	2	100
1980–1989	8	2	25	3	2	67
1990–1999	30	9	30	27	8	30
2000–2009	35	7	20	28	7	25
2010–2012	16	3	19	13	3	23
Total	102	28	27	77	26	34

out of 27 electorally induced changes in leadership, eight or 30% were followed by coup attempts. And while the problem has slightly improved since the turn of the century, it has by no means disappeared with close to a quarter of all electoral power transfers still engendering coup attempts. Table 2.3 presents a full breakdown of constitutional and electoral changes of leadership and subsequent coup attempts by decade.

Approximately 58% of these constitutional power transfers (62% of electoral transfers) involved a change in the ethnicity of leadership. In the highly diverse context of African societies, this is both expected and normatively desirable. Power should routinely change hands between leaders drawn from different ethnic communities and real democracy requires that this be possible. Yet, these ethnic power transfers have systematically provoked coups. Tables 2.4 and 2.5 depict the relationship between ethnic changes in leadership, the tendency of previous leaders to build coethnic armies, and coup attempts. Where leaders had successfully constructed coethnic armies and constitutional processes then brought to power new leaders from different ethnic backgrounds, those ethnic armies reacted by seizing power 66.7% of the time. Restricting the sample to electoral transfers of power reinforces these findings. When elections change the ethnic identity of the head of state, and the prior leader had constructed a coethnic army, soldiers rebelled 72.2% of the time. That power cannot safely change hands between leaders hailing from different

TABLE 2.4. *Dismantling Ethnic Armies and Coup Attempts:*
All Constitutional Transfers of Power

		Prior Ethnic Army	
		no	yes
Power Transfer	ethnic continuity	0% (n = 18)	31.8% (n = 22)
	ethnic change	14.7% (n = 34)	66.7% (n = 21)

Cells contain the percentage of countries experiencing a coup attempt in the four years following the power transfer. Missing Observations: Algeria (1999), Comoros (1990, 1996, 1998, 2006, 2011), Malawi (2012). Bivariate logit (coup ~ ethnic change x prior ethnic army) = 2.8167 ($p \leq 0.001$). T-test (ethnic change & prior ethnic army v. all other groups) = 5.0096 ($p \leq 0.001$).

TABLE 2.5. *Dismantling Ethnic Armies and Coup Attempts:*
Electoral Transfers of Power

		Prior Ethnic Army	
		no	yes
Power Transfer	ethnic continuity	0% (n = 12)	46.7% (n = 15)
	ethnic change	18.5% (n = 27)	72.2% (n = 18)

Cells contain the percentage of countries experiencing a coup attempt in the four years following the power transfer. Missing Observations: Algeria (1999), Comoros (1990, 1996, 1998, 2006, 2011). Bivariate logit (coup ~ ethnic change x prior ethnic army) = 2.4960 ($p \leq 0.001$). T-test (ethnic change & prior ethnic army v. all other groups) = 4.2872 ($p \leq 0.001$).

ethnic communities, without army intervention, deeply threatens African liberalization.

These findings likely underestimate the relationship between dismantling ethnic armies and soldier rebellion. First, other types of violent reactions from the military can occur, involving similar ethnic dynamics. For example, the 1993 elections in the Central African Republic led to the transfer of executive power from Andreé Kolingba, of the southern Yacoma, to Ange-Félix Patassé, of the northern Gbaya ethnic group. Patassé quickly implemented new policies that provided patronage positions in his administration to coethnics and fellow northerners. When he extended these inclinations to the military, blatantly purging southern soldiers, he sparked three army mutinies.[38] Second, the military can also annul election results before a power transfer even occurs, as happened in Nigeria in 1993. After Moshood Abiola, a southern Yoruba, decisively won the presidential elections, the northern Hausa-Fulani-dominated officer corps canceled the results on spurious claims of fraud. Ultimately, a coup unseated the transitional civilian leader and Nigeria returned to military governance.[39] These anecdotes suggest that restricting the analysis to actual power transfers, and the outcome variable to coup attempts, may significantly understate the extent to which prior ethnic armies undermine democratization.

Regression Analysis

These cross-national patterns lend preliminary support to the argument that the construction and dismantling of ethnic armies during decolonization and later democratization have provoked soldier rebellion. Descriptive statistics do not, however, control for potentially confounding variables, test alternative explanations, or rigorously estimate uncertainty. I thus now turn to regression analysis.[40]

Two distinct models are leveraged to further test the hypotheses. First, I have argued that countries choosing to build ethnic armies despite diverse officer corps' should experience greater relative instability following independence. To test this implication of the theory, I employ a negative binomial model using the total count of military coup attempts in the 15 years following independence.[41] Second, I have argued that countries whose leaders have employed ethnic stacking policies in the past are vulnerable to military reactivity when processes of democratization bring new leaders to power from different ethnic groups. I analyze this hypothesis using logit regression on the same coup variable constructed for the descriptive democratization data: whether a coup attempt occurred in the

---

38 Minority Rights Group 2010.
39 Adeakin 2015, 70; Bratton & van de Walle 1997, 216; Campbell 1994, 182 & 186; Lewis 1994, 326–327; Mahmud 1993, 88–90.
40 All statistical models were run in R version 3.4.0 using the Zelig package version 5.1.2 (Choirat et al. 2017; Imai, King, & Lau 2008).
41 A negative binomial model is employed as the variance-to-mean ratio of this dependent variable, 3.1, suggests over-dispersion. Also, 24 of 53 countries experienced no coup attempts in this time period, for a 0 rate of 45.3%, which does not necessitate a zero-inflated model.

four years following a constitutional transfer of executive power. This analysis is run on both versions of the data: all constitutional changes in leadership and only electoral successions of power.

The small size of each data set, ranging from 48 to 80 observations after accounting for missing data, grants very low power for testing hypotheses. Thus only a limited number of variables could be included and no interaction effects.[42] For the decolonization data, I work around this problem by including the *Ethnic loyalty* and *Umatched officer corps* variables in the baseline negative binomial regression and then later simulate the interaction to generate predicted coup counts with confidence intervals for each group in Table 2.1: a choice of ethnic loyalty given an ethnically matched officer corps, ethnic loyalty with an unmatched officer corps, inclusive loyalty given an ethnically matched officer corps, and inclusive loyalty with an unmatched officer corps. A similar approach is used in the democratization models. I include the variables *Ethnic change* and *Prior ethnic stacking* without the interaction effect and then simulate the interactions to generate predictions with confidence intervals for each of the groups in Tables 2.4 and 2.5: an ethnic change in leadership given a prior ethnic army, an ethnic change in the absence of a prior ethnic army, ethnic continuity in leadership given an ethnic army, and ethnic continuity absent a prior ethnic army.

The control variables were also carefully selected on the basis of theoretical significance. Complete descriptions, sources materials, and summary statistics are contained in Appendix D. As discussed in the previous chapter, ethnic politicization in the pre-independence period weakly shaped leaders' choices to build ethnic or inclusive security institutions. Such politicization may also have made it more difficult for leaders to sustain inclusive practices, as ethnic tensions within the military could spiral into fear-based anticipatory coups. In both the decolonization and democratization models, I thus include the *Ethnic parties* variable, which captures whether at least one political party or anti-colonial movement in the immediate pre-decolonization period was formed on an exclusive ethnic basis (see Appendix A).

Scholars have also linked broader social ethnic diversity directly to coup propensity. Greater ethnic heterogeneity may increase inter-group tensions and competition, undermining state strength and encouraging

---

[42] Due to the high degree of multicollinearity between the dichotomous independent variables, including interaction effects inflated the standard errors to exceptionally high-levels.

violent challenges to government power, including in the form of coups.[43] Numerically dominant groups could also capture the state and exclude others from power via democratic means, prompting coups by smaller groups as violence becomes their only recourse to political power.[44] Although statistical results across studies have returned ambiguous and often contradictory results,[45] measures for *Ethnic diversity* and dominance were included as controls, primarily in the robustness checks.

In weak states, foreign protection of the incumbent regime and the intervention it promises in the face of a coup, make the attempt a known folly. Even given fervent motivations to seize power, soldiers will likely avoid the risk of overt rebellion if they think their efforts will bring them into confrontation with a formidable foreign military. Such external guarantees have thus constituted a key strategy by which African regimes have attempted to underwrite their stability.[46] Indeed, in the immediate postcolonial context, there were good reasons to think that the former colonial powers would intervene to stabilize African governments. In 1964, the United Kingdom forcibly suppressed the East African mutinies that threatened Kenya, Uganda, and Tanzania.[47] That same year, France utterly crushed a coup attempt in tiny Gabon, deploying troops with fighter aircraft support from bases in Dakar and Brazzaville.[48]

Foreign protection, however, must be credible. The potential intervening power must not only harbor the desire to stabilize the current regime, it must also possess the local military capabilities to do so. In an era where strategic airlift was still in its infancy, that usually meant prepositioning military resources on the ground. Paper guarantees were "given teeth" through stationing combat troops and maintaining military bases on African territory.[49]

Arguably, protection against coups could also be ensured through foreign dominance of the officer corps. Potentially outnumbered and subject to constant foreign observation, local officers would find it difficult to successfully plot and organize a coup. This was, however, a

---

43 Kposowa & Jenkins 1993; Rabushka & Shepsle 1972.
44 Brass 1985; Jackman 1978.
45 Collier & Hoeffler 2005; Collier & Hoeffler 2007; Jackman 1978; Jackman et al. 1986; Jenkins & Kposowa 1990; Jenkins & Kposowa 1992; Kposowa & Jenkins 1993.
46 Decalo 1991, 73.
47 Luckham 1982, 65.
48 Crocker 1968, 24.
49 Decalo 1991, 73.

ubiquitous condition immediately following decolonization.[50] It was also a situation that changed in a fairly uniform manner, with Africanization of the officer corps largely controlled by the former colonial powers until the mid-1960s, when political pressures caused the mass exodus of seconded European officers across the continent. The only countries that did not rely excessively on foreign officers in the first years of independence were those that fought anti-colonial insurgencies and thus had built military forces of their own. These countries are, however, captured by the *Anticolonial insurgency* variable in the robustness checks. *Foreign military protection* is thus coded 1 if a military base or combat troops were initially maintained in the country, and 0 otherwise.

Extant studies of military coups also indicate the potential importance of economic development and coup history. It has consistently been found that overall indicators of relative wealth, especially GDP per capita, are negatively correlated with both successful coups and coup attempts, as well as with democratic instability.[51] The log of GDP per capita, measured in the year of independence or the year of a power transfer, is thus included (*Ln GDP/k*). It is also reasonable to think that economic shocks, understood as sharp downturns in a country's economic well-being, may increase coup risk. As public support for the incumbent government declines, recessions increase popular protest and civil unrest, creating opportunities for many types of violence, including coups.[52] For the democratization models, an *Economic shock* variable was coded 1 if, in any year during the four-year period following the leadership transition, the country experienced a negative growth rate of 1% or more, and 0 otherwise.[53] Unfortunately, measuring economic shocks in the 15 year

---

[50] At the time of independence, the most progressive countries in terms of Africanization could still only count about 25% of their officers as native (Clayton 1989, 160). Welch argues that this nearly uniform European dominance of the officer corps explains why Africa first witnessed a wave of mutinies, demanding Africanization along with pay raises, before the coup attempts began (1967, 306–308 & 317).

[51] Bell & Sudduth 2017; Collier & Hoeffler 2005; Collier & Hoeffler 2007; De Bruin 2017; Houle & Bodea 2017; Johnson & Thyne 2018; Londregan & Pool 1990; O'Kane 1981; Przeworski et al. 1996. McGowan argues that Africa's general poverty has made it easier to gain wealth through the government then by private enterprise, enticing politicians and soldiers to fight for control over the state (2005, 10).

[52] Alesina et al. 1996; Galetovic & Sanhueza 2000; Kim 2016. Additionally, Svolik 2008 finds that only economic recessions predict the timing of autocratic reversals, often due to coups, in democratizing countries.

[53] If during the four-year period of observation there was a coup attempt or another constitutional change in leadership, the period was truncated so as not to introduce reverse causality.

period following independence would introduce severe reverse causality problems as coups and instability engender economic crisis as well as potentially being caused by them. This variable is thus excluded from the decolonization models.

Many scholars have also argued that a past history of coups leads to future military intervention. The seizure of power by force undermines alternative principles of legitimacy – might makes right – easing the way for additional coups. Past coup history, whether measured by the number of past attempts, volume of past successes, or time since last coup, consistently predicts future coups.[54] *Prior coups*, measured as the count of total coup attempts in the ten years prior to the constitutional or electoral transfer of power, is thus included in the democratization models. Since colonial territories did not experience coups, no control for prior coup history is included in the decolonization models.

Lindberg and Clark have argued that the legitimacy accrued through processes of political liberalization may serve to inoculate regimes against military overthrow.[55] This insight is drawn from liberal democratic theory, which posits that democratic regimes enjoy legitimacy in both the eyes of the general population and amongst important elites such as military actors. Thus, as a state travels from authoritarianism through the various stages of democratic transition and liberalization towards consolidated democracy, its legitimacy should correspondingly grow, decreasing its susceptibility to military overthrow.[56] Trajectories of increasing liberalization should thus correlate with reduced coup risk while trajectories toward authoritarian regression may have the opposite effect.

Measuring legitimacy, however, is inherently difficult as it is a subjective and contextually dependent phenomenon.[57] Survey data, such as that provided by Afrobarometer, may ultimately provide the best measure but is currently unavailable across enough countries and years to systematically assess trajectories of legitimacy. Alternatively, I employ

---

54 Belkin & Shofer 2003; Bell & Sudduth 2017; Collier & Hoeffler 2005; Collier & Hoeffler 2007; De Bruin 2017; Marcum & Brown 2016; McGowan & Johnson 1984; O'Kane 1981; Powell 2012a; Wig & Rød 2016.

55 Clark 2007; Lindberg & Clark 2008. Decalo also considers government legitimacy as protection against coup attempts, although he maintains that such legitimacy can exist outside of a democratic or liberalizing context (1991, 73–74).

56 Lindberg & Clark 2008, 89. See also Sutter 1999, who argues that democratic legitimacy will induce non-cooperation by civilians in the event of a military takeover, thereby incentivizing soldiers to remain in the barracks.

57 Clark 2007, 143.

the following imperfect proxy in the democratization models: if theories of democratic legitimacy are correct, then general trajectories of state legitimacy should track changes in the rights and freedoms afforded to society. I thus include a measure, *Change in civil liberties*, coded as the difference in a state's Freedom House civil liberties score between the year in which a constitutional power transfer occurred and the end of the observation window. Such data is, unfortunately, unavailable for the immediate postcolonial years.

For the logit models on electoral transitions only, three additional control variables are considered. First, closely contested elections may increase the probability of a violent military response by those officers sympathetic to the losing side. Drawn from Lindberg's data on African elections, *Margin of victory* is measured by subtracting the vote share of the second place candidate from that of the winner.[58] Second, continuity in leadership may exist despite a change in the chief executive. If the new leader held a significant post in the old regime, or if the same political party maintains power, then military officers may not fear restructuring despite the transition. Following Lindberg again, *Regime continuity* is coded 1 if the pre- and post-transition leaders belong to the same political party or if the post-transition leader held an integral post in the prior administration, such as the vice-president, foreign minister, or secretary of state. Finally, past success with peaceful, electoral transfers of power could encourage the military to refrain from intervention. *Prior successful transfer* is coded 1 if at any point in the past, no matter how long ago, executive power was transferred constitutionally or electorally without a subsequent successful coup attempt, and 0 otherwise.

Findings: Constructing and Dismantling Ethnic Armies Provokes Instability

The regression analysis confirms the findings of the descriptive statistics: building and dismantling ethnic armies provokes political instability. In the decolonization context, countries whose leaders chose to build ethnic armies despite facing an existing, diverse officer corps tended to face substantially more coups: over four times as many, with a predicted 2.48 attempts in the 15 years following independence versus 0.56 for leaders who recruited inclusively and inherited a matched officer corps. See Table 2.6 for the full regression results and Figure 2.1 for the simulated

[58] Lindberg 2006.

TABLE 2.6. *Regression Results: Decolonization, the Construction of Ethnic Armies, and Coup Attempts*

	coup attempts in 15 years following independence (negative binomial)
Ethnic Loyalty	0.3959
	(0.3956)
Unmatched Officer Corps	1.1017**
	(0.3778)
Ethnic Parties	1.4893**
	(0.4844)
Ethnic Diversity	−0.3050
	(0.7321)
Foreign Protection	−0.0929
	(0.4141)
Ln GDP/k	−0.6336†
	(0.3444)
Intercept	3.0374
	(2.3089)
N	48

***$p \leq 0.001$, **$p \leq 0.01$, *$p \leq 0.05$, †$p \leq 0.10$

interaction effects between the loyalty choice made at independence and the ethnic diversity of the late colonial officer corps.

Interestingly, the inclusive loyalty & unmatched group did not fare substantially better, with a predicted 1.65 coup attempts following decolonization. Breaking down the data, the coup prone countries in this group comprise Burundi, Congo-Brazzaville, Ghana, Madagascar, and Nigeria.[59] These countries were attempting to build inclusive security institutions in a context of high ethnic politicization: all but Burundi had ethnic political parties competing in pre-independence elections and all but Madagascar had experienced ethnic violence in the run-up to decolonization (see Appendix A). Diversity in the inherited officer corps

---

[59] These countries experienced four to seven coup attempts in the 15 years following decolonization while no other country in the inclusive and unmatched set experienced more than one attempt.

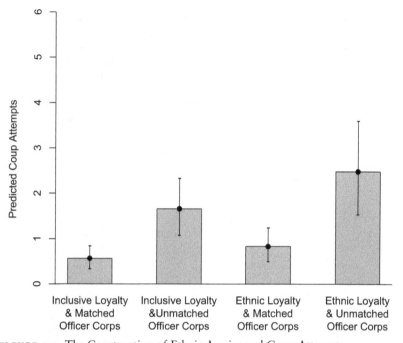

FIGURE 2.1. The Construction of Ethnic Armies and Coup Attempts

Note: Each bar represents the predicted number of coup attempts in the 15 years following independence for a country fitting that category. Predictions based on 100,000 simulations with 90% confidence intervals shown.

meant that the developing ethnic struggle for power could be brought into the military, destabilizing civil-military relations and making the quest for inclusivity difficult. Indeed, many of these countries quickly switched to ethnic stacking practices shortly after independence, including Burundi in 1965, Ghana in 1963, and Nigeria in 1966. That prior ethnic politicization would undermine efforts to build inclusive security institutions is further supported by the positive and statistically significant result for *Ethnic parties*. Merely having at least one ethnically-based political party competing in pre-independence elections increased the predicted number of coup attempts fourfold, from 0.5 to 1.9. While ethnic politicization did not determine leadership choices, it certainly impacted their ultimate success and contributed to political instability. No other control variables were statistically significant.

In the democratization context, the threat of dismantling ethnic armies engendered by ethnic turnovers in power greatly increases coup risk.

TABLE 2.7. *Regression Results: Determinants of Military Coups after Constitutional Transfers of Power*

	coup attempt after power transfer (logit)				
	all constitutional	electoral only			
Ethnic Change	1.5718 (1.1417)	4.1004* (1.8148)	4.1390* (1.8316)	4.2638* (2.1283)	4.0607* (1.8148)
Prior Ethnic Stacking	1.8459* (0.7331)	2.0763* (0.9063)	2.0736* (0.9052)	2.2706 (1.2243)	2.0109* (0.9515)
Ethnic Parties	−0.3232 (0.7608)	−0.9395 (0.9352)	−0.9193 (0.9414)	−0.9091 (1.0551)	−0.8926 (0.9562)
Ethnic Diversity	−0.8835 (1.8804)	−5.6509* (2.6859)	−5.7192* (2.7214)	−4.7654 (2.9780)	−5.6545* (2.6870)
Ln GDPk	−0.2652 (0.4684)	0.2539 (0.5812)	0.2372 (0.5888)	0.3686 (0.7353)	0.2621 (0.5773)
Economic Shock	0.4074 (0.8569)	0.8058 (1.0554)	0.8513 (1.1008)	0.4126 (1.2633)	0.7409 (1.0909)
Prior Coups	0.5571* (0.2569)	1.0383** (0.3676)	1.0408** (0.3677)	1.0218* (0.4951)	1.0052* (0.3928)
Δ Civil Liberties	−0.6485 (0.4971)	−0.7039 (0.5912)	−0.6962 (0.5932)	−0.0624 (0.7745)	−0.6882 (0.5935)
Margin of Victory		0.0032 (0.0216)			
Regime Continuity			−0.1693 (1.3805)		
Prior Successful Electoral Transfer				−0.2540 (1.1864)	
Intercept	−1.4299 (3.2612)	−3.9784 (4.0340)	−3.9522 (4.0114)	−5.46830 (5.05599)	−3.8567 (4.0305)
N	80	63	63	49	63

*** = p ≤ 0.001, ** = p ≤ 0.01, * = p ≤ 0.05

Table 2.7 presents the regression results for both the full set of constitutional power transfers as well as the elections only data. Figure 2.2 shows the simulated interaction effect between the *Ethnic change* and *Prior ethnic stacking* variables. While both the ethnic continuity & stacking and ethnic change & inclusive categories are associated with increased

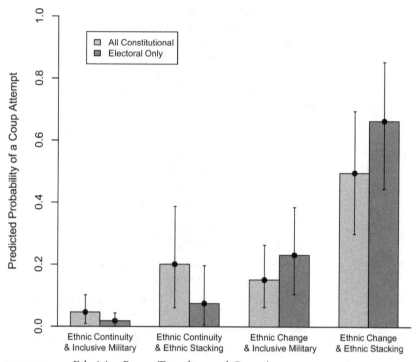

FIGURE 2.2. Ethnicity, Power Transfers, and Coup Attempts

Note: Each bar represents the predicted probability of a coup attempt in the four years following a constitutional or electoral transfer of executive power fitting that category. Predictions based on 100,000 simulations with 90% confidence intervals shown.

coup risk, the magnitude of the effect is comparatively small: 15–23% risk compared to the 2–6% risk of the baseline category (ethnic continuity & inclusive military). The ethnic change & stacking category, on the other hand, has a drastically higher predicted coup risk: 50% for all constitutional power transitions and 66% when elections are involved, all else being equal. Ethnic armies pose a significant threat to democratization.

Few of the control variables attained statistical significance. *Prior coups* is positive and significant as expected. Within the electoral data, experiencing 2.3 coup attempts in the ten years prior to the power transfer (the mean plus one standard deviation) increases coup risk to 35%, from 7% with no prior coups and 13% with the mean number of attempts (0.8). Ethnic diversity is also significant but runs counter to theoretical expectations: greater diversity, after accounting for ethnic practices within the military itself and ethnic dynamics between civil and military authorities, seems to substantially decrease coup risk. Surprisingly, neither general wealth levels nor economic shocks impacted coup risk. Nor did ethnic politicization under late colonialism continue to exert a significant impact on coup attempts during democratization. This raises some hope that the legacies of ethnic political party formation can be overcome. Benin and Ghana, for example, have maintained fairly liberal political systems replete with free and fair elections and multiple turnovers of power since they democratized in 1991 and 2000, respectively, without military interference. Both overcame long histories of ethnic politicization and frequent coup attempts.

Additional Alternative Explanations and Robustness Checks

A number of additional statistical tests were conducted to check the robustness of the findings. Across all tests, the results remain consistent: ethnically manipulating the military provokes political instability. Ethnic politicization and prior coups also continued to strongly shape coup risk. Full results, as well as variable descriptions and sources, are contained in the Online Supplementary Materials, Appendix D.

Two concerns arise with the comparability of observations. First, substantial variation exists in the reasons behind Africa's constitutional and electoral power transfers. Transitions following the deaths of leaders while in office or their retirement after decades of rule may engender different civil-military dynamics than regular alternation of power through elections. A separate analysis was thus conducted on the most homogeneous subset of electoral transitions: those regularly scheduled or occurring through planned democratization efforts. The *Ethnic change* and *Prior ethnic stacking variables* remain consistently positive and of generally similar magnitude but drop in statistical significance to the $p \leq 0.10$ level, which is expected given the small number of observations ($N = 42$).

Second, ethnically homogeneous or nearly homogeneous countries have perfectly ethnically stacked militaries and yet such stacking is meaningless in a context where this entails no discrimination or exclusion. In case their inclusion biases the findings, robustness checks were run on all three base models dropping the ethnically homogeneous countries (Cape Verde, Lesotho, São Tomé and Príncipe, Seychelles, Swaziland, and Tunisia). The results remain the same.

Several new variables were introduced to capture additional alternative explanations. Former French colonies were slightly more likely to build ethnic armies immediately following independence (see Chapter 1). France was also far more likely to intercede within its former African territories. Drawing lessons from World War II, following decolonization,

France conceived of Africa as vital to its strategy of defense in depth and maintained bases across the continent that were integral to its global military logistics and communications infrastructure.[60] France also supported a complex web of mutual defense agreements in Francophone Africa that provided for military assistance and training as well as for direct French intervention in the event of either external or internal challenges to standing governments. These had no British, Belgian, or Portuguese equivalents.[61] Indeed, in the first two decades following independence, France intervened at least 18 times to assist African governments, almost always due to domestic turmoil.[62] The United Kingdom, in contrast, only directly intervened once: sending troops to East Africa in 1964 to suppress the army mutinies in Kenya, Tanzania, and Uganda.[63] Understanding France's interest in stability and their capacity to quickly deploy troops, Francophone militaries may have been less likely to attempt coups, even given threats to their corporate interests or government efforts to engage in ethnic stacking. A control variable for French colonialism is thus included in all models.

Many scholars have also articulated a potential relationship between natural resources and conflict, including coups. Natural resource rents could stabilize governments by providing fiscal revenue, independent of citizens, that can be used to increase the repressive capabilities of the state, including coup-proofing.[64] Other scholars propose an alternative mechanism: that revenues from the sale of natural resources increase the potential rewards of state control, thereby encouraging attempts to seize power.[65] We thus have two mechanisms, pulling in opposite directions. For the negative binomial model, I include a dummy variable for whether oil constituted a principal export at independence. For the logit models on democratization, I include measures for oil production, diamond production, and whether the country was either an oil or diamond producer.

Certain characteristics of military organizations may also influence coup risk. Plotters in large militaries must coordinate across greater

---

[60] Luckham 1982, 60.
[61] Crocker 1968, 20–21; Crocker 1974, 283–284.
[62] Nonetheless, France had a mixed track record of responding to coup attempts. While preventing coups in Gabon (1964) and Niger (1973), France failed to assist Congo-Brazzaville's leader, Fulbert Youlou, who was removed in a coup in 1963 – even though they had troops stationed only 300 meters down the road. Togo's leader, Sylvanus Olympio also failed to receive help when he was toppled that same year (Decalo 1991, 76; Welch 1967, 317).
[63] Luckham 1982, 55 & 65.
[64] Ross 2004.
[65] Collier & Hoeffler 2005, 4–5; Humphreys 2005, 519.

numbers of officers, increasing the risk of detection. Low military spending may create a myriad of grievances and motivate soldiers to seize power to increase their resources.[66] In contrast, high military spending may buy off the military by giving soldiers individual perks or prestigious weaponry.[67] Counterbalancing, or expanding the number of military and paramilitary organizations, may raise the difficulty of coup coordination or directly create forceful opposition to coup attempts.[68] Large-scale purges may also motivate soldiers to intervene in government decision-making to preserve the integrity and size of the armed forces.[69] While comprehensive data is currently not available to account for all of these factors, I introduced controls for military spending, military expenditures, expenditures per soldier, and changes to all three following constitutional power transfers.

Domestic turmoil may also create the motivation and opportunity for a coup. Popular dissent may signal government weakness and facilitate elite coordination, increasing the likelihood of regime change via coups.[70] Civil wars may similarly weaken the government or create grievances within the military.[71] For example, in 2012, Mali's army toppled one of Africa's few solidly democratic regimes while in the midst of fighting the Tuareg rebellion. The complicit soldiers claimed that poor leadership had resulted in inadequate combat supplies, including food, arms, and medical care, resulting in unnecessary battlefield defeats and fatalities.[72] On the other hand, fighting interstate wars, or even engaging in militarized international disputes, could depress coup risk by impeding the military's ability to plot and execute coups as organizational resources are channeled externally, soldiers deployed to far away borders, and personnel reorganized for combat.[73] Robustness checks were conducted for popular unrest, including antigovernment demonstrations, riots, and strikes,[74] as well as concurrent civil and international wars.

Variables were also included for Herbst's measurement of difficult geography, to control for spatial-demographic ungovernability;[75] contemporary efforts to deter coups by the African Union via member

---

[66] Leon 2014; Powell 2012a.; Thompson 1980.
[67] Powell et al. 2018; Wang 1998.
[68] De Bruin 2017: Powell 2012a; Powell 2012b.
[69] Sudduth 2017b.
[70] Aksoy et al. 2015; Casper & Tyson 2014, 548; Johnson & Thyne 2018.
[71] Bell & Sudduth 2017.
[72] Vinter 2012.
[73] Arbatli & Arbatli 2016; Piplani & Talmadge 2016.
[74] Drawn from Banks 2001; Salehyan et al. 2012
[75] Herbst 2000, 139–172.

expulsions and sanctions following the Lomé Declaration of 2000;[76] and anti-colonial war fighting. Anti-colonial insurgencies could have served to build and unify the nation while granting the new leadership vital experience in exerting control over the armed forces, thereby dampening both ethnic conflict and civil-military strife.[77] Alternatively, fighting a rural insurgency may have created norms of violent resistance instead of the more democratic legacies created by non-violent urban protest movements against colonialism.[78] Further robustness checks were conducted by substituting alternative measures for several of the control variables including ethnic fractionalization and dominance,[79] economic shocks,[80] prior coups,[81] and legitimacy.[82] Whether countries experienced ethnic violence in the years preceding decolonization and the vote share captured by ethnic political parties in pre-independence elections were also substituted for *Ethnic parties* to further capture ethnic politicization.

None of these robustness checks meaningfully change the results. During the decolonization period, the ethnic loyalty, unmatched officer corps, and ethnic parties variables retain their direction, general magnitude, and statistical significance. Alternative measures for ethnic politicization indicate that while the vote share captured by ethnic political parties shaped later instability, prior ethnic violence did not. This suggests that the merging of ethnic politics and democratic competition may be more

---

[76] Powell & Lasley 2012; Shannon et al. 2015 find that international reactions are particularly strong when coups target democracies.

[77] Feaver 1999, 223; Robinson 2014.

[78] Wantchékon & García-Ponce 2014.

[79] Competing ethnic fractionalization measures were drawn from Alesina et al. 2003; Fearon 2003; Posner 2004a. Two measures for ethnic dominance were also constructed from Fearon's data: the percent share of the largest group in the total population and whether any group constituted more than 50% of the population.

[80] 3% and 5% economic shock variables were coded in a parallel manner to the original 1% control variable to capture increasing levels of crisis severity. An alternative measure using the country's lowest (i.e., worst) current account balance (CAB) as a percentage of GDP was also constructed. Large current account balance deficits tend to cause, or at least reflect, greater financial struggles as well as a government's inability to pay its employees, including the military.

[81] Alternative measures include the count of prior successful coups in the ten years prior to the power transfer, whether a coup directly led to the power transfer, and the number of years elapsed since the last coup attempt at the time of the transition.

[82] Including Freedom House's raw civil liberties score (2016b); polity and polity squared (Marshall, Gurr, & Jaggers 2016); whether the country was liberalizing or an electoral democracy at the time of the power transfer, following Lindberg and Clark (2008); and whether the Geddes, Wright, & Frantz 2014 project on regime types codes the country as a democracy in the year following the power transfer.

dangerous for political stability than communal violence. The outbreak of civil armed conflict in the immediate years following independence also greatly increased coup risk: from an expected 0.76 coup attempts to 5.22. None of the other controls reached conventional levels of statistical significance, including oil exportation, French colonialism, or fighting an anti-colonial war.

Similarly, the robustness checks for the democratization period did not meaningfully change the results of the baseline models. The prior ethnic stacking and prior coup attempts variables were stable in their direction, magnitude, and statistical significance and all of the alternative measures for prior coups were positive and statistically significant. Indeed, leaders seemed particularly vulnerable to military overthrow when a recent coup instigated the elections that brought them to power. If a coup caused the power transfer, coup risk increased from around 6–7% to 76–77%, all else being equal. Contrary to some recent claims in the coup literature, this suggests that coups do not initiate meaningful and lasting democratic change. The ethnic change variable intermittently gained or lost statistical significance, but was also generally consistent in its direction and magnitude. Few of the other added control variables or alternative measures were significant. Across both the all constitutional and electoral transfers models, expansion of military personnel counter-intuitively increased coup risk. Moving from the mean increase in the number of soldiers to one standard deviation above the mean increased the probability of a coup attempt from 12–13% to 24–25%. Perhaps this measure is capturing the creation of paramilitary or counterbalancing forces by the new leader, which could inspire a coup attempt by the regular armed forces to prevent their overshadowing.[83] For electoral transfers only, oil production, popular unrest, and democracy (as coded by Geddes, Wright, and Frantz),[84] all attained statistical significance and decreased coup risk. Oil wealth may indeed enhance coup-proofing capabilities. The result for popular unrest is counterintuitive and difficult to explain. More internal tumult should increase coup risk rather than dampen it. None of the other controls attained conventional levels of statistical significance, including most of the measures for political legitimacy, natural resources, characteristics of military organizations, French colonialism, or being a member of the African Union.

[83] See De Bruin 2017.
[84] Geddes, Wright, & Frantz 2014

CONCLUSION

The empirical findings of this chapter support the argument that the construction and dismantling of ethnic armies in Africa have led to widespread soldier rebellion, fomenting coups and undermining political stability. In the immediate post-decolonization period, many independence leaders chose to construct military loyalty on ethnic grounds, recruiting coethnics into the security forces. Where the construction of such ethnic armies ran up against existing diversity in the officer corps, losing factions violently resisted their marginalization. Such countries experienced nearly four times as many coup attempts in the first 15 years following decolonization. In the later context of democratization, ethnic armies continued to challenge African political stability when faced with their own dismantling. Where elections or other constitutional means brought to power leaders who no longer ethnically matched the armies they inherited, coup risk increased from under 25% to 50–66%.

Ethnic politicization was also found to strongly shape coup risk, at least in the immediate years following independence. Where political parties had formed and campaigned on an exclusive ethnic basis during the prelude to decolonization, coup attempts were more numerous, increasing by a factor of four. Even leaders who initially sought to build inclusive security institutions struggled in these contexts, often abandoning their efforts and turning to ethnic stacking practices.

Statistical analysis of observational data, however, is subject to limitations. While revealing important, generalizable correlations between theoretical concepts, it cannot itself establish causal effect or account for many important contextual nuances. Thus, while these results strongly support the notion that ethnic politics and practices within military institutions drive many coup attempts, to develop a causal account I now turn to in-depth case study analyses. The following three chapters use process tracing to understand why and how the construction and dismantling of ethnic armies leads to political instability.

3

Building Ethnic Armies: Cameroon and Sierra Leone

Who sai dem tie cow nar day e go eat.

– Sierra Leonean proverb[1]

The goat eats where it is tethered.

– Cameroonian proverb[2]

Building systems of ethnic privilege into important state institutions provokes discontent and even rebellion as non-favored groups resist their declining status. Within security institutions, constructing ethnic armies threatens soldiers disadvantaged by the new recruitment and promotion policies. At best, their career prospects decline as officers of favored groups are promoted above them. Often, they also face purges and mass arrests as the officer corps is ethnically restructured. These soldiers have strong incentives to rebel, staging coups to prevent or reverse their diminishing fortunes. Yet, some diversity must exist for this to occur. If the preexisting officer corps is already dominated by the favored group, or if there is no officer corps to speak of, then there is no one to resist.

This chapter compares two cases where newly independent African states chose to build military loyalty on the basis of ethnic identity, with contrasting results. While Sierra Leone experienced four destabilizing coup attempts in the ten years following independence, Cameroon escaped any such turmoil during this period.[3] I propose that this

---

[1] As quoted in Kpundeh 1994, 146.
[2] As quoted in Bayart 2009, 235.
[3] Cameroon has experienced one failed coup attempt in its post-independence history, in 1984 after the first successful transfer of power.

divergence in civil-military relations is primarily a result of the varying initial conditions that they faced. Though the leaders of each state made similar choices when it came to building a new military, they inherited colonial armies with different ethnic compositions. Colonial officials in Sierra Leone had intentionally created a tribally diverse officer corps, one in which all of the politically relevant ethnic groups were represented. In Cameroon, on the other hand, colonial officials had failed to train native officers prior to the devolution of internal autonomy. They then assisted the government of Ahmadou Ahidjo, which would take up the reigns of power upon independence, in constructing an officer corps of co-ethnics. Thus, when Ahidjo continued to build an ethnic army in the post-independence period there was no minority faction in the officer corps to resist. When the leadership of Sierra Leone, however, attempted to implement the same policies, they faced stiff resistance from ethnic groups already in the military who were to be disenfranchised. Heightened ethnic antagonisms within the military, combined with bitterly contested elections between ethnically-based political parties, tumbled the country rapidly toward instability.

Within each case study, I first discuss the rise of the post-decolonization leader and the context of ethnic politicization they encountered. In both countries, political parties had formed along ethno-regional cleavages and, in Cameroon, the government also faced an ethnically-based insurgency that had been excluded from pre-independence elections. Given this backdrop, I then analyze the choice of each leader to build military loyalty on ethnic grounds and how they attempted to restructure security institutions to favor coethnics. I next examine the potential for resistance, both the composition of the late colonial officer corps as well as any foreign protection that may have existed. Finally, I analyze the path of stability or instability that each country traveled, focusing on the interplay of ethnic military recruitment policies and soldier support for the regime. Here is where the cases sharply diverge: while delving into the mechanisms of stability in Cameroon, in Sierra Leone we are taken on a tumultuous journey of mutinies, plots, coups, and counter-coups.

STABILITY IN CAMEROON

Cameroon has experienced little political instability since independence. Apart from the last gasps of a dying, ethnically-based, anti-colonial rebellion in the early 1960s and a failed military coup attempt in the mid-1980s, Cameroon has escaped the violence that seems endemic to other African countries. What explains this remarkable stability? At root, it can be traced back to the decisions of colonial French administrators who enabled Ahmadou Ahidjo to build strong, authoritarian institutions backed by ethnically loyal security forces. Unlike Sierra Leone, where the departing British colonizers had created a diverse officer corps, the French administrators in Cameroon first neglected to train an officer corps until the very end of colonialism and then supported Ahidjo as he recruited the initial cohort of officer cadets from his own region and ethnic group. Following independence, as he continued to build an ethnic army, Ahidjo unsurprisingly encountered no military resistance. Relying on ethnically loyal security institutions, Ahidjo was then able to centralize his power over the state while coopting the leaders of other ethnic groups through civilian appointments and patronage opportunities. This combination of ethnically inclusive and exclusive practices proved remarkably endurable. Although Ahidjo's retirement and the subsequent transition of power did spark a coup attempt, the new president, Paul Biya, was able to reconstitute Ahidjo's system of rule under a new dominant ethnic group. His government has survived to this day, without incurring much instability and even resisting the heavy pro-democracy pressures of the post-Cold War period.

The Rise of Ahmadou Ahidjo amidst an Ethnically-Based Anti-Colonial Insurgency

Ahmadou Ahidjo was not an obvious or natural choice to lead Cameroon to independence. He had poor nationalist credentials and was from the marginalized Muslim north of the country. Neither he nor his political party commanded a territory-wide following. Nor was he favored by the power brokers of Paris, who tended to prefer his predecessor. Rather, a unique confluence of contingent events and decisions conspired to hand Ahidjo power on the very eve of independence and amidst a serious ethnically-based uprising in the south.

Indeed, the insurgency spearheaded by the Union des Populations du Cameroun (UPC), with its purported ties to international communism, strongly shaped France's decolonization practices in Cameroon. Founded in 1948, and led by Ruben Um Nyobè, the UPC advocated for rapid and total independence, including from French economic domination, as well as the unification of the British and French administered Cameroons.[4] In

---

4 Following World War I, colonial administration over German Kameroun had been split between the two powers under League of Nations trusteeship.

the mid-1950s, the French colonial state turned a strong, repressive hand against the UPC, resulting in a series of riots across the territory. Blaming party militants for the violence, French administrators banned the UPC, prevented its members from running for office in the 1956 parliamentary elections, and pushed the organization underground.[5] In reaction, the UPC formed an armed wing, the Armèe de Liberation Nationale Kamerun (ALNK), that was dominated by members of the southern Bamiléké and Bassa ethnic groups, and began establishing military bases in the jungles of the Sanaga-Maritime region. The ALNK launched its insurgency just prior to the scheduled elections, blocking roads and railways, cutting telephone lines, and assassinating elites, including two legislative candidates.[6] By 1959, a state of emergency had been declared across the entire south of the territory and by 1960 the conflict had spread to the British Cameroons as insurgents fled across the poorly guarded border.[7]

The UPC adopted a socialist leaning ideology and its military wing received training and support from various communist governments, including both China and the USSR. British military intelligence reports are filled with references to the communist funds, arms, and advice flowing to the "terrorist" ALNK.[8] French administrators were also wary of growing communist influences in Africa and saw the UPC as a pro-communist revolutionary organization.[9] Given the escalating Cold War context of the 1950s, these ties furthered Western perceptions that the insurgency represented an extreme security threat. France regarded Cameroon as strategically vital to its interests: the territory was the geographic hinge between French West Africa and French Equatorial Africa and the deep water port at Douala provided waterway access to the natural resources of the central African interior. The UPC insurgency thus threatened not only France's interests in the territory itself, but also in the broader region.

But perhaps more importantly, French administrators viewed the Cameroonian insurgency as tightly linked to events transpiring in Algeria. As Atangana, a historian of Cameroon's decolonization, argues, "...the

---

[5] Atangana 2010, 17; Awasom 2002, 7.

[6] Atangana 2010, 16–24; Minority Rights Group 2010; Stark 1980, 276.

[7] Awasom 2002, 9; Harkness & Hunzeker 2015, 787.

[8] TNA WO 208/4386 52A, "Annex A to 1 King's Own Border Group Perintrep 8/61: Overseas Training ALNK Terrorists," May 1–15, 1961; TNA WO 208/4386 80A, "Notes on the Gren Gds Stay in the Cameroons," October 16, 1961; TNA WO 208/4385 57A, "1 Kings Own Border Group Intelligence Review, Southern Cameroons," June 21, 1961.

[9] Awasom 2002, 9.

outbreak of the Algerian revolution in 1954 was considered by France to be not only a new challenge, but also a gangrene whose spread had to stop immediately. It was essential for the French authorities that the request of independence by the UPC should not create a precedent in Black Africa."[10] Negotiation with the UPC, let alone political inclusion, carried the risk of setting expectations for the Algerian insurgents – a territory that French leaders and many citizens held to be an integral part of the metropole. These considerations of the broader, international ramifications of policy towards Cameroon only served to redouble France's efforts to exclude the UPC and its sympathizers from the government.

Fearing the loss of Cameroon to the Soviet bloc, as well as the precedent that devolving power onto an active insurgency would set for Algeria, the French marginalized the UPC from pre-independence elections and searched instead for a moderate government that would maintain strong ties with the French community, preserve French economic interests and access to natural resources, adopt a gradual approach to independence, and shun communist overtures.[11] Initially, in May 1957, when the French still retained broad powers over territorial governance, the High Commissioner appointed André-Marie Mbida as the first Prime Minister of Cameroon. Mbida was the leader of the moderate Démocrates Camerounais political party and was associated with the cohesive Catholic center of the political spectrum.[12]

The appointment of a new High Commissioner, Jean Ramadier, upended these arrangements. Arriving within a year of Mbida's appointment, Ramadier decided his leadership was detrimental to both the future of Cameroon and French interests. Hoping to avoid an expansion of the insurgency and an increase in France's troop commitments, Ramadier sought a political solution to the conflict. He considered Mbida too autocratic and too ruthless to make the necessary compromises. Indeed, Mbida had publicly proclaimed that "the whole of Cameroon will come together to exterminate the Bassa."[13] Such rhetoric not only further enraged the UPC, but alienated the populations of the British Cameroons, who were scheduled to vote on unification in 1960. This undermined another important French goal, in Ramadier's opinion.[14] He thus began searching for a new prime minister, turning to the

---

10 Atangana 2010, 14.
11 Mbaku 2003, 44
12 Atangana 2010, 40–41.
13 Mbida as quoted in Atangana 2010, 56.
14 Atangana 2010, 64–66.

remaining moderates in the legislature: Ahmadou and the Groupe d'Union Camerounaise, a northern Muslim political party dominated by the Peuhl and Fulani, which had previously publicly opposed demands for immediate independence.[15] Together, Ahidjo and Ramadier manufactured a cabinet crisis that resulted in the fall of Mbida's government and allowed Ramadier, as High Commissioner, to promote Ahidjo as Prime Minister. This was orchestrated without metropolitan approval and Ramadier was subsequently recalled to France to face disciplinary action for insubordination.[16]

The French thereby created a potentially combustible situation: installing a government that was ethnically, religiously, and regionally distinct from an ongoing insurgency. While communal violence was not yet a reality in Cameroon, its specter hung over the new government. Although the UPC had originated as an anti-colonial uprising, targeting the French colonial state, it considered Ahidjo and his political party illegitimate and vowed to continue fighting. It was in this context that Ahmadou Ahidjo made his choices over how to construct the new national army.

Building an Ethnic Army: Northern Fulani and Peuhl Dominance

Ahidjo's ascendency immediately preceded deep political upheaval in France, caused by the protracted and bloody counterinsurgency in Algeria. In 1958, France's military commanders revolted, resulting in the collapse of the Fourth Republic and the return of Charles de Gaulle to power. Bent on retrenching the French empire, de Gaulle immediately accelerated decolonization processes envisioned to last more than a decade, rapidly devolving powers of self-government to overseas territories. In Cameroon's case, this encompassed full control over legislative and regulatory matters, from the appointment of ministers to the management of the civil service. It also included power over internal defense, which at the time entailed creating a national army and training an officer corps as France began dissolving its regional security forces and transferring their constituent units to the territories.[17] Ahidjo thus gained broad discretion in the early construction of Cameroon's military and officer corps while still under French colonial rule.

---

[15] Ibid., 38; Joseph 1978, 52.
[16] Atangana 2010, 74.
[17] Ibid., 98.

Using his powers over the transitional state, Ahmadou Ahidjo built a coethnic army and presidential guard who benefited not only from preferential recruitment and promotion policies but also gained access to extensive patronage. Ahidjo hailed from the Muslim Fulani people of the northern reaches of Cameroon.[18] Reflecting this, the initial cohorts of native Cameroonian army officers, trained at the newly established cadet school in Yaounde, were recruited extensively from the north and from the Fulani and Peuhl ethnic groups in particular. These coethnic recruitment practices continued in subsequent cohorts.[19] Shortly following independence, Ahidjo also founded an elite paramilitary presidential guard unit that was charged with his protection and operated outside the normal command structure of the army. Into this elite unit, who received the highest patronage rewards available in the security sector, Ahidjo exclusively recruited not merely coethnics, but coethnics from his hometown.[20] Ahidjo thus used his powers over the formation of the new national army and other paramilitary organizations to recruit officers that matched his own identity as well as the ethnic power base of his political party.

Low Potential for Resistance: Absence of a Colonial Officer Corps and French Protection

At the time that Ahidjo rose to power and began to influence officer recruitment, the native Cameroonian officer corps was practically nonexistent, giving him a free hand to construct an ethnically-based army without opposition. The first cohorts of native Cameroonian officers only began graduating from the Yaoundé cadet school post-independence, in 1960–1961, being shortly thereafter integrated into active military units.[21] Even with this influx, only 54 of 175 officers were Cameroonian, the rest being seconded from the French military. Of these, only one Cameroonian had achieved a rank higher than lieutenant (a captain). Most graduating cadets received the lowest commissioned rank of second lieutenant.[22] Similarly, the Gendarmes, an elite force of rural military

---

[18] The Fulani are also variously called Fulbe or Fula and span many contemporary Sahelian states in sub-Saharan Africa (Konings 1996, 247).

[19] Minorities at Risk 2009; Minority Rights Group 2010.

[20] DeLancey 1987, 17.

[21] TNA WO 208/4386 71A, "MILO Report No. 16," August 28, 1961.

[22] TNA WO 208/4386 1A, "Appendix to Perintemp 4/60: A Short Up to Date Survey of the Cameroun Republic," November 1, 1960; TNA WO 208/4386 65A, "MILO Report No.15," July 26, 1981; TNA WO 208/4386 80A "Notes on the Gren Gds Stay in the Cameroons," October 16, 1961.

policeman, possessed only 39 Cameroonian officers for a force larger than the army in 1961.[23] Thus, unlike in much of West Africa where a small group of commissioned officers existed prior to decolonization, and could thus be promoted to fill part of the field grade and senior ranks, in Cameroon the officer corps was being constructed from a blank slate. Without any preexisting faction available within the officer corps to resist ethnic restructuring, Ahidjo could manipulate recruitment and promotion as he saw fit without fearing a revolt.

In addition to the opportunities afforded by the absence of a preexisting officer corps, Ahidjo also benefited from extensive French military support and protection in the early years of his rule. First, the dearth of native officers resulted, correspondingly, in a preponderance of seconded French military personnel following independence. In 1961, 69% of army officers were French.[24] By 1971, a majority of senior military officers were still on loan from the French government.[25] Even as late as 1981, there were around 70 French military personnel advising and training the Cameroonian army.[26] With so many Frenchmen in key command and control positions in the immediate postcolonial period, the ability of disgruntled Cameroonian officers to covertly organize and stage a mutiny or coup was low.

Due to the ongoing insurgency in the south, moreover, Ahidjo had requested and been granted the continued assistance of French combat troops. Even though independence had been the primary war aim of the UPC/ALNK, its granting did not end hostilities but rather intensified the conflict. Because the UPC had been banned from participating in the 1956 elections, they considered Mbida's and then Ahidjo's government unrepresentative and illegitimate. After de Gaulle devolved powers of internal governance to Cameroon and made a firm commitment to rapid independence, the UPC did temporarily suspend military operations. They simultaneously called for new elections to form a properly representative government prior to decolonization. Neither Ahidjo's government nor the French, however, wanted to risk such elections. The issue was brought before the United Nations, where Cameroonians possessed the right to raise matters as a trustee territory. Yet, the vote fell along typical Cold War lines and the UN ultimately backed France's decision not to hold new,

[23] TNA WO 208/4385 60A, "MILO Report No. 13," June 28, 1961.
[24] TNA WO 208/4386 80A, "Notes on the Gren Gds Stay in the Cameroons," October 16, 1961.
[25] Joseph 1978, 16.
[26] Takougang 1993, 280.

territory-wide elections prior to independence. This effectively politically marginalized the UPC and the south in general. The UPC relaunched the insurgency, accusing Ahidjo's government of being nothing more than a French puppet.[27]

Facing mass violence in the south, Ahidjo turned to the French for continued security assistance. He signed a military cooperation agreement with France at the end of 1959 and then, in early 1960, requested two full strength combat battalions to aid in suppressing the UPC/ALNK.[28] By the eve of independence, one such battalion was already deployed in the south, remaining until 1964.[29] Thus, Ahidjo had two sources of French military protection in the early years after independence: seconded officers to command the regular army and combat troops to help quell internal dissent. This provided him ample protection, given continued French support for his regime, to restructure Cameroonian institutions as he saw fit.

Resulting Stability: An Ethnic Army and Secure Authoritarian Rule

Decolonization thus entailed handing power to a northern-dominated and western-friendly government led by Ahmadou Ahidjo, backed by a coethnic army comprised predominantly of northern Fulani and Peuhl. Because Ahidjo was able to exert control over military recruitment prior to the existence of a native officer corps, there was no possible intra-military resistance to his construction of an ethnic army. French protection provided a further defense against military challenges. This sequencing of events marks a critical difference from cases like Sierra Leone, where the same policies were attempted but against a diverse, preexisting officer corps who could rebel.

Through a combination of ethnic loyalty and patronage, Ahidjo maintained strong control over security institutions. From the time the Ahidjo government attained significant powers of self-government in 1958, until Ahidjo retired in 1982, members of the northern Fulani and Peuhl groups were recruited extensively into the army and presidential guard.[30] Ahidjo also personally appointed all high-ranking military officers, privileging personal loyalty over merit and even seniority.[31] Such

---

[27] Atangana 2010, 102–107.
[28] Awasom 2002, 18; Takougang 2003b, 85.
[29] Atangana 2010, 124; TNA WO 208/4386 24A, "MILO Report No. 6," February 18, 1961.
[30] Minorities at Risk Project 2009.
[31] Takougang 2003a, 102.

ethnic and personal loyalty were further combined and reinforced with extensive patronage benefits. Senior officers were granted lucrative private business opportunities, in addition to their salaries and other perks, and even rank-and-file soldiers were routinely granted pay raises.[32]

Unchallenged control over the security sector provided Ahidjo a power base from which to enact other institutional changes that reinforced the autocratic stability of the Cameroonian state. First, Ahidjo designed and redesigned the constitution to prevent the rise of legal, democratic challenges to his reign. Just prior to decolonization, the parliament granted emergency powers to Ahidjo and permitted him nearly exclusive jurisdiction over the drafting of the original constitution.[33] The result was a unitary state with power concentrated in the presidency.[34] After the British Cameroons united with the French Cameroons, Ahidjo then dissolved congress with the help of the army, further concentrating constitutional powers in his own hands. He now fully controlled the appointment and termination of ministers, judges, and governors. He also dominated the procedures for introducing new legislation and could veto bills with no option for an override. The constitution additionally permitted its own easy amendment and, as a last resort, allowed the president to rule by decree if necessary.[35] Finally, in 1972, the Unitary Constitution was adopted which abolished the remaining autonomy of state and local institutions.[36] Cameroon had virtually no institutional checks left against presidential power.

Second, Ahidjo transformed the electoral system such that no opposition leader or party could realistically challenge him. Rather than directly outlaw opposition parties, Ahidjo implemented a winner-take-all, single-list system with the entire country constituting the sole electoral district. Winning more than 50% of the national vote thus granted the victorious political party both the presidency and every seat in the legislature. Given Ahidjo's vast incumbency advantages, including control over the media and use of the security services to harass and repress the opposition, no other party could hope to win. As head of the reconstituted Union Nationale Camerounaise (UNC), Ahidjo also presided over the composition of his party's election lists, allowing him to manipulate the distribution of legislative seats. This created strong incentives for

[32] Takougang 1993, 276–277; Takougang 2003b, 76–77.
[33] Awasom 2002, 14.
[34] Ibid., 24.
[35] DeLancey 1987, 11–12; Stark 1980, 281.
[36] DeLancey 1987, 6; Takougang 1993, 273.

legislators to cooperate fully with his agenda, lest they find themselves replaced with more pliable candidates. Thus, although opposition parties remained legal and could compete in elections, a de facto one-party state was fully entrenched by 1966.[37]

Finally, Ahidjo used government resources to coopt the leaders of important ethnic groups, tying them and their constituents to the state through extensive patronage. Cameroon is an ethnically complex society, comprised of more than 200 groups and subgroups that are nested and intermingled in intricate ways.[38] Using a sophisticated "ethnic arithmetic," that was sensitive to preserving ethnic and regional balance, Ahidjo included important identity groups within the civilian side of the administration by appointing tribal and ethnic leaders as ministers, legislators, and managers of state-owned enterprises.[39] With these positions came access to funds and projects that could then be distributed amongst their clients and within their ethnic homelands. Groups thus felt represented in government, though certainly not democratically, and that they had some recourse to power.[40]

Continued access to government resources depended on cooperation within the system and dissent resulted not only in expulsion from the government's largesse, but repression. Violence was often used against those who could not be coopted, with military troops directly deployed to extinguish the remnants of the UPC rebellion in the 1960s and to suppress protests and demonstrations throughout the 1970s.[41] Ethnic groups relegated outside of the cooptation system would also find themselves at the mercy of the state's northern-dominated security institutions, who were used to dampen dissent when it arose.[42] Those included in the system faced weighty incentives to remain loyal while repression by the ethnic army and presidential guard was levied against those who resisted cooptation.

Thus, the power generated by an ethnic army allowed Ahidjo to build other self-reinforcing institutions of dominance that, together, perpetuated his rule for over 20 years. The stability of these institutions

---

37 DeLancey 1987, 5–12.
38 Gros 1995, 115.
39 There is some evidence that Ahidjo did prefer fellow Fulani in the allocation of resources and opportunities, especially those from his hometown of Garoua, and that the Bamiléké received privileged business opportunities (Konings 1996, 249).
40 Konings 1996, 248; Takougang 1993, 271–275; Takougang 2003b, 76.
41 Takougang 1993, 278; Takougang 2003b, 77.
42 DeLancey 1987, 5–6 &15–16.

was remarkable. As repeated coups felled regimes and rebellions and civil wars broke out across Africa, following independence Cameroon definitively defeated the UPC rebellion and steered clear of any civil-military instability for over two decades.

After Ahidjo: The Coup Attempt and the Reconsolidation of Stability under Biya

Further evidence that Cameroon's stability was fundamentally grounded in the coethnic patronage ties between Ahidjo and his security institutions can be found in the momentary instability following his departure from office. Convinced of his own severe illness and pending mortality, in 1982, after 22 years of rule, Ahmadou Ahidjo retired. Following constitutional procedures, he was succeeded by his hand-picked successor, Paul Biya. Although a Christian southerner from the ethnic Bulu subgroup of the Beti, Biya was a long time regime insider and had served as prime minister under Ahidjo from 1975 until his promotion to vice president.[43] In January 1984, Biya secured his presidency by winning his first full term in a carefully controlled, and by no means democratic, national election.

Shortly thereafter, Biya began to take actions against both the former president and his military. In February, Ahidjo was convicted and sentenced to death in abstentia by the Yaoundè military court for subversion and conspiracy to carry out revolution.[44] In April, Biya announced that he would soon begin transferring northerners out of the elite Republican Guard to other military units. At the time, the Republican Guard numbered around 1000 soldiers and was still strongly dominated by northern Fulani and Peuhl.[45] Although the reporting is scarce and unreliable, Biya may have been motivated by earlier rumored assassination plots that suggested a northern-based conspiracy against his rule.[46]

The day after Biya proclaimed his intentions to move against the Republican Guard, on April 6th, the unit mounted a coup attempt against him. The rebels took control of the radio station, attacked the presidential palace in Yaoundè with artillery, seized the airport, and severed communication links with the outside world. It took nearly four days of intense fighting for loyal troops to put down the rebellion. It was claimed, at the time, both by the Minister of State for the

---

[43] Konings 1996, 250; Takougang 1993, 269.
[44] BBC 1984 (March 1).
[45] *Keesings* 1984, v.30 (September).
[46] Takougang 1993, 284.

Armed Forces, Gilbert Andze Tsoungui, and by the Army Chief of Staff, General Pierre Semengue, that all of the rebels were northern Muslims.[47] Subsequent analyses have concurred that the coup attempt was conducted predominantly by northern Muslims, although the loyalist soldiers who defended Biya hailed from all regions, including the north.[48]

Using the failed coup attempt to his advantage, Biya then reconstituted Ahidjo's system of governance under Beti dominated security institutions. Following the coup, a police state was imposed with areas of the north subjected to a six-month "military clampdown," involving roadblocks and security checks, while the northern-dominated Republican Guard was disbanded, its loyal members retained and placed under the command of the Gendarmerie.[49] Biya then moved forward with discriminatory recruitment and promotion policies of his own: southerners, especially the Beti ethnic group and the Bulu clans within it, came to dominate the military and disproportionately hold key command positions in the officer corps.[50] Biya also maintained the accustomed financial perks of officership, reinforcing once again ethnic loyalty with material patronage benefits.[51]

On the civilian side, Biya has kept some of the ethnic and regional balancing in government appointments characteristic of the Ahidjo regime.[52] Accusations of Beti favoritism, however, abound. To consolidate his power, Biya seems to have granted disproportionate business opportunities as well as ministerial and civil service positions to the so-called "Beti Mafia."[53] According to Takougang, 37 of 47 senior prefects, 75% of the directors and managers of state-owned corporations, and 22 of 38 high-ranking bureaucrats in the prime minister's office were ethnically Beti by the early 2000s.[54] This suggests a heavier reliance on systems of ethnic privilege, in both civilian and military institutions, than even Ahidjo maintained.

Once again, the stability generated by such practices of ethnic loyalty and patronage seems remarkable. Biya has not faced any subsequent coup attempts nor has the regime confronted a significant insurgency. Nor did Cameroon's autocratic institutions succumb to democratization pressures following the end of the Cold War, even given significant domestic protests

47 *Keesings* 1984, v.30 (September).
48 Gros 1995, 115; Takougang 1993, 284.
49 *Keesings* 1984, v.30 (September); Konings 1996, 251.
50 Gros 1995, 122; Minorities at Risk 2009; Minority Rights Group 2010.
51 Takougang 1993, 289.
52 Ibid., 287.
53 Konings 1996, 251.
54 Takougang 2003a, 108.

and a partial return to multiparty politics. In 1991, a national movement calling itself Opération Villes Mortes (Operation Ghost Town) attempted to shut down the towns and cities until Biya authorized a constitutional conference and embarked on true democratization. Despite widespread participation, the campaign did not seriously endanger the regime nor provoke any threat of military insubordination.[55] Notwithstanding competitive multiparty elections in 1992, moreover, Biya not only survived an election noted for the emergence of ethnic political parties, but was able to reconsolidate his power in its aftermath.

Throughout this period of democratization pressures, the military was used extensively to repress demonstrations and dissent.[56] Indeed, Gros writes that "the support of the military and the security forces for the Biya government was probably the single most important domestic factor behind the failure of transition to multiparty politics."[57] Biya's ethnic army has played a fundamental role in guaranteeing regime stability and survival.

That this stability is rooted in Biya's personal and centralized control over the political system and his reliance on an ethnically loyal and patronage spoiled military, creates worries for the future. President Biya is not a young man, having now ruled Cameroon for over three decades. Another leadership transition is imminent, whether by autocratic or democratic means. If a northerner returns to power, or perhaps even if a rival southern group claims the presidency, then this next transition could engender another moment of potential institutional crisis – creating opportunities for political change as well as the danger of destabilization.

Alternative Explanations

Alternative theories emphasize economic factors and general practices of ethnic exclusion, but neither predict the occurrence or timing of Cameroon's one coup attempt. Important ethnic groups were generally granted access to patronage resources, through the civilian side of the government, under Ahidjo and in the early years of the Biya government. Indeed, it was only after the coup attempt that evidence emerges of Beti favoritism and this did not result in additional coup attempts. Ethnic exclusion on the military side was constant under Ahidjo and, later,

55 Gros 1995, 117–120.
56 Takougang 1993, 296.
57 Gros 1995, 121.

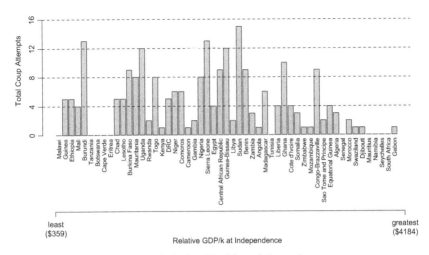

FIGURE 3.1. Relative Wealth and Coup Attempts

under Biya. These long periods of exclusion also failed to result in soldier rebellion. It was only in the transitionary period, when Biya attempted to dismantle Ahidjo's coethnic presidential guard, threatening the privileged position of its members, that rebellion unfolded.

Typical economic explanations also poorly explain Cameroon's coup history. Cameroon gained independence with below average wealth, even for Africa, and a similar GDP per capita level to Sierra Leone (see Figure 3.1). Cameroon's economy was also highly dependent on exports, mostly agricultural products such as cocoa, coffee, bananas and palm oil, creating high exposure to global market fluctuations. The discovery of oil in the mid-1970s also added a lucrative, non-agricultural, natural resource into the mix.[58] Yet, Cameroon has experienced relatively few coup attempts despite its poverty and vulnerable economy. Cameroon's only coup attempt, moreover, transpired during a period of strong growth and no coups occurred amidst Cameroon's long and severe recession between the mid-1980s and mid-1990s (see Figure 3.2).

Here, ethnic manipulations within the military, specifically the attempted dismantling of the ethnically-based presidential guard, provide a far more compelling explanation for Cameroon's coup attempt than economic structural risk factors. Ethnic loyalty works when leaders can build from a blank canvas: when there are no existing soldiers to rebel

---

[58] Konings 1996, 246; Takougang 2003a, 112.

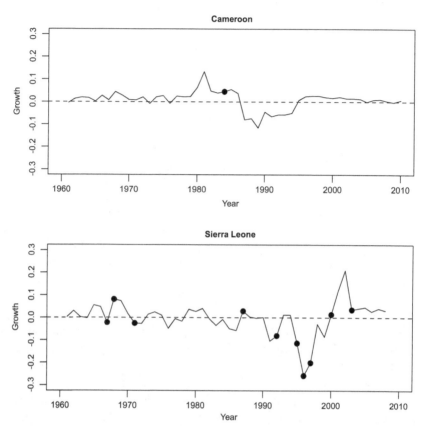

FIGURE 3.2. Economic Growth and Coup Attempts: Cameroon and Sierra Leone

as in Ahidjo's case. Deconstructing ethnic armies, however, provokes rebellion as soon-to-be disadvantaged soldiers resist their downgrading and fight to preserve their privileged position. The presidential guard attacked Biya precisely because he threatened to undo its existing ethnic basis.

INSTABILITY IN SIERRA LEONE

Sierra Leone's democratic future looked bright as independence neared. The colony had a long history of local elections and participation in politics, at least within Freetown, dating back to the early nineteenth century. As the franchise was extended outward to the provinces in the run-up to decolonization, the historic cleavage between Creoles and other ethnic groups softened and a strong but seemingly loyal opposition party emerged. And apart from a series of strikes and anti-tax riots in 1955, the road to independence was generally peaceful.[59] Despite these promising circumstances, within a decade the country had witnessed three successful military coups and had reached the brink of widespread ethnic conflict more than once. The root of this instability can be traced back to the government of Sir Albert Margai and his efforts to build a coethnic, Mende-dominated army, despite inheriting an ethnically diverse officer corps from the departing British. Sir Albert's military restructuring inspired a failed coup plot by Temne and other northern officers, leading to subsequent purges. Fearing the loss of their newly acquired dominance, Mende officers then intervened in elections when it became apparent that the northern-based political party had won. More plots, coups, and counter-coups followed as ethnic tensions within the military spiraled out of control. Stability was only achieved after a mutiny turned coup imprisoned the entire officer corps and immediately handed power back to a civilian regime, under the leadership of Siaka Stevens. Benefiting from both a non-existent officer corps and protection from Guinean bodyguards and combat troops, Stevens then successfully built coethnic security institutions dominated by the northern Limba. Civil-military strife abated for almost two decades under these arrangements until both external and internal wars destabilized the regime.

The Rise of Sir Albert Margai amidst Growing Ethnic Politicization

Sierra Leone gained independence in 1961, under the leadership of Prime Minister Milton Margai and the Sierra Leone People's Party (SLPP), with a robust opposition based in the north. Margai hailed from the southern Mende ethnic group and the Mende were also perceived to dominate the leadership of the SLPP and the growing civil service.[60] Although Milton's government extended patronage to northern chiefs and some northern leaders were coopted into his government,[61] an opposition party quickly gained ground amongst the northern ethnic groups, especially the Temne. Due to the early Islamization of the north, Christian missionaries had worked primarily amongst the animists in the southern reaches of the territory, granting the Mende and Sherbro an advantage in educational attainment and, as a result, in economic,

---

[59] Clapham 1976, 13–14; Cole 2013b, 163.
[60] Bebler 1975, 64; Cartwright 1972, 73.
[61] Kandeh 1992, 91.

civil service, and political leadership opportunities. Infrastructure such as roads, rails, and schools were also concentrated in the south, generating relative deprivation inspired grievances amongst northerners. Abuses by northern chiefs combined with perceptions of Mende domination and advantage, fueled the rise of the All People's Congress (APC) as the primary, if regionally and ethnically-based, opposition to the SLPP.[62]

During his mere three years of rule, Milton Margai paid little heed to the new national army, leaving the force essentially in the hands of the British. British officers not only continued to command the force, constituting the majority of the officer corps, but they also managed rank-and-file recruitment, trained and commissioned the small but growing pool of native officers, and stood as the final arbiters over promotions.[63] It was thus not Milton Margai who shaped the loyalty basis of the army, or influenced its later role in politics, but his successor.

Milton Margai's death in 1964 resulted in a contentious internal SLPP process of determining the next party and government leader. Milton's brother, Sir Albert Margai, emerged victorious over his principal rival, Dr. John Karefa-Smart (a northerner), ensuring continuity of Mende leadership and heightening beliefs of southern Mende dominance over the government. Sir Albert further fed into these perceptions by requiring demonstrations of personal loyalty in order to gain appointment to office, which sometimes included an ethnic dimension. He also diminished the number of Temne ministers in his cabinet by half. Albert Margai's government, from the beginning, thus faced increasing opposition from non-Mende ethnic groups, particularly in the north.[64]

Building an Ethnic Army: Mende Dominance

Within this context, Sir Albert had begun questioning both the continued role of the British in officering Sierra Leone's military and the loyalty basis of his security institutions. Many of Margai's domestic policies faced stiff opposition, particularly his proposal to transform the government into a one-party state – which only furthered fears of Mende domination.[65] Albert had also taken to using the military and police to intimidate dissidents and his growing number of political opponents. He often

[62] Cartwright 1972, 73–74; Kandeh 1992, 86.
[63] Cox 1976, 54 & 73.
[64] Clapham 1976, 14–15; Hayward 1984, 23; Kandeh 1992, 93.
[65] *Keesings* 1967, v.13 (April).

traveled with detachments of soldiers to rural areas, harkening back to the colonial practice of "showing the flag": regularly parading military troops through the districts in order to demonstrate the strength of the state and deter rebellion.[66] This increased reliance on the military for internal security, in a context of growing ethnic tensions, raised questions as to its future loyalty. A military coup that same year in nearby Ghana, as well as outcries across the region against the slow Africanization of military command hierarchies, further generated fears of mutinies and coups from the very institutions that were supposed to protect the government.[67]

In response to these events at home and abroad, Sir Albert decided to bind military officers to civilian authorities through ethnic loyalty. In 1965, when operational command of the Sierra Leone military was transferred from the British, it was vested in Brigadier David Lansana, an ethnic Mende and relative of Albert Margai by marriage.[68] Lansana then oversaw the restructuring of the officer corps after Margai dismissed most of the seconded British officers and assumed control over military recruitment and promotion in mid-1966. A local officer training academy was also established in March 1966, allowing complete circumvention of the British in selecting and training new officers.[69] This opened the door to full ethnic stacking.

Lansana quickly began recruiting fellow Mendes to replace the departing British officers, gaining a reputation within the military for allowing "political and tribal affiliations" to heavily affect his recruitment and promotion decisions.[70] The military at this time remained small: a single infantry battalion based in Freetown and a company stationed on the Guinean border, collectively comprising 1300 men with only about 50 officers and NCOs.[71] Rapid changes in force composition were thus easily achieved. Within a year, Sir Albert had doubled Mende representation in the officer corps. According to Cox, a historian of the Sierra Leone

---

[66] Cole 2013a, 7.

[67] Cox 1976, 73.

[68] The National Archives of the UK (TNA), Foreign and Commonwealth Office (FCO) 38/28 24, "Sierra Leone: The Internal Situation and the Possibility of an Army Mutiny or Coup d'Etat (second draft)," February 3, 1967; Cole 2013b, 166.

[69] Cox 1976, 74.

[70] TNA FCO 38/28 24, "Sierra Leone: The Internal Situation and the Possibility of an Army Mutiny or Coup d'Etat (second draft)," February 3, 1967. See also Cox 1976, 73; Kandeh 1992, 93.

[71] Bebler 1975, 71.

military, Mende identity became "the sole basis for one's recruitment as an officer."[72] He further documents that:

Between mid-1964 and mid-1967 – Sir Albert Margai's period of tenure – the African contingent of the Sierra Leone officer corps more than doubled in size from an establishment of thirty-four men to one of seventy-nine. Whereas Mendes represented some 26 percent of the total at the time of Sir Milton's death, by mid-1967 their proportion of the entire officer corps had reached approximately 52 percent, well over the Mende proportion of the population as a whole. Furthermore, of the forty-five officers commissioned in that three-year period, some twenty-nine or 64 percent were Mendes.[73]

Additionally, Lansana selected a group of junior officers and NCOs, all of Mende identity and trained by Israeli security experts, to serve as a personal guard for himself and Prime Minister Margai.[74] Thus, within only a few years, rapid Africanization of the officer corps was combined with disproportionate Mende recruitment to create a Mende-dominated officer corps and praetorian guard.

High Potential for Resistance: Ethnic Diversity in the Officer Corps and the Absence of British Protection

Unlike in Cameroon, Sir Albert attempted to build this ethnic army against a backdrop of existing diversity amongst Sierra Leone's officers. There had long been an official policy of tribal balance amongst the rank-and-file in the colonial military, although recruitment difficulties outside the south had created some concerns about Mende overrepresentation. This meant that there was an ethnically diverse pool of NCOs from which to draw potential officers as Africanization of the officer corps began. Such Africanization had progressed extremely slowly, mostly due to Milton Margai's fervent gradualism. At the time of independence, there were only six African officers out of 60.[75] In April 1964, the closest point of available data prior to the start of Sir Albert Margai's military restructuring, there were still only a total of 34 African officers: 26% of whom were Mende, 12% Temne, and the remaining 64% were drawn from other tribes, mostly from the Muslim north.[76] Even after significant

---

72 Cox 1976, 73.
73 Ibid., 75.
74 TNA FCO 38/29 66, "Attempted Coup by Group of Sierra Leone Army Officers," February 10, 1967; TNA FCO 38/34 42, "Freetown Despatch No. 4, Sierra Leone: National Reformation Council: The First Month," April 26, 1967.
75 Cole 2013b, 159 & 165.
76 Cox 1976, 54.

changes in recruitment had already taken place, the middle officer ranks at the end of 1966 included only four Mendes out of a total of 13.[77] When ethnic restructuring began, there were thus many non-Mende officers within the army that were capable of organizing resistance against practices that threatened to increase Mende domination.

Combining rapid Africanization with coethnic recruitment also meant that Sir Albert and Brigadier Lansana largely forewent any British protection from which they might have benefited. Under Milton Margi, the British had maintained a strong contingent of seconded officers immediately following decolonization. The official handover day for the Sierra Leone army preceded independence by roughly two years. According to British military documents, at that time 51 British officers and 46 NCOs were to remain with the force. Pay scales had also yet to be constructed for higher ranking African officers, indicating that the few current native officers were of low rank.[78] As previously noted, by independence these numbers had hardly improved and the army still relied heavily on seconded British officers and NCOs.

By the time Albert Margai had assumed power and begun his construction of a Mende-dominated force, however, the British presence had significantly declined. In 1963–1964, the number of seconded British officers had been reduced to around 15 out of 50, reliance on British NCOs had decreased to 20 out of 132, and British financial support of the military budget had shrunk from 71% to 25%.[79] Native officers had also been promoted to some of the higher ranks, including the position of force commander. Prior to the start of restructuring, then, the British presence in the Sierra Leone military had already greatly diminished. The final departure of the British, which had concluded by December 1968, however, overlapped with the beginning of Albert Margai's ethnic restructuring efforts. Unfortunately, hard data is unavailable for 1965–1966, limiting our ability to understand the interaction between declining British involvement and the original implementation and escalation of ethnic recruitment practices.

What can be pieced together is that the British likely afforded a minimal deterrent to military plotting in 1966, a deterrent that almost completely ceased to exist by early 1967. First, the British draw down was rapid, with only eight seconded officers and four other ranks remaining

---

[77] Ibid., 78.
[78] TNA CO 968/681 22A, "Paying the Difference," December 10, 1958.
[79] Cox 1976, 41–45; Kandeh 1992, 93.

by the beginning of 1967. Their duties primarily concerned training and administration.[80] By the end of the year, only three British officers remained and they departed soon thereafter.[81] Moreover, as the British withdrew, they increasingly held relatively unimportant positions, such as bandmaster and force paymaster, and ceased holding field command or general staff positions.[82] This limited their ability to directly interfere with a coup plot. Finally, the terms of officer secondment furthermore proscribed the use of British officers during any hostilities, including internal conflict, without the explicit consent of the United Kingdom government. The British representatives were insistent on this point and, during later troubles, the High Commissioner repeatedly informed the Sierra Leone government that there would be no British intervention or assistance forthcoming in the event of a military coup.[83] It thus seems reasonable to conclude that what influence the British retained at the start of the restructuring period, which they curtailed through their own policies, had fully dissipated within a year. The Sierra Leone government was thus afforded little opportunity for protection were they to encounter a challenge from their own military.

The Resulting Instability: Coups and Counter-Coups

The instability that followed Prime Minister Margai and Brigadier Lansana's military restructuring exhibits both the dynamics of out-group officers resisting the construction of an ethnic army and in-group officers fighting to maintain their established privileges. Fueled by fears of exclusion, non-Mende officers hatched a coup plot in early 1967. Foiled by incompetence and leaked information, the failed plot was met with purges and further Mende domination. Having only just gained preeminence over the military, the Mende officers then witnessed their leader and political party lose narrowly at the polls. No sooner had

---

[80] TNA FCO 38/28 5, "Request for British Assistance in the Event of an Army Mutiny or Coup d'Etat," February 1, 1967.

[81] TNA FCO 65/498 8, "Round-up as at 6 December," December 6, 1968; Kandeh 1992, 93.

[82] Cox 1976, 61.

[83] The National Archives of the UK (TNA), Dominions Office (DO) 118/315, "Exchange of Letters Concerning the Arrangements for the Secondment of Personnel of the Armed Forces of the United Kingdom to Serve with the Royal Sierra Leone Military Forces," January 21, 1965; TNA FCO 38/28 11, "Telegram from Commonwealth Office to Freetown," February 1, 1967; TNA FCO 38/30 43, "Note for the Secretary of State: Sierra Leone: The General Election," March 22, 1967.

Siaka Steven's and the northern-based APC been sworn into office, than Brigadier Lansana seized power. His coup rapidly unleashed discontent, a counter-coup, and the establishment of a military junta that turned to northern officers and soldiers for support. Mende resistance to this turn of fate resulted in frequent rumors of coup plots, arrests, and the heightening of ethnic tensions within the ranks. This, combined with poor pay and living conditions and the increasing graft of senior officers, resulted in a rank-and-file mutiny. Having arrested the entirety of the officer corps, the mutineers handed power over to Siaka Stevens as the declared winner of the last election. Now unencumbered by an existing officer corps, Stevens was able to create a northern-dominated military without facing resistance. However, his later attempts to narrow the ethnic base of the military even further, to just fellow Limba, inspired one last failed coup attempt by Temne officers resisting their exclusion. Thereafter, the state was stabilized under Stevens' coethnic Limba army aided by the protection of foreign Guinean troops. In Sierra Leone, officers resisted the construction of ethnic armies until there were quite literally none left to rebel.

The January 1967 Coup Plot

Margai and Lansana's efforts to build a Mende-dominated army were first met by overt resistance in January 1967.[84] At that time, Captain Seray-Wurie approached a senior government official and related details of an imminent coup attempt planned, he said, by Temne officers. The Captain had lost his stomach for the operation when high-level ministers were targeted for assassination.[85] The dissidents, led by Colonel Bangura, had already held multiple meetings and were purportedly recruiting support on ethnic grounds, particularly amongst northern tribes. Taped

---

[84] Two strands of evidence attest to the veracity of this coup plot. First, court records from later treason trials concerning a different coup were leaked to local newspapers, containing details of the 1967 plot. The trials were conducted by the APC, whose hold on power at the time was tenuous and who could be implicated in this plot. Their interest would thus have been to suppress information on the 1967 plot, not fabricate evidence of its existence (Cox 1976, 100–102). Second, at this time, the British still maintained a good intelligence network on the ground in Sierra Leone, including seconded officers within the military. On February 15, 1967, just after the plot had been publicly announced and arrests made, the British West and General Africa Department, within the Commonwealth Office, noted that they had "no reason to doubt that there was a genuine plot or that the government are correct in claiming that the situation is under control" (TNA FCO 38/28 61, "Sierra Leone Memo from West and General Africa Department, Commonwealth Office," February 15, 1967).

[85] Cox 1976, 100–102.

phone conversations revealed that even after being discovered and placed under house arrest, having nothing left to lose, the rebellious officers continued plotting.[86] According to Police Commissioner William Leigh, who had infiltrated the army with special branch informants, the plot culminated in a meeting of some 300 non-Mende officers and NCOs, held at Aberdeen on the night of February 5th. Fearing that Mende domination of the army was about to be irrevocably imposed, they sent an emissary to the opposition leader, Siaka Stevens, and the APC requesting arms. Apparently, Stevens turned them down.[87]

In response to the unfolding plot, Brigadier Lansana issued guns and ammunition to select Mende soldiers and arrested eight suspects, including Colonel Bangura, the 2nd in command of the army. Those arrested represented a multi-ethnic coalition, mostly northern but also inclusive of two southern Sherbro officers and one Creole officer. Unsurprisingly, no Mende officers were central to the plot or suspected of it.[88] The loss of these officers only reinforced Mende domination of the battalion. Indeed, after the arrests and subsequent purges, only one non-southern officer remained in the upper echelons of the officer corps with a rank of Major or above.[89] The failed coup plot thus reinforced the existing tendencies of the government toward consolidating their power with the backing of an ethnic army.

The March 1967 General Elections

The general elections of March 1967 posed a threat to Sir Albert Margai's government and to Mende dominance in both civilian and military institutions. The opposition party, the APC, was popular and nationally competitive but drew its support predominantly from the northern ethnic groups, including the Temne, Suso, Loko, and Mandingo.[90] According to Kandeh, the Temne even viewed the APC as their political party and one that would save them from Mende domination.[91] Albert and

---

[86] TNA FCO 38/28 35, "Telegram from Freetown to Commonwealth Office," February 7, 1967; TNA FCO 38/29 66, "Attempted Coup by Group of Sierra Leone Army Officers," February 10, 1967.

[87] TNA FCO 38/29 76, "Note of Meeting with Commissioner of Police by R.J.S. Thomson," February 20, 1967.

[88] TNA FCO 38/29 66, "Attempted Coup by Group of Sierra Leone Army Officers," February 10, 1967; TNA FCO 38/29 76, "Note of Meeting with Commissioner of Police by R.J.S. Thomson," February 20, 1967.

[89] Cox 1976, 106.

[90] Minority Rights Group 2010.

[91] Kandeh 1992, 91.

the incumbent SLPP thus faced an opposition that was, in essence, anti-southern and anti-Mende.

To preserve their power, the SLPP engaged in widespread election fraud. Neither political party played by the rules either in their campaigning or on the day of the vote. The APC was guilty of several irregularities, including anti-SLPP violence and voter intimidation in their strongholds, backed by a paramilitary force that Siaka Stevens had trained and was holding in reserve over the Guinean border.[92] Nonetheless, as the party in power, the SLPP had greater resources and latitude to cheat. The British Governor-General, the High Commissioner, and the Commissioner of Police all alleged that Albert's government was to blame for most of the irregularities. There were reports of "gross intimidation" and violence against voters in some constituencies as well as numerous cases of SLPP supporters found with illegally large supplies of ballot papers, presumably to stuff the ballot boxes. Bribes were offered to independent candidates in the hope of convincing them to declare for the SLPP.[93] Independent and APC candidates were also intimidated and sometimes prevented from campaigning while local chiefs in SLPP strongholds threatened non-Mende's with the withdrawal of their mining and marketing licenses if they voted for the opposition.[94]

Despite Margai's efforts to rig the election, the APC eked out a win by the narrowest of margins. The Dove-Edwin Commission, later appointed to investigate electoral irregularities and the outcome of the vote, found that the final results were 31 seats for the APC, 28 seats for the SLPP, and seven independents. The balloting also demonstrated a clear polarization of the country along ethnic lines, with the SLPP dominating in Mende constituencies and throughout the south and the APC dominating the northern and western constituencies.[95]

Events, however, had eclipsed the final tallying. Initially, the Governor-General requested the two political parties form a coalition government. Siaka Stevens and the APC politely refused. Then, despite the close seat totals between the two parties, the small but important

---

92 Allen 1968, 218; Kposowa 2006, 37.
93 TNA FCO 38/30 33, "Telegram from Freetown to Commonwealth Office," March 21, 1967; TNA FCO 38/30 68, "Freetown Despatch No. 3 Sierra Leone – The Lost Elections: Summary," April 6, 1967; TNA FCO 38/31 71, "Elections – Freetown Despatch No. 3," May 18, 1967.
94 Allen 1968, 218; Bebler 1975, 66.
95 TNA FCO 38/30 68, "Freetown Despatch No. 3 Sierra Leone – The Lost Elections: Summary," April 6, 1967; TNA FCO 38/31 71, "Elections – Freetown Despatch No. 3," May 18, 1967.

number of undeclared independents, and the fact that the results of the Paramount Chiefs' elections had yet to be counted, the Governor-General declared Siaka Stevens and the APC victorious and asked them to form an exclusively APC government.[96]

The general election thereby switched the ethnic identity of the civilian regime, from Mende to a coalition of northern groups. This left Sierra Leone in a dangerous predicament: the recently established Mende-dominated officer corps faced potential restructuring under a political party and leader who were unlikely to tolerate the continued existence of such a threat to their rule.

The March 1967 Coups and the NRC

The situation did not take long to unravel. Around noon on March 21st, within hours of being sworn in as prime minister, Siaka Stevens sent two emissaries to the British High Commissioner pleading that the military command would not favor his government and requesting the protection of British combat troops. He was rebuffed.[97] Within hours, Brigadier Lansana had seized power, declared martial law, and erected barricades throughout Freetown with the intention of restoring Albert Margai and his Mende-dominated civilian government to power.[98] Such a rapid response was enabled by prior planning. Sensing the likelihood of an SLPP loss, Lansana had mobilized the army strategically during the elections to facilitate his coup. In critical units, only Mende soldiers were issued arms and ammunition. Small units commanded by Mende lieutenants were deployed, in advance, as sentries to the Sierra Leone Broadcasting Service and to the Goderich Transmitting site, the capital's radio and television stations, as well as to guard State House, the seat of executive power.[99] The coup was quick and relatively bloodless, resulting in nine fatalities and 54 other casualties, all civilians with rifle wounds.[100]

Merely two days later, another coup attempt unseated Brigadier Lansana. Internal frictions amongst the officers over the restoration of Sir

---

[96] TNA FCO 38/30 36, "Telegram from Freetown to Commonwealth Office," March 21, 1967; TNA FCO 38/33 79, "Annex: Letter from Governor General to the Queen," April 5, 1967; *Keesings* 1968, v.14 (May).

[97] TNA FCO 38/30 35, "Telegram from Freetown to Commonwealth Office," March 21, 1967; TNA FCO 38/30 43, "Note for the Secretary of State: Sierra Leone: The General Election," March 22, 1967.

[98] TNA FCO 38/30 47, "Telegram from Freetown to Commonwealth Office," March 22, 1967; Minorities at Risk Project 2009.

[99] Cox 1976, 106–107 & 117.

[100] TNA FCO 38/33 97, "The Army Coup in March, 1967," July 18, 1968.

Albert Margai fueled this reshuffling of power, which is best understood as a continuation of the original coup. Both Margai and Lansana were deeply unpopular, even with many Mende army officers, who saw the upheaval of the coup as a prime opportunity to rid themselves of these two powerful leaders without necessarily jeopardizing Mende-domination of the army. The three leaders of this second coup – Major Charles Blake, Lieutenant-Colonel Genda, and the Commissioner of Police William Leigh – had all supported the initial coup but strongly opposed restoring Margai to power.[101] Blake even publicly asserted that, in addition to preventing the escalation of ethnic hostilities and violence, the officers had arrested Lansana and divested him of power in order to prevent the reimposition of Sir Albert as Prime Minister.[102] Personal distaste for Lansana ran even deeper. Just a month prior, Leigh had told the British High Commissioner during one of their frequent sit-downs that all military officers disliked Lansana and feared his complete dominance over the army. He further asserted that Lansana had no friends amongst the officers, not even the Mende, and that he was "an incompetent drunkard, full of arrogant ambition and said he felt nothing but contempt for him."[103] Indeed, there was no resistance to this second coup, a bloodless affair that established the National Reformation Council (NRC), headed by Brigadier Juxon-Smith who had been called back from training in Britain to lead.[104]

If Mende officers had acted to preserve their privileged position within the army, as the evidence suggests, then they were quickly disabused of such hopes under the NRC. The initial military council was both multi-ethnic and regionally representative.[105] This did not, however, prevent Juxon-Smith from succumbing to ethnic favoritism. Although of creole descent himself, Juxon-Smith quickly turned to the northern

---

[101] Allen 1968, 324.

[102] TNA FCO 38/30 68, "Freetown Despatch No. 3 Sierra Leone – The Lost Elections: Summary," April 6, 1967.

[103] TNA FCO 38/29 76, "Note of Meeting with Commissioner of Police by R.J.S. Thomson," February 20, 1967.

[104] *Keesings* 1967, v.13 (April).

[105] The original NRC was comprised of: Colonel Juxon-Smith (Western Area, Creole), Police Commissioner Leigh (Western Area, Creole), Lieutenant Colonel Blake (Southern Province, Sherbro), Major Kai Samba (Eastern Province, Kono), Major Jumu (Southern Province, Mende), Major Turay (Northern Province, Temne), Mr. Kamara (Northern Province, Temne), and Captain Foya (Eastern Province, Kissi). TNA FCO 38/33 96, "Western European Union Ministerial Meeting, Rome, April 4–5, 1967: Brief No. 4 The Situation in Sierra Leone," [undated]; TNA FCO 38/34 42, "Freetown Despatch No. 4 Sierra Leone – National Reformation Council: The First Month," April 26, 1967.

factions of the military for support. He first released and reabsorbed into the officer corps the northern soldiers who had earlier been arrested for the January 1967 coup plot; a move Leigh characterized as creating a strategic counter-balance to the Mende officers.[106] As early as July 1967, he then began selecting his confidants and personal guards from amongst the northern officers and rank-and-file.[107] By September, reports flowed in that northern soldiers were being used to spy on the Mende troops, with their movements and even their homes watched for subversive activity.[108]

Such northern favoritism, combined with the extensive investigation and prosecution of the Margai government for corruption, led to renewed Mende unrest in the army. Rumors of coup plots and other Mende intrigues raged throughout September. The High Commissioner noted heightened ethnic tensions in Freetown, widespread fears that Mende officers might be plotting to overthrow the government, and loose talk amongst soldiers that a plan had coalesced amongst southern sympathizers.[109] Other rumors suggested that Sir Albert and other SLPP politicians distributed large sums of cash amongst Mende discontents in the army to stir up trouble.[110] While these remained whispers and innuendos, precautionary measures were taken by the NRC against a possible Mende uprising. All ammunition was removed from the battalion and, on September 16, four Mende men connected with the army were arrested on conspiracy charges: two sergeants, a rank-and-file driver, and a civilian. All four were later released for lack of concrete evidence.[111]

While none of the reports or evidence amount to a confirmed coup plot, Juxon-Smith's leadership and reliance on northern officers certainly heightened ethnic and regional tensions within the military and alienated

---

[106] TNA FCO 38/35 58, "National Reformation Council," May 11, 1967.

[107] TNA FCO 38/36 115, "Freetown Despatch No. 6: Sierra Leone: Assessment of the National Reformation Council," July 19, 1967.

[108] TNA FCO 38/36 159, "Telegram from Freetown to the Commonwealth Office," September 18, 1967; TNA FCO 38/36 161, "Sierra Leone Intelligence Reports," September 16, 1967; TNA FCO 38/36 186, "Defence Adviser's Quarterly Report," September 30, 1967.

[109] TNA FCO 38/36 150, "Letter from the British High Commission to the Commonwealth Office," September 2, 1967; TNA FCO 38/36 159, "Telegram from Freetown to the Commonwealth Office," September 18, 1967.

[110] TNA FCO 38/36 161, "Sierra Leone Intelligence Reports," September 16, 1967; TNA FCO 38/43 100, "The Army Mutiny," May 4, 1968.

[111] TNA FCO 38/35 69, "Telegram from Freetown to the Commonwealth Office," June 1, 1967; TNA FCO 38/36 161, "Sierra Leone Intelligence Reports," September 16, 1967; TNA FCO 38/36 179, "National Reformation Council," October 6, 1967.

Mende soldiers. He went so far as to publicly proclaim that "you Mendes are to stop causing discontent" in an address to assembled troops.[112] The NRC thus failed to resolve the underlying issues created by Sir Albert Margai and David Lansana's attempts to create a Mende-dominated army and even sharpened unrest as they began demonstrating northern favoritism. Ethnic factionalism within the officer corps also contributed, if only indirectly, to further unrest the following year.

The 1968 Mutiny Turned Coup

On April 17, 1968, rank-and-file soldiers mutinied at Daru, an up-country military base. The senior officer on site quickly telegrammed his superiors that dissension had broken out in the ranks over demands for higher pay. Overnight, the rebellion spread to the Freetown barracks where soldiers burst into the armory and stole weapons and ammunition, including heavy machine guns and explosives. By that evening, nearly the entire officer corps, including the NRC leadership, had been arrested and was under close guard at the Pademba Road Prison. What began as a spontaneous mutiny thus rapidly spiraled into a rare successful coup by privates and NCOs. While there were a handful of fatalities and casualties, mostly the damage was contained to bands of soldiers firing in the air, looting, and being generally ill-disciplined.[113]

Although the 1968 coup has been characterized as a plot by northern NCOs to restore Siaka Stevens to power,[114] there is little evidence that this was initially the case.[115] Unlike most coups, there was no plan and no initial intent to seize power. Soldiers later interviewed vehemently denied any premeditated plotting, at any level. It is even questionable how involved the Warrant Officers (WOs) and other NCOs were until relatively late in the coup. The British Defense Advisor, who witnessed events in the Freetown barracks, claimed that the NCOs not only had not planned the mutiny, but that they ran as hard as the commissioned officers when it

---

112 TNA FCO 38/36 161, "Sierra Leone Intelligence Reports," September 16, 1967.
113 TNA FCO 38/43 53, "Report on events in Sierra Leone," April 18, 1968; TNA FCO 38/43 100, "The Army Mutiny," May 4, 1968.
114 Bebler 1975, 79; Cox 1976, 198.
115 Much of the following account on motivations is drawn from a report compiled by the British High Commissioner in Freetown, which was based on personal observations, the observations of the British Defense Advisor (who was physically with Sierra Leonean military officers at the time of the coup), and on interviews conducted by the Defense Advisor with both Mende and Temne sergeants and privates in the immediate aftermath of the coup (TNA FCO 38/43 100, "The Army Mutiny," May 4, 1968).

started. Faced with the choice of joining their officers in jail, or backing the mutineers, the NCOs ultimately collaborated with the rebellion.[116]

The motivations of the mutineers also, at least initially, transcended ethnic divisions and there was broad participation of rank-and-file soldiers across the northern versus Mende divide.[117] Individual motivations for participation naturally varied widely, but it appears that four main factors drove the mutiny: first, the already discussed politicization of the officer corps along ethnic lines undermined the rank-and-file's faith in their leadership. Second, the soldiers began to doubt whether the NRC was ever going to retreat to the barracks as promised. A civilian committee had been established by the NRC to investigate and recommend a pathway back to civilian rule. The committee had recently issued its findings, which included rejecting the NRC's preferred mechanism of holding new elections. Instead, they proposed forming a national government within three months based on the 1967 election results, with the exception that those found guilty of corruption under the NRC commissions would be disqualified and by-elections held to fill their seats.[118] Juxon-Smith disparaged the committee and had already implied that the NRC was going to dismiss the report and hold onto power.[119] Third, there was growing resentment over unearned promotions and financial corruption within the officer corps. Under the NRC, officers had promoted themselves against standing norms and regulations. Amongst the rank-and-file, there was also widespread talk of corruption: that the NRC was just as bad as those convicted by its own, politically motivated corruption investigations.[120] Finally, ordinary soldiers had been caught up in austerity measures, imposed by superiors who were all the while apparently enriching themselves. The rank-and-file had not received a pay increase in some time, their facilities, living quarters, and uniforms were becoming "shabby," and they felt generally neglected by the regime

---

[116] TNA FCO 38/43 10, "Telegram from Freetown to the Commonwealth Office," April 18, 1968; TNA FCO 38/43 97, "Letter from Ted Edwards, Defense Advisor to Sierra Leone, to Lesley," April 26, 1968; TNA FCO 38/43 100, "The Army Mutiny," May 4, 1968.

[117] TNA FCO 38/43 61, "Telegram from Freetown to the Commonwealth Office," April 19, 1968.

[118] TNA FCO 38/38 331, "Telegram from Freetown to the Commonwealth Office," March 5, 1968; TNA FCO 38/38 342, "Telegram from Freetown to the Commonwealth Office," March 20, 1968.

[119] TNA FCO 38/38 331, "Telegram from Freetown to the Commonwealth Office," March 5, 1968; TNA FCO 38/43 100, "The Army Mutiny," May 4, 1968.

[120] TNA FCO 38/43 100, Annex A, "Note by D.A., Mutiny in Sierra Leone Army," May 4, 1968.

they had helped to put in power.[121] Left out of the prosperity of the officer corps, suffering declining living standards, and rent by the ethnic animosities of their superiors, the common soldiers rose up in unity and unseated the military regime.

The mutineers established an interim council and then rapidly handed power over to Siaka Stevens and the APC. In their short reign, the military council immediately gave NCOs a 15% pay raise, privates a 10% raise, and reversed all officer promotions granted by the NRC that were contrary to established military rules and regulations.[122] Having achieved those corrections, less than 10 days after the coup, Siaka Stevens was brought back from exile and sworn in as prime minister.[123]

The 1968 mutiny-turned-coup demonstrates important limitations to the theory. Coups are tactics. Soldiers seize power for many reasons beyond resisting or preserving systems of ethnic privilege within the military, even in contexts where ethnic armies are prevalent. Although ethnic tensions and the prior struggle for power between Mende and northern officers contributed to soldier motivations here, the rank-and-file banded together across these ethnic divides. They also, at least in part, rose up to put an end to ethnic conflict in the military. This suggests that other identity cleavages can be mobilized for action and that cross-cutting cleavages, such as the economic and class interests reflected in the officer versus rank-and-file divide, may sometimes supersede ethnic motivations. This also offers hope that these dynamics are not inescapable; that ethnic armies can be dismantled and soldiers can decide that they would be altogether better off in a fair and non-discriminatory institution. One should not, however, overestimate the ease with which the yoke of ethnic exclusion and conflict can be thrown off. Despite their best intentions, the rank-and-file soldiers of the Sierra Leone army failed to prevent full ethnicization of the military under their chosen leader.

Stabilization under the APC: Guinean Troops and the Ethnic Homogenization of the Military

Siaka Stevens and the APC consolidated power under their rule, and ended military rebellions for over twenty years, through a combination

---

[121] TNA FCO 38/43 34, "Telegram from Freetown to Commonwealth Office," April 20, 1968; TNA FCO 38/43 100, "The Army Mutiny," May 4, 1968.

[122] TNA FCO 38/43 36, "Telegram from Freetown to the Commonwealth Office," April 21, 1968; TNA FCO 38/43 97, "Letter from Ted Edwards, Defense Advisor to Sierra Leone, to Lesley," April 26, 1968.

[123] TNA FCO 38/43 74, "Telegram from Freetown to the Commonwealth Office," April 27, 1968; *Keesings* 1968, v.14 (May).

of successfully imposing ethnic homogenization on the officer corps and relying on foreign troops for protection. Although this was facilitated by the nearly officer-less state of the military, Siaka's efforts to construct an ethnic army did not go unchallenged, particularly when he moved from northern domination to specifically Limba domination of security institutions. Other northern ethnic groups, and especially the Temne, resisted but failed to stop this narrowing of the ethnic basis of the state.

Upon gaining power, Stevens inherited a military with neither officers nor discipline. The soldiers were still keeping a round-the-clock guard on Pademba prison and refusing to allow the release of any of their former commanders. Over 100 army and police officers had eventually been detained, including all of the army's officers except for four, three of whom had been abroad at the time of the coup.[124] In a small military such as Sierra Leone's, which at this time still comprised a mere battalion of around 1500 men, this lack of leadership enabled both the breakdown of discipline and a continued coup threat from the NCOs, who now held any remaining command authority.

Mende discontent over the wholesale granting of power to Stevens, combined with the APC's struggle to regain civil authority over the military, led to pervasive fears of a Mende counter-coup. In their reports, the British gloomily noted that "the whole government is morbidly suspicious, finding dark shadows round every corner and vindictive in pursuing old animosities."[125] Any small gathering of Mendes was disbanded to thwart plotting, while APC supporters were allowed to organize mass gatherings.[126] The Mende soldiers and NCOs that had once served as Lansana and Margai's personal guards fell under the greatest suspicion and were taken into custody. More arrests of Mende politicians, soldiers, and NCOs soon followed, including many who had actively helped restore Stevens to power.[127] Through these purges, the Mende were expelled not only from the officer corps (which was practically non-existent anyway) but also from the non-commissioned and other ranks of the military.

---

[124] TNA FCO 38/51 57, "Army and Police," May 18, 1968; TNA FCO 65/507 23, "The Sierra Leone Army – Twelve Months of Turmoil," March 26, 1969.

[125] TNA FCO 38/45 28, "The Situation in Sierra Leone," June 26, 1968.

[126] TNA FCO 38/47 10, "Round-up of Recent Events," June 7, 1968.

[127] TNA FCO 38/45 28, "The Situation in Sierra Leone," June 26, 1968; TNA FCO 38/47 10, "Round-up of Recent Events," June 7, 1968; TNA FCO 38/51 57, "Army and Police," May 18, 1968; TNA FCO 38/51 59, "Telegram from Freetown to the Commonwealth Office," May 29, 1968.

Siaka Stevens then constructed a northern-dominated military while gaining some protection from his personally loyal paramilitary force. While exiled in Guinea, Stevens had recruited and trained an irregular band of soldiers thought to number around 150–300 men. This force accompanied Stevens on his return to Sierra Leone, taking up residence in Freetown with their weapons guarded by "specially selected Temne soldiers."[128] This paramilitary then operated as a counterweight to the army, facilitating its restructuring along northern lines. In November and December 1968, a large recruiting drive brought 257 new recruits into the ranks of the army. Ethnic quotas were set in advance, stipulating that no more than 20% of the recruits were to be drawn from the south, with the remaining 80% drawn from northern ethnic groups. The seconded British officers noted this influx of northerners into the army, especially Temnes, while the Minister of Finance complained that many of the recruits arriving in Freetown hailed from the extreme north of the country, from the Yalunka and Limba tribes.[129] The new officer corps quickly took on a northern cast as well. Although initially a small number of army NCOs and WOs were promoted and commissioned as 2nd lieutenants, with careful balance kept between ethnicities, this balance was soon lost. Not only were Mende officers later arrested or purged, but subsequent efforts to rebuild the officer corps showed a distinctive northern bias. In December, as the rank-and-file was still being flooded with northerners, 19 officers were released from detention and reinstated in the army, the great majority of whom were northern.[130] Indeed, Stevens gained a reputation for selectively stacking the officer corps with Limba and Temne officers in particular.[131]

The construction of a northern army coincided with, and indeed facilitated, the consolidation of the northern-dominated APC's political power. The APC moved quickly and strongly towards a de facto one-party

---

[128] TNA FCO 65/507 14, "Defense Adviser's Report for the Quarter Ending 31st December, 1968 – Sierra Leone," December 31, 1968; TNA FCO 38/43 100, "The Army Mutiny," May 4, 1968.

[129] TNA FCO 65/498 8, "Round-Up as at 6 December," December 6, 1968; TNA FCO 65/507 6, "Extract from B.H.C. Freetown," November 23, 1968; TNA FCO 65/507 8, "Round-Up as at 6 December," December 6, 1968; TNA FCO 65/507 14, "Defense Adviser's Report for the Quarter Ending 31st December, 1968 – Sierra Leone," December 31, 1968.

[130] TNA FCO 38/52 81, "Telegram from Freetown to the Commonwealth Office," August 8, 1968; TNA FCO 38/52 85, "Round-Up as at 16 August, 1968," August 16, 1968; TNA FCO 65/507 14, "Defense Adviser's Report for the Quarter Ending 31st December, 1968 – Sierra Leone," December 31, 1968; TNA FCO 65/507 23, "The Sierra Leone Army – Twelve Months of Turmoil," March 26, 1969.

[131] Kposowa 2006, 40.

state. SLPP members of the newly reinstated parliament were systematically unseated through court petitions that alleged fraud in the 1967 elections. The by-elections for their seats were then rigged. Twenty-six such petitions were lodged in the courts against the SLPP, each and every one of which was successful. During the resulting by-elections, army and paramilitary units were used throughout the country to intimidate voters and harass SLPP candidates. The APC won the vast majority of the contested seats, even in traditional SLPP strongholds in the Mende areas of the south. Indeed, in the Bo-Kenema by-elections, the APC won a remarkable half of the former SLPP seats, granting them more than a two-thirds parliamentary majority and thus the ability to pass any legislation they wished.[132]

Stevens then endeavored to further narrow the ethnic base of the military, from a coalition of northern factions that had opposed Mende domination to his own Limba group. In 1970, serious divisions emerged between Siaka Stevens and both Temne civilian administrators and military officers. These frictions led Temne political leaders to withdraw their support from the APC and form a new opposition party, which was almost immediately banned. Stevens then employed Limba soldiers, and allies amongst the Yalunka and Koranko, to arrest Temne army officers and NCOs and purge them from the military.[133] To add insult to injury, Stevens had contracted out his personal protection to Guinean bodyguards and had begun bringing Guinean combat troops into Freetown to protect his regime from internal and external challenges.[134]

In response, Temne military officers led by Brigadier Bangura tried to seize power. Two failed attempts were made on Stevens' life, the first during the night of March 22–23 and the second around lunchtime the following day. His Guinean bodyguards proved instrumental in fending off the attacks. Cuban trained, professional, and efficient, six of them managed to hold off the army and hustle Stevens to the Guinean Embassy for further protection.[135] With Stevens in hiding, the military split into factions with Creole and Limba soldiers refusing to follow the northern coup leaders' orders. Assisted by Guinean troops and the repeated buzzing

[132] TNA FCO 65/497 1, "Round-Up as at 1 November, 1968," November 1, 1968; TNA FCO 65/497 12, "Sierra Leone – Background to the Internal Security Situation," November 25, 1968; TNA FCO 65/499 11, "Internal Security and Political Scene," March 22, 1969; TNA FCO 65/507 14, "Defense Adviser's Report for the Quarter Ending 31st December, 1968 – Sierra Leone," December 31, 1968; Hayward 1984, 25; Kposowa 2006, 40.
[133] Minorities at Risk Project 2009.
[134] TNA FCO 65/1041 38, "Situation in Sierra Leone," March 31, 1971.
[135] TNA FCO 65/1041 40, "Disturbances," March 26, 1971.

of Freetown by Guinean aircraft, the loyal elements of the army eventually prevailed. Within two days, Stevens was at least loosely back in control. He then signed a defense agreement with Sékou Toreé of Guinea and requested more combat troops. On March 29th, a second detachment arrived, bringing the numbers of Guinean soldiers up to as many as 150. They were seen cordoning off Steven's house and taking over key facilities and check points across Freetown. By March 30th, the situation was firmly in hand, with Bangura and the other coup leaders under arrest. Despite the intense fighting, fatalities from the coup were only estimated at four or five soldiers and two civilians.[136]

After the failed coup, Stevens' regime continued both its purges of Temne officers and its growing reliance on Guinean protection. 200–300 Guinean troops were soon estimated to be in Sierra Leone, serving as an additional counterweight to the regular army. Some 40,000 leones (Sierra Leone's currency) also exchanged hands, compensation convincing the remaining loyal soldiers not only to accept this influx of foreign troops, but to allow their own disarmament.[137] Stevens then continued his restructuring of the armed forces such that all commanders of the army and police were soon Limba. Additionally, he created a predominantly Limba paramilitary, known as the Internal Security Unit (ISU), that was used to inflict violence on domestic opponents and eventually grew to be more powerful and better equipped than the regular army.[138] The coups and coup attempts ceased thereafter.

After Siaka Stevens finally stepped down, the regime and security apparatus he developed persisted. In 1985, Stevens handed over power to his hand-picked successor, a coethnic and the current head of the military, Major-General Joseph Saidu Momoh. Under Momoh, most officers continued to be recruited from the north, and particularly from

---

136 TNA FCO 65/1041 1, "Telegram from Freetown to the Commonwealth Office," March 23, 1971; TNA FCO 65/1041 2, "Telegram from Freetown to the Commonwealth Office," March 23, 1971; TNA FCO 65/1041 14, "Telegram from Freetown to the Commonwealth Office," March 25, 1971; TNA FCO 65/1041 25, "Telegram from Freetown to the Commonwealth Office," March 26, 1971; TNA FCO 65/1041 26, "Telegram from Freetown to the Commonwealth Office," March 29, 1971; TNA FCO 65/1041 27, "Telegram from Freetown to the Commonwealth Office," March 30, 1971; TNA FCO 65/1041 31, "Situation in Sierra Leone (Summary)," March 29, 1971; TNA FCO 65/1041 38, "Situation in Sierra Leone (Speaking Note)," March 29, 1971. See also Minorities at Risk Project 2009.

137 TNA FCO 65/1042 47, "Sierra Leone's Fourth Coup," April 2, 1971; TNA FCO 65/1042 63, Untitled Report written by SJL Olver the British High Commissioner to Sierra Leone, April 1, 1971.

138 Cox 1976, 106–107; Davies 2000, 352–353; Horowitz 1985, 477–479; Kandeh 1992, 94; Minorities at Risk Project 2009.

the Limba. The civilian administration also gained a reputation for nepotism and tribalism. Key ministerial and other positions were held by Limbas and by the so-called "ekutay group," whose members hailed from Binkolo, the hometown of the President.[139] Momoh ruled without civil-military strife until he later became embroiled in both internal and external wars in the 1990s.[140]

A long hiatus from civil-military instability was thereby achieved when, through the destructiveness and violence of a series of coups and counter-coups, Sierra Leone's security institutions were finally homogenized under Limba domination. This stabilization was greatly facilitated by the prior decimation of the officer corps combined with imported Guinean troops to protect the president. The price of this stability, however, was high: the nearly total ethnicization of the state, reliance on paramilitary units, rampant corruption, erosion of civil liberties, and economic stagnation under Steven's and then Momoh's rule set the stage for later civil war.[141]

Alternative Explanations

Alternative theories of ethnic exclusion and structural economic weakness provide less convincing accounts of Sierra Leone's early postcolonial instability. With regard to general practices of ethnic exclusion, although Mende representation in government and the security sector was increasing under Albert Margai, other ethnic groups, including from the north, still had access to power. The APC was a strong opposition party, well represented in parliament, and able to advocate for non-Mende interests. The military also included significant numbers of non-Mende soldiers. After the 1967 coups, as the military council began favoring northern ethnic groups, diversity and inclusion were nonetheless still pervasive.

---

[139] Kandeh 1992, 93–94; Kpundeh 1994, 140 & 150–151.

[140] The 1992 coup that unseated Momoh embodied a different logic than resistance to the creation or dismantling of ethnic armies. At the time of the coup, Sierra Leone was fighting both a civil war and an external war against Charles Taylor's Liberia. Soldiers on the front lines faced poor logistical and material support, dreary living conditions, and significant pay arrears. The coup leader, Captain Valentine Strasser told of being operated on without anesthesia after fighting with "obsolete guns that will not fire" (as quoted in Zack-Williams & Riley 1993, 94). Seeking redress, a convoy of soldiers drove from the front to Freetown. Upon seeing the heavily armed troops approach, the APC leadership panicked. They lost the resulting battle and fled to Guinea, leaving the military in control of the government. See Kpundeh 1994, 141; Kandeh 1996, 390.

[141] Kposowa 2006.

It was during these periods of relative inclusion that soldier rebellions increasingly destabilized the political system. Indeed, the violence ceased only after Siaka Stevens achieved widespread ethnic exclusion under a coethnic Limba army and government. It was the struggle for ethnic domination of the government – resistance against the construction and feared dismantling of systems of ethnic privilege – that fueled violence, not existing exclusion.

Standard economic explanations could plausibly explain some of Sierra Leone's coup history. Sierra Leone was a poor country following independence, despite its natural resource wealth, with below average GDP per capita levels even for Africa (see Figure 3.1). Sierra Leone was also heavily dependent on mineral exports, especially diamond mining, adding a lucrative incentive to controlling state power as well as exposing the economy to commodity price fluctuations. Growth rates were also weak following decolonization, with two recessions occurring in the 1960s. All of these factors predict instability. Yet, many African countries poorer than Sierra Leone experienced far fewer coup attempts, including Cameroon. Sierra Leone has also experienced coups during periods of both positive and negative economic growth, with such growth having little predictive power (see Figure 3.2). Moreover, the initial 1967 coups and coup plots all occurred during a period of strong economic growth and, while the 1971 coup did take place during a recession, the recession itself was most likely a result of the already unbridled government instability.

The timing of the coup attempts is thus better explained by the preceding analysis of ethnic politics. Attempting to build ethnic armies despite existing diversity in the officer corps sparked great civil-military strife in Sierra Leone. Coups, counter-coups, coup plots, and mutinies proliferated as the political competition between Mendes and northern ethnic groups was channeled into the military by Sir Albert Margai and his successors. Their attempts to construct ethnic armies provoked active resistance from officers who saw their groups being purged from the ranks. Only after the complete decimation of the officer corps was Siaka Stevens able to build a northern, Limba-dominated army and even then he faced a last gasp of resistance from fellow northern but ethnically Temne officers.

CONCLUSION

Both Sierra Leone and Cameroon achieved independence under leaders who decided to build military loyalty on the basis of ethnic identity:

to create officer corps' stacked with coethnics as a bulwark against potential challenges by other ethnic groups. Yet, despite the inherently exclusionary design of such policies and the threat they posed to groups left outside of the most important power structures of the state, this choice only had destabilizing consequences in Sierra Leone. While a series of ethnically motivated coups and counter-coups in Sierra Leone hardened ethnic sentiments and led to a Limba-dominated state, which would later break down into further violence and eventually civil war, Cameroon has largely escaped from any civil-military instability in its post-independence history.

The key difference between these two cases lies in the officer corps they each inherited from their departing colonizers. In Sierra Leone, the British had constructed a diverse officer corps, inclusive of all the major ethnic groups competing for power in the pre- and post-independence elections. Thus, when Prime Minister Albert Margai began to ethnically restructure the military – to recruit co-ethnic Mendes in disproportionate numbers – there existed a faction of threatened, non-Mende officers in the military to resist. Then, when the Mende lost their hold over civilian power in the 1964 elections, and in all probability fearing that they would be treated as they had treated others, they used their foothold in the military to stage a coup attempt and spark a series of ethnic coups and counter-coups. In Cameroon, on the other hand, the French had neglected to build a native officer corps prior to Ahmadou Ahidjo's rise to power, allowing him to implement discriminatory recruitment policies and construct an ethnic army without intra-military resistance.

4

Creating Inclusive Armies: Senegal and Ghana

I prefer small successes to a Pyrrhic victory.

– Léopold Senghor[1]

I watched the seed of tribal conflict being slowly sown by the actions of the Busia regime and with the blood of millions of our Nigerian brothers to warn us I acted to nip the threat in the bud.

– Lieutenant-Colonel Ignatius Acheampong[2]

If building ethnic armies provokes resistance from officers threatened by the new promotion and recruitment practices, then constructing inclusive militaries should ameliorate the dangers of political instability. This chapter compares Senegal and Ghana, both of whose initial leaders attempted to create diverse security institutions. Absent the construction of ethnic armies, both cases should thus have avoided soldier rebellion. Senegal cleanly follows this prediction, remaining inclusive and coup-free throughout its post-independence history. Ghana, on the other hand, quickly succumbed to a series of destructive coups and counter-coups. I trace this divergence in trajectories to a sharp reversal in Kwame Nkrumah's policies: although originally committed to diversity and building a non-tribal nation, after two assassination attempts he abandoned inclusivity and began targeting coethnics for army recruitment. This led to stiffened resistance amongst non-favored ethnic factions within the military and, ultimately, to a successful coup by Ewe officers facing exclusion. Repeated purges of military officers, further ethnic manipulations of the

[1] As quoted in Markovitz 1969, 104.
[2] As quoted in Smock & Smock 1975, 249.

army, and repeated counter-coups ensued. Building an ethnic army against the reality of a diverse officer corps once again provoked violence.

That Kwame Nkrumah abrogated his original, inclusive practices raises the question of why he failed where others succeeded? Rather than personal fault, the comparison with Senegal points to the critical importance of early political party formation. While prior ethnic violence did not condition the choice to construct ethnic armies, deep ethnic politicization nonetheless makes diverse militaries difficult to sustain. In Senegal, pre-independence political parties developed around a strong urban–rural divide, between the French assimilated communes and the agricultural hinterlands. Léopold Senghor's party, overwhelmingly dominant by independence, coopted the rural vote through the Muslim brotherhoods, who issued religious edicts mandating their followers' support in return for peanut farming subsidies. Early political parties thus entirely eschewed mobilizing voters on an ethnic basis, restricting identity to a negligible role in politics. Senghor was thus able to consistently recruit inclusively into the military without encountering social or political resistance.

On the other hand, while Kwame Nkrumah's party attempted to transcend ethnic divisions, other Ghanaian political parties garnered support by directly appealing to ethnic interests and historic rivalries, especially amongst the Asante and Ewe. The deep ethnic politicization engendered by pre-independence elections, which even turned violent in Asante territory, undermined Nkrumah's early attempts to build nation-ally representative institutions. Instead of support, he faced factional ethnic resistance to his policies, culminating in the two assassination attempts that spurred his turn towards building a coethnic army. Deep ethnic politicization may thus condition the capacity of leaders to build inclusive security institutions even where the political will exists.

The case studies proceed as follows: first, I examine the rise of the independence era leader and the degree of ethnic politicization they faced, contrasting Senegal's non-ethnic political competition to the divide between nationalist and ethnic parties in Ghana. Given this context, I then analyze how each leader initially chose to build military loyalty on inclusive grounds as well as Nkrumah's turn toward ethnic loyalty and the motivations behind it. I then discuss the potential for resistance, focusing on the ethnic composition of the officer corps and the degree of foreign protection. Finally, I analyze the path of stability or instability that each country traveled, tracing how ethnic recruitment practices shaped soldiers' propensity for violence. Here is where the cases depart: while probing the mechanisms of stability in Senegal, in Ghana we follow a chaotic story of plots, coups, and counter-coups within a military riven by ethnic factionalism.

STABILITY IN SENEGAL

Senegal has avoided much of the political instability faced by other African countries. While there has been a small separatist movement in the Casamance that turned violent in the 1990s, the country has never experienced large-scale ethnic violence, a coup attempt, or military governance. I argue that this stability is rooted in Senegal's long tradition of ethnic inclusivity. No effort has been made to construct ethnically exclusive civil or military institutions, obviating the need to rebel against either their construction or maintenance. Indeed, Senegal's independence leader, Léopold Senghor, was committed to preserving diversity in the military as a foundation for nationalism – a practice enabled by the country's low level of ethnic politicization. These traditions of inclusivity have persisted to the present day, facilitating continued stability and contributing to current democratization efforts.

Political Party Formation and the Rise of Léopold Senghor

Unlike in so much of sub-Saharan Africa, early Senegalese political leaders forewent building their parties by appealing to ethnic constituencies and interests. As a result, the political parties that contested pre- and post-independence elections did not mirror the ethnic cleavages of Senegalese society. This lack of ethnic politicization cannot be reduced to anything unique or atypical about the country's ethnic composition. Like so many other African societies, Senegal is comprised of multiple ethnic groups, none of which constitute a majority.[3] Rather, Senegal's low level of ethnic politicization resulted from the constituency building strategies of early political parties; strategies that cross-cut ethnic cleavages rather than reinforcing them.

Stark contrasts in French colonial policy between the communes and the rest of the territory led politics to coalesce, initially, around a strong

---

3 According to a census conducted in 1960, the ethnic breakdown of Senegal's population around the time of decolonization was 36% Wolof, 19% Serer, 14% Toucouleur, 7.5% Peul, 7% Diola, 5% Manding, 2% Sara-kolé, 1.5% Bambara, 1.5% Lébou, and 6.5% other groups (Dresch et al. 1977).

urban–rural divide. French administrators had created four communes in the urban areas: Saint-Louis, Dakar, Gorée, and Rufisque. Native Senegalese born within the communes were considered citizens of France and granted equivalent legal status as Frenchmen. They were expected to give up their traditions and become, culturally and educationally, French. In return, they were granted privileges denied to nearly all of colonized Africa outside of the white settler communities. As far back as the early 1800s, the communes had been allowed limited forms of democratic self-government, including civic associations and political parties. By 1914, local politics in the communes were firmly controlled by Senegalese politicians.[4] In contrast, the remainder of the territory was governed like any other colony, autocratically through the appointment of local chiefs and administrators. The rural areas were also subjected to military law and the labor corvée (forced, unpaid manual labor duties). Thus, a strong political, cultural, and educational divide developed between the urban communes and the rural hinterlands.[5]

Given such policies, Senegal's earliest political parties naturally took root within the urban communes. The first such party was an offshoot of the Paris-based French Socialist Party (Section Française de l'Internationale Ouvrière or SFIO), which established a Senegalese branch in the 1930's. French assimilationist policies firmly rested on the assumption of eventual colonial incorporation. In due time, and when proper political and cultural maturity had been attained, colonial possessions would be fully integrated into French laws and political structures.[6] Congruent with this policy, under France's Third Republic (1870–1940), the communes could elect one representative to the metropolitan lower Chamber of Deputies. The constitution of France's 4th Republic (1946–1958) established even greater colonial representation in the National Assembly, with full voting privileges. In the first legislature of the 4th Republic, 11.8% of deputies were elected from overseas territories, including 30 from sub-Saharan Africa and 30 from Algeria (half of whom were elected by enfranchised Muslim Algerians rather than French settlers).[7] France's multi-party system was also highly fragmentary, with no single-party controlling more than 28.6% of parliamentary seats at any point during the 4th Republic.

4 Barry 1988, 272–273; Galvan 2001, 57; Morgenthau 1964, 127.
5 Galvan 2001, 57.
6 Smith 1978, 74.
7 Data compiled from the archives of the French National Assembly, available at www.assemblee-nationale.fr/histoire.

Colonial deputies thus became very important to the major French political parties, incentivizing the establishment and maintenance of party branches in the overseas territories.[8] Under the local leadership of Lamine Guèye, the SFIO came to monopolize Senegalese electoral politics by the end of World War II.[9]

In 1948, SFIO party members, disaffected with the subordination of African deputies to the French metropolitan center, split and formed a new party, eventually known as the Parti Socialiste du Sénégal (PS), under the leadership of Léopold Sédar Senghor.[10] While the metropolitan SFIO leaders may have valued and sympathized with Senegalese interests, their primary objectives and loyalties were always understood in terms of French interests. As a key player in Paris, fending off challenges from both the right and the left, the SFIO could hardly support radical changes in colonial policy that would have alienated both their moderate coalition partners and French voters. Indeed, it was an SFIO led government in 1946–1947 that elected to fight nationalist insurgent forces in Indochina, affirming the principle of empire, rather than begin decolonization.[11] To gain real representation for local interests, Senghor founded a party that would be responsible solely to Senegalese voters.

As the SFIO was firmly entrenched in the communes, Senghor turned to the newly enfranchised rural masses to garner support.[12] Even though ethnic and tribal categories were more salient in the countryside than within the assimilationist communes, the PS nonetheless still built a political following without appealing to ethnic identity. Rather, they tapped into existing patronage networks between the state and the Sufi brotherhoods to mobilize mass support. As the brotherhoods were ubiquitous, influence over them carried with it large voting blocks and thus potential political power. At the time of decolonization, around 90% of Senegalese Muslims, who constituted over 80% of the population, belonged to one of the two dominant Sufi brotherhoods, the Tijaniyya and the Mourides.[13]

---

[8] Lewis 1998, 281.
[9] Smith 1978, 81.
[10] The party was originally named the Bloc Démocratique Sénégalais (BDS) and then went through two interim names: the Bloc Populaire Sénégalais (BPS) and the Union Progressiste Sénégalais (UPS). For clarity and consistency, I refer to the party in each of its phases as the Parti Socialiste du Sénégal (PS).
[11] Smith 1978, 81.
[12] Foltz 1965, 58–59.
[13] Clark 1999, 160; Foltz 1965, 58–59.

Understanding the evolution of the Islamic brotherhoods as, simulta-neously, religious orders able to control the political behavior of their fol-lowers, important agricultural producers in the groundnut export sector, and large-scale recipients of colonial subsidies, illuminates why garnering their support was such a compelling and successful electoral strategy. One that, moreover, obviated the need for other mass mobilization measures, including ethnic appeals.

Although Islam had made peaceful inroads into West Africa as early as the tenth century, it touched the lives of few Senegalese until the middle of the nineteenth century. In 1854, the jihads raging further north reached the upper Senegal valley when Al-Hajj Umar Tal of the Sufi Tijaniyya brotherhood launched an attack against the French-supported, non-Muslim tribes of that region. Then, in 1886, as the Tijaniyya were gaining influence and gathering supporters in the north and east of the colony, Amadu Mamba founded the Muridiyya brotherhood (or the Mourides) in the heart of Wolof territory toward the west.[14] Unlike earlier Islamic influences, the Tijaniyya and Muridiyya brotherhoods represented reform movements that sought a direct relationship with their adepts. Before, the Sufi religious leaders, or marabouts, had confined themselves to the royal courts and to giving spiritual guidance to the princely families. Both brotherhoods now sought conversion of the peasantry to Islam. Their efforts coincided with the French conquest of the Senegalese interior and the resulting destruction of traditional states and their customary ways of ordering political and religious life. The brotherhoods welcomed the refugees of this destruction, playing an intermediary role in rebuilding society under colonialism while rapidly converting followers.[15] The Sufi orders thus achieved great success in proselytization while developing a close alliance with the conquering French.

The relationship between the marabouts and their adepts, or talibés, was grounded in a strong, theologically motivated exchange. For the talibé, entrance to paradise could only be gained through the direct intervention of the marabout and his prayers, which were secured by working for the marabout, paying tithes, and following religious edicts. Disobeying an edict was thus tantamount to sacrificing one's afterlife.[16] Through this religious relationship, the marabouts gained a significant degree of control over the personal and political choices of the vast majority of Senegal's rural population.

[14] Clark 1999, 152–156; Markovitz 1970, 83–85.
[15] Galvan 2001, 58; Markovitz 1970, 85.
[16] Foltz 1965, 115; Markovitz 1970, 86; Villalón 1999, 133–136.

At the same time as the Sufi brotherhoods were developing as religious communities, they were also evolving as agricultural producers, recipients of patronage, and important mediators between the colonial state and the peasantry. Initially, both the brotherhoods and the French were engaged in violent conquests of the same lands, leading to clashes. Given their compatible end goals, however, they were eventually able to develop a mutually supportive coexistence: the French aspired to political supremacy while the brotherhoods sought cultural and spiritual domination. Colonial administrators then helped the marabouts transform their religious schools into profitable plantations. By the time of decolonization, the marabouts controlled peanut cultivation, which accounted for approximately 80% of Senegal's gross domestic product. The Mourides alone managed over half of all groundnut production.[17] In exchange for seeds, market access, transportation infrastructure, security, and other agricultural inputs, the marabouts collected taxes and issued religious edicts to ensure the population's adherence to colonial laws. Amadu Mamba himself issued a fatwa in 1910 justifying obedience to French rule.[18] The marabouts were thus transformed into an agrarian elite, dependent on the colonial state for continued access to resources, but remarkably powerful in their ability to control the rural population and economy.[19]

As the French devolved increasing powers of self-governance to Senegal and extended political rights to the countryside, which was enfranchised in 1946, this preexisting social order structured by the Sufi brotherhoods allowed the PS to gain an electoral advantage without itself engaging in mass mobilization. Rather, Senghor approached influential marabouts for their endorsement. Through this strategy, in 1951, the PS was able to win both of Senegal's National Assembly seats over the previously dominant SFIO. With the devolution of agricultural policy, the new PS controlled government also carefully maintained the existing colonial patronage structures, substituting themselves as the principal source of financial and material support for the brotherhoods and their peanut plantations. By the late 1950s, the PS were thus perfectly positioned to offer the marabouts continued state patronage in exchange for their intercession with the peasantry. The marabouts would issue religious edicts commanding their followers to vote for the PS and the PS would continue to buttress the marabouts' control over peanut

[17] Fatton 1986, 65–66; Markovitz 1970, 92.
[18] Clark 1999, 156.
[19] Boone 2003, 51–60; Clark 1999, 153–154; Galvan 2001, 58; Markovitz 1970, 89.

production.[20] This strategy was so effective that in the 1959 legislative assembly elections, the PS won roughly 83% of the vote, granting them an overwhelming majority in Parliament and allowing Senghor to assume the presidency after the short-lived Mali Federation had collapsed.[21]

This ability to garner such a commanding victory at the polls, by working through the marabouts and existing patronage structures, allowed the PS to forego expensive and time-consuming direct mass mobilization tactics. It was also a superior strategy to ethnic mobilization. Senegal's largest ethnic group, the Wolof constituted merely 36% of the population around the time of decolonization.[22] Although comparatively much greater than any other ethnic group, the next largest groups being the Serer and Toucouleur constituting approximately 19% and 14% of the total population, respectively, it still would have trailed the 50% needed for political control by a substantial margin.[23] A mobilization strategy organized around Wolof interests would thus have failed to gain a majority; an unlikely strategy in any case given Senghor's descent from the Serer. Given the small size of Senegal's ethnic groups, even an electoral strategy integrating multiple groups would have fallen well short of the overwhelming victory produced by the collaboration with the marabouts.

Senegal's two main political parties at the time of decolonization thus reflected the primary divide in French colonial policy: with the SFIO representing the interests and aspirations of an educated and assimilated elite in the communes and the PS seeking a following amongst the traditionally subjugated peasantry. Moreover, neither party turned to ethnicity as a source of voter mobilization. The SFIO was guided by an overarching concern for French politics and interests and the communes themselves were dominated by an assimilationist mentality that eschewed tribal heritage in favor of French education and identity. The PS, on the other hand, relied on the Sufi brotherhoods to gain votes and never needed to explore other mobilization strategies, such as ethnicity. Léopold Senghor thus led Senegal to independence while minimizing the role of ethnicity in politics.

---

[20] Beck 2008, 73–74; Boone 2003, 60–63; Foltz 1965, 115–116; Galvin 2001, 58.
[21] Nunley 2011. Indeed, the exchange of agricultural patronage for votes continued for over 25 years, ensuring continued PS dominance of Senegalese politics under a one-party state.
[22] Dresch et al. 1977. The Wolof's share in the total population has grown to roughly 44% today (Minority Rights Group, 2010).
[23] Dresch et al. 1977.

Building an Inclusive Army: Nation before Ethnicity

After the Mali federation collapsed just a few months after independence from France, in 1960, Senghor became the president of Senegal and the architect of its new national military. Reflecting his belief in a nationalism that would transcend, but not end, ethnic and tribal identities, Senghor continued French military recruitment practices that had always reflected Senegal's great ethnic diversity. Senghor chose an inclusive rather than an ethnic army.

Léopold Senghor envisioned that Senegalese nationalism would develop, however slowly, by protecting local communities within federal institutions and winning their loyalty over time. To Senghor, the nation was an artificial construction that must be built through the unification of what he termed the "fatherlands," or Senegal's various tribes and ethnic groups. The nation would not replace prior identities but unify their loyalties within a shared political community. Unlike many nationalisms that claim ownership over the state on behalf of a particular identity group, Senghor viewed the state as belonging to everyone. The Senegalese nation-building project thus did not entail capturing and then homogenizing governing institutions along ethnic lines. Instead, the state could both tolerate the continued existence of local and regional identities and share power with them.[24] Indeed, Senghor had pushed for and joined the Mali Federation precisely because he believed federalism would protect Senegal from the worst depredations of the modern, centralized nation-state:

> ... we shall take care not to succumb to one of the temptations of the nation-state: the uniformization of people within the fatherland... Wealth springs from the diversities of countries and persons, from the fact that they complement each other. We shall always remember a truth often expressed by Father Teilhard de Chardin: Races are not equal but complementary, which is a superior form of equality. Whence the superiority of the federal over the unitary state. I shall go even further. There is but one way to reduce the tyranny of the state, to ward off its diseases, as the socialist Proudhon said, and that way is through federalism – in other words, the decentralization and deconcentration of its economic and political institutions.[25]

Protecting Senegal's diverse ethnic and tribal communities was thus central to Senghor's nationalism. Federal institutions would garner the

[24] Markovitz 1969, 113.
[25] Senghor as quoted in Markovitz 1969, 111.

loyalties of all citizens and would not belong to any particular ethnic group.

Consistent with these beliefs, under Senghor's leadership, the Senegalese military continued colonial practices of recruiting broadly from across Senegal's ethnic and tribal communities. While data on the exact numbers of commissioned officers, broken down by ethnic group, is unavailable throughout this period, we do know that officer recruitment operated first by random draw and then by voluntary enlistment. Historical sources also unanimously concur that the military was ethnically heterogeneous, that no group held noticeable numerical or command hierarchy advantages, and that intra-military tensions were focused on non-ethnic criteria such as technical expertise, foreign education and exchange opportunities, and training cohorts.[26] Given these seemingly unbiased recruitment practices, combined with Senghor's known beliefs on protecting ethnic diversity, it is reasonable to assume that he intentionally built a heterogenous and representative military, both amongst the rank-and-file and the officer corps.

Low Potential for Resistance: Continuity in Diverse Recruitment Practices and French Protection

Senghor's policies were unlikely to provoke discontent within the officer corps, let alone overt resistance, because they both continued existing recruitment practices and benefited from external French protection. Known as the Tirailleurs Sénégalais, France's West African colonial troops were drawn from across the region and integrated into a single fighting force that could be deployed wherever needed. The Tirailleurs even served on the front lines in Europe in World War I, in North Africa during World War II, and in Indochina and Algeria during those anti-colonial insurgencies.[27] While recruitment for the Tirailleurs across broader West Africa sometimes followed British martial race doctrine, excluding politically unreliable groups or those deemed unfit for military service,[28] within Senegal itself the French practiced near universal male

---

[26] Diop & Paye 1998, 319; Keegan 1983, 514–515; Nelson 1974, 340.

[27] Echenberg 1991.

[28] For example, the forest peoples of lower Côte d'Ivoire were declared "too feeble and unwarlike" to serve. French administrators also often exempted Saharan and Sahelian tribes from military service because sending draft boards so far into the interior carried a high cost and because they worried that Arab tribesmen would disobey the orders of

conscription. From 1912 to 1960, in times of both war and peace, all Senegalese ethnic groups were subject to the draft.[29]

According to Echenberg's rich historical study of the Tirailleurs Sénégalais, based on the total number of recruits the colony was to contribute towards the inter-territorial force, each of Senegal's administrative units, or cercles, was allotted a yearly quota reflecting its population density. Because Senegal's ethnic groups are geographically concentrated, this resulted in recruitment patterns that generally reflected the territory's underlying ethnic diversity (see Figure 4.1).[30] Although the records are partially incomplete, in the decade prior to independence, military recruitment continued to draw broadly from across these old cercles, by that time subdivided into smaller recruitment areas. Draft board lists survive from everywhere but Djoloff and the sparsely populated eastern areas of Matam, Bakel, Kédougou, and Tambacounda.[31] We can thus be fairly confident that Senegal's rank-and-file, at independence, reflected the country's ethnic diversity.

As with the rest of Africa, Senegal faced a dearth of African officers as decolonization approached. Although France had begun promoting African soldiers to officer rank as early as the 1910s, usually for valor during battle, a serious Africanization program for the officer corps was not launched until after World War II. The program failed to achieve any significant progress until the mid-1950s: in 1956, there were still only 85 African officers in all of French West Africa.[32] As a core French colony and the backbone of the colonial army, however,

---

Black NCOs. Other groups were excluded based on similar social and cultural appraisals (Ibid., 63).

[29] Ibid., 4.

[30] Ibid., 47–57.

[31] Archives Nationales du Sénégal (ANS), Fonds Sénégal Colonial (FSC) 11D1/0106, "Diourbel, Army Recruitment Tables 1955–60"; ANS FSC 11D1/0130, "Diourbel, Army Recruitment 1958"; ANS FSC 11D1/0172, "Casamance & Bignona, Military Journal of Mobilization 1952"; ANS FSC 11D1/0225, "Oussaye, Military Recruitment 1934–64"; ANS FSC 11D1/0256, "Velingara, Military Affairs 1947–60"; ANS FSC 11D1/0331, "Zinguinchor, Military Recruitment 1926–55"; ANS FSC 11D1/0386, "Zinguinchor, Military Recruitment 1946–52"; ANS FSC 11D1/0707, "Bas-Sénégal, Military Recruitment 1954–60; ANS FSC 11D1/1024, "Noro, Gendarmerie and Military Recruitment 1953–59"; ANS FSC 11D1/1088, "Sine-Saloum & Foundiouge, Military Recruitment 1953–64"; ANS FSC 11D1/1186, "Koolack, Military Classes 1957–58"; ANS FSC 11D1/1265, "Cayor-Tivaouane, Military Recruitment 1948–59,"; ANS FSC 11D1/1305, "Mbour, Military Recruitment 1945–60"; ANS FSC 11D1/1426, "Thies, Military Recruitment Tables 1952–54"; ANS FSC 11D1/1436, "Thies, Military Class 1954"; ANS FSC 11D1/1443, "Thies, Military Recruitment Tables 1955–56."

[32] Echenberg 1991, 118.

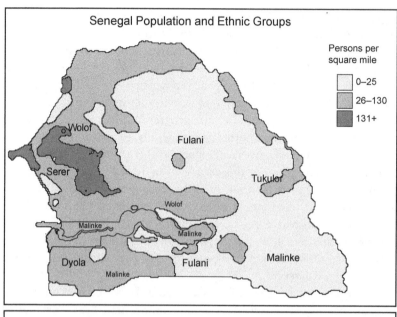

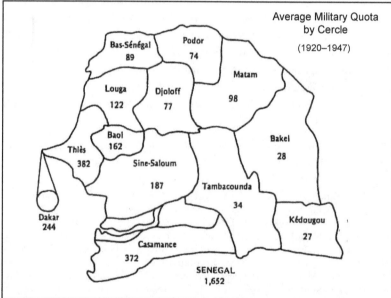

FIGURE 4.1. Colonial Military Recruitment in Senegal

Top: Based on "Senegal and Gambia: Population and Ethnic Groups 1972," courtesy of the University of Texas Libraries, The University of Texas at Austin. Bottom: "Average Military Quota by Cercle," from *Colonial Conscripts: The Tirailleurs Sénégalais in French West Africa, 1857–1960.* Copyright ©1991 by Myron Echenberg. Published by Heinemann, Portsmouth, NH. Reprinted by permission of the Publisher. All rights reserved.

Senegal did disproportionately benefit from this Africanization program with many of the Tirailleurs officers' and NCOs hailing from the territory.[33] Although exact ethnic breakdowns for this growing officer corps are unavailable – French records fail to note ethnicity – officer promotion and transfer registers from the time period contain last names representative of a wide diversity of Senegalese ethnic groups.[34] Senghor thus inherited an ethnically diverse military, including amongst its officers. Merely continuing these longstanding recruitment practices, in a context of low ethnic politicization, was unlikely to provoke resistance from unthreatened officers.

Senghor's government also benefited from a high degree of French protection, although such protection seems superfluous. Even after independence, Africanization proceeded gradually, leaving many French soldiers in field command positions until around 1974, when most seconded officers had finally been reduced to entirely advisory positions.[35] Additionally, Senegal sustained close ties to France and allowed the French to maintain a strong military presence in the country, not just during the immediate postcolonial period, but consistently up until the present day. Senghor developed the idea of independence through interdependence: since the modern state could not achieve economic self-sufficiency, it would always be partially dependent on others. Independence must thus be realized through alliances and coalitions, both with other African states and with France.[36] Senghor also believed in the gradual evolution of Senegalese political institutions toward greater autonomy rather than a sharp break with French rule. Gradualism was preferred to radicalism because it avoided the dangers of rapid change, of progress towards democratic socialism being abandoned for destruction and dictatorship in the name of independence.[37]

When presented with the option of immediate independence, the PS even supported continued colonial rule over rupturing relations with France. In 1958, the French army in Algeria revolted, leading to the collapse of the Fourth Republic and the return to power of Charles de Gaulle. A constitutional referendum was quickly held across the colonies, offering a choice between continued subordination to France within a federal constitutional framework or full independence replete with

33 Ibid., 19–20.
34 ANS FSC 11D1/0213 "Garde Républicaine Personnel, 1959–1963."
35 Nelson 1974, 334–336.
36 Young 2001, 270.
37 Markovitz 1969, 104.

expulsion from the Francophone community. Senghor and the PS rallied Senegal's voters to reject independence on such terms. Instead, Senegal prioritized close economic and political relations with France, even after independence had finally been granted.[38]

Such close relations allowed France to retain its strong military position in Senegal. In addition to seconding many officers to the Senegalese army and providing extensive aid and training, France maintained a garrison of around 2,250 combat soldiers near Dakar. Even after formally transferring this base to Senegal in 1974, France preserved its strategic presence by continuing to station a battalion of marines near the capital.[39]

Close relations combined with this direct French military presence may have aided Senghor in preserving political stability while constructing the inclusive military he desired. As Diop and Paye note, this "strategically placed French military unit at the Dakar support base, and French oversight of the Senegalese army, brought a presumption that any coup d'état would fail."[40] The French were, however, highly inconsistent in their willingness to intervene on behalf of the governments of their former colonies, despite defense pacts and security guarantees specifying otherwise. In the 1960s alone, the French government allowed successful coups to stand in Benin, Burkina Faso, the Central African Republic, Congo-Brazzaville, and Mali.[41] Relying on French protection was an uncertain gambit. Yet, Senegal was considered a core former colony and the potential for French intervention may nonetheless have aided Senghor in avoiding potential conflicts with the military.

Resulting Stability: Inclusive Security Institutions and Gradual Liberalization

An ethnically diverse army, facilitated by low ethnic politicization, has allowed Senegal to avoid much of the political destabilization encountered by other African countries. There have been no incidents of ethnically motivated soldier rebellion, either mutinies or coups. Indeed, there has only ever been one incident of the Senegalese military intervening directly in politics, which occurred shortly after independence.

---

[38] Foltz 1965, 91–94; Smith 1978, 89.
[39] Keegan 1983, 514–515; Luckham 1982, 64; McCoy 1994, 42; Crocker 1968, 22; Nelson 1974, 337.
[40] Diop & Paye 1998, 329.
[41] See, for example, Decalo 1991, 76; Welch 1967, 317.

Sometimes characterized as a failed coup attempt, there was no intention to seize power, no resulting purges or changes in recruitment practices, and no slide toward instability. Instead, Senegal remained a stable one-party state under Senghor's leadership until he began to slowly open the political system to multiparty competition. Since the 1990s, Senegal has become a success story of African democratization, peacefully transferring the presidency between leaders of different political parties and ethnic backgrounds. Throughout, Senegal's inclusive military has not only refrained from seizing power but has stood behind liberalization and discouraged leaders from defying the constitution.

Despite a general pattern of military respect for civilian rule and abstinence from politics, Senegal's armed forces did meddle in domestic political struggles during the constitutional crisis of 1962. Considered by many as a coup attempt, there is actually little evidence that any military faction desired power or thought they were doing anything other than their constitutional duty. Nonetheless, the army interposed itself decisively on the side of the president and his parliamentary allies, shifting the balance of domestic power and further consolidating one-party rule under Senghor. This sole instance of direct military intervention contained no ethnic dimension and stands in stark contrast to the ethnically driven instability of cases like Sierra Leone and Ghana.

The roots of the 1962 constitutional crisis lay in the collapse of the Mali Federation mere months after independence. To cope with this sudden change in governing institutions, Senegal's territorial Prime Minister, Mamadou Dia, declared a state of emergency. He thereby evoked temporary powers which would allow Senegal's leaders to alter the constitutional arrangements underpinning the now defunct federation. A hybrid parliamentary and presidential system was adopted with executive powers shared between Prime Minister Dia and the newly established office of the president, to be held by Senghor. Dia was made head of the national assembly as well as minister of defense, and charged with the day-to-day affairs of the administration. Senghor primarily held responsibility for foreign affairs.

That the PS controlled both positions masked an underlying division between conservative and radical economic interests that would propel these arrangements of shared executive authority into crisis. Senghor continued to work closely with the marabouts, supplying patronage in return for political support. He thus represented the interests of traditional forms of peanut production within the government. Dia, on the other hand, envisioned a complete transformation of colonial social and economic structures. His was a vision more in accord with the socialism that the PS purportedly represented and Dia garnered the radicals' support within the party.[42]

Tensions developed as Dia failed to lift the state of emergency he had imposed for nearly two and a half years, using his emergency powers to implement agricultural reform. He aimed explicitly to undercut the authority of the marabouts, diversify the rural economy, and eventually nationalize peanut production. First, Dia proposed the creation of a Supreme Islamic Council, which would disrupt traditional relations between the marabouts and their adepts, potentially bypassing the marabouts as intermediaries altogether. Second, he reduced the subsidies and loans available to the marabouts and declared his intention to functionally nationalize all commercial agriculture, placing it under the direction of educated bureaucrats. Finally, Dia began seizing lands traditionally cultivated by the marabouts and establishing farmer's cooperatives in their place.[43] These measures severely alienated the Sufi brotherhoods and their political allies, including Senghor. Combined with the extended use of emergency powers, the radical economic reform program led over 40 deputies in the National Assembly to sign a motion of censure against Dia.

Under the constitution, however, a motion of censure was technically illegal during a state of emergency. On these grounds, Dia denied the motion a parliamentary vote when it was brought before the full assembly in December 1962. Senghor then threw the full weight of his political authority into the dispute, backing the petitioners and advocating for a vote despite its illegality. The executive committee of the PS intervened between the factions but was unable to broker a compromise. The Prime Minister then drastically escalated the crisis. Using his prerogatives as the Minister of Defense, Dia ordered the gendarmerie and police to evacuate and seal off the National Assembly building, physically preventing any vote on the censure motion. His forces also occupied the radio station and cut the telephone lines to the presidential palace where Senghor and his supporters had gathered.

The conflict may have been forcefully resolved in Dia's favor at that moment if it were not for the split authority over the security forces written in the constitution. Observing the police and gendarmerie stationed around the capital, Colonel Jean Alfred Diallo deployed army units on Senghor's behalf as the President and Commander-in-Chief.

---

[42] Barry 1988, 280; Fink 2007, 24–25 & 34.
[43] Fink 2007, 25; Loimeier 1996, 186.

Parachute troops surrounded the presidential palace to protect Senghor and other troops were ordered to face off against Dia's units outside the main administration building. A military stand-off ensued. Not wanting to shoot at each other, many emergency meetings were called throughout the night, both between military and police officers and with the powerful marabouts, who naturally threw their support behind Senghor. The crisis passed without violence in the wee hours of the night when the top military brass decided to fully back Senghor. The following morning, Dia and several of his closest associates were arrested and the censure motion vote was allowed to proceed and passed. The office of prime minister was then abolished, consolidating full executive authority under Senghor's presidency. There was no interruption in civilian rule and the military retreated to the barracks as soon as the political crisis had abated. Moreover, while the commander of the armed forces was dismissed and placed under house arrest, there were no further arrests or purges of military officers.[44]

Following this single instance of military intervention in politics, Senegal has maintained political stability and gradually traveled down a path of increasing electoral competition and democratization. One-party rule was legally established in 1966 under Senghor and the PS, but the political system was reopened to multiparty competition in 1976,[45] well before the third wave of democratization reached the rest of Africa. In 1980, Senghor became the first African head-of-state to retire voluntarily from politics, relinquishing power to his handpicked successor, Abdou Diouf. Within a year, Diouf lifted the remaining restrictions on opposition parties. Then, in 1985, profound economic difficulties culminated in IMF mandated structural adjustment programs, severely restricting the available resources for agricultural subsidies and credits. This undercut the patronage system that had for decades tied the marabouts to the PS. With the loss of their financial support, the marabouts stopped issuing religious edicts and adopted a stance of political neutrality. Thereafter, the vote share of the PS steadily declined, from 80–83% in the 1983 elections, to 71–73% in 1988, to 56–58% in 1993.[46] By the 1990s, a more transparent electoral code had also been adopted and opposition politicians had gained many seats in parliament. In 2000–2001, the PS

---

44 Fatton 1986, 67; Fink 2007, 34–36; *Keesings* 1963, v.9 (January); Nelson 1974, 344.
45 Albeit constrained within a predetermined ideological range, with Senghor's PS representing the moderate socialists, the Senegalese Democratic Party representing a more centrist but still liberal alternative, and the African Independence Party representing a radical but still non-communist left.
46 Nunley 2011; Villalón 2015, 312.

was finally defeated at the polls in both the executive and legislative elections – a watershed moment that brought about Senegal's first democratic transfer of power.[47]

By all accounts, throughout both the periods of PS rule and the later democratic transition, there have been no attempts by Senegal's soldiers to rebel or seize state power. Rather, they have become a model of civil-military stability. As will be shown in the following chapter, Senegal's inclusive military has even become a bulwark against authoritarian regression and a staunch advocate of constitutionalism.

Alternative Explanations

Alternative theories such as standard economic explanations do not fair well in explaining Senegal's lack of political instability. Although Senegal was relatively wealthy, for sub-Saharan Africa, at the time of independence it was still a remarkably poor country with an average annual per capita gross domestic product of only $1241, comparable to that of Ghana, Congo-Brazzaville, and Equatorial Guinea, all of which were subjected to multiple coups after decolonization. Senegal was also heavily dependent on the export of a single commodity, peanuts, which created intense vulnerability to international price fluctuations. Moreover, Senegal faced poor average growth rates, the worst of the four cases analyzed here: just 0.8% on average in the five years immediately following independence. Senegal has also experienced high volatility in growth rates and frequent, deep recessions, particularly from the late 1960s to the mid-1980s (see Figure 4.2).[48] Even during the worst of these economic times, the military refrained from intervention. Neither poverty, commodity dependence, nor poor growth – all common explanations for coups – led to instability in Senegal.

Ethnic exclusion arguments are more difficult to dismiss. The fact that no system of ethnic privilege has ever been constructed within Senegal's military logically entails that none has been perpetuated. Both absences of cause predict not only the lack of rebellion, but also the absence of each theory's causal mechanisms. We thus cannot use the timing of violence, since there is none and both theories predict none, to differentiate between the arguments. Indeed, it is nearly impossible to disentangle the theories within any negative case, a failure not remediable by case selection:

---

[47] Galvan 2001, 52–59; Kelly 2012, 122; Villalón 2015, 312.
[48] All economic data derived from The Maddison Project (2013 version).

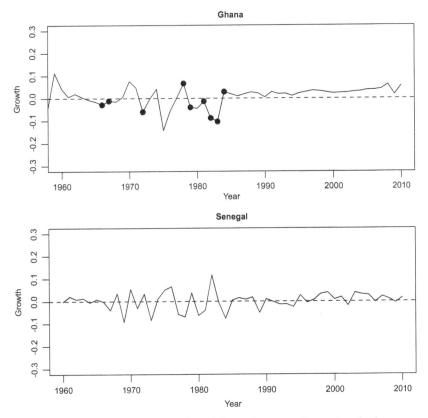

FIGURE 4.2. Economic Growth and Coup Attempts: Senegal and Ghana

any context lacking the construction of institutional ethnic privilege would also lack its continued existence. The strength of the evidence thus rests on the between-case comparisons. The case of Ghana will demonstrate that it was the choice to turn away from inclusive practices, and toward the construction of an ethnic army, that provoked soldier rebellion. Senegal's commitment to diversity, facilitated by its low level of ethnic politicization, was thus vital to maintaining peace and political stability.

INSTABILITY IN GHANA

Ghana witnessed an extraordinary degree of political instability following independence. Between 1966 and 1984, the country experienced ten coup attempts, many of which were successful. I argue that this instability resulted from Kwame Nkrumah's turn toward constructing systems of ethnic privilege within the military, after having initially committed himself to an inclusive nationalism that built ethnic diversity into the army. Facing discrimination and exclusion, Ewe and Ga officers seized power, provoking fears of reciprocal exclusion amongst Akan officers. The resulting struggle for dominance between the Ewe and Akan, over both civilian and military institutions, repeatedly degenerated into violence and spurred coups, counter-coups, and preemptive coups.

Nkrumah's fateful choice was conditioned by the preexisting high degree of ethnic politicization in Ghana. Early political parties formed largely along ethnic lines and pre-independence elections were marred by ethnic violence. Nkrumah thus interpreted two assassination attempts against his life in ethnic terms, leading him to seek military loyalty through coethnicity. This points to a crucial difference with Senegal, where political parties formed along non-ethnic lines and ethnicity exerted a minimal influence on politics. Ethnic politicization limits the ability of political leaders to build inclusive militaries, even where the will to do so exists.

The Politicization of Ethnicity and the Rise of Kwame Nkrumah

Ghana's early political parties developed along both ethno-regional and nationalistic lines. The two main political parties that spearheaded Ghana's independence movement were the National Liberation Movement (NLM)[49] and the Convention People's Party (CPP). Their leaders drew inspiration from Mahatma Gandhi and Martin Luther King Jr. as well as from West Africa's own history of non-violent colonial reform movements, notably the Aborigines Rights Protection Society and the Congress of British West Africa. Both parties eschewed violence and openly pledged to struggle for decolonization through constitutional means.[50]

Despite these shared beliefs and inspirations, however, the NLM and CPP approached their ethnic recruitment and representation efforts quite differently. Ghana is a remarkably diverse country with over 50 distinct identity groups, divided into four major regional ethno-linguistic clusters: the Akan of the center and south (44.1% of the total population), the

---

[49] Originally named the United Gold Coast Convention (UGCC). For clarity and consistency, I refer to the party by its later name throughout.
[50] Morrison 2004, 423.

Mole-Dagbani of the north (15.9%), the Ewe of the southeast (13%), and the Ga-Adangbe of the eastern coastal region (8.3%).[51] Founded in 1949, the CPP was led by Kwame Nkrumah, who hailed from one of Ghana's smallest ethnic groups, the Nzima of the southwest. Perhaps because of his outsider status to Ghana's primary ethnic cleavages, Nkrumah and the CPP welcomed all Ghanaians into their ranks, regardless of regional or ethnic identity. Indeed, the party purposefully appealed to a nationalism that cut across ethnic lines and sought support and representation across all parts of the colony.[52] Conversely, the NLM framed itself as an Akan and Asante political party, the Asante[53] comprising an important and large ethnic subgroup of the Akan. Formed in 1946 and led by J.B. Danquah and Kofi Busia, the party was dominated by Akan merchants, businessmen, and intellectuals. Party recruitment efforts, moreover, focused on coopting rural Akan chiefs and capturing the urban votes of the cities in the Akan region of south and central Ghana.[54]

During the pre-independence elections, several smaller political parties also formed, mainly along ethno-regional lines. The Northern People's Party (NPP) represented the Mole-Dagbani, an alliance of small northern identity groups that shared linguistic and cultural traits (although to treat them as a unified ethnic group would betray the complexity of group and sub-group relations in northern Ghana). The Togoland Congress (TC) drew on Ewe support in the southeast and campaigned explicitly for the unification of Ewe peoples, who were divided across British-French colonial borders. The Muslim Association Party represented Muslim immigrants to Ghana's large towns and urban areas and allied itself with the NPP. Thus, by the time of the 1954 elections, three of Ghana's four principal ethno-regional groups had formed political parties expressly representing their narrow ethnic interests.[55]

This already worrisome degree of ethnic politicization was deepened during the 1954–56 legislative and presidential elections, when party competition turned violent. Considered "widespread and persistent," the violence was concentrated in the Asante homelands and occurred primarily between CPP and NLM supporters. These clashes resulted in several deaths and the destruction of many homes. CPP leaders and

[51] See Adekson 1976, 252; Minority Rights Group 2010.
[52] Adekson 1976, 252–254; Minorities at Risk Project 2009.
[53] Also referred to as the Ashanti.
[54] Morrison 2004, 422–425.
[55] Adekson 1976, 252; Asante & Gyimah-Boadi 2004, 233; Mazrui & Tidy 1984, 87–88; Morrison 2004, 422–423.

politicians were also precluded from campaigning in or even visiting Kumasi, the regional capital, for fear of their personal safety. Asante ethnic politicization had thus taken a violent turn prior to independence.[56]

Despite the proliferation of ethnic political parties and violence, however, the CCP easily won the 1956 legislative and presidential elections. Kwame Nkrumah thereby assumed the presidency just prior to decolonization and commanded a clear majority in the Legislative Assembly, with the CCP controlling 71 of 104 seats.[57]

Foundations of Military Loyalty: From Inclusivity to Ethnic Manipulation

Nkrumah initially rejected ethnicity as a cornerstone of politics and attempted to build a national and inclusive military. Nkrumah abhorred what he pejoratively called tribalism, viewing it as "the canker-worm which, unless removed, may destroy the solidity of the body politic, the stability of the government, the efficiency of the bureaucracy and judiciary, and the effectiveness of the army and police."[58] He saw no place for ethnic considerations or competition in any part of the government and especially not within the state's security institutions. Rather, he believed the military could be used to overcome the tribal divisions adversely affecting Ghanaian society and corrupting its political parties. Through rigorous training and education, recruits of diverse backgrounds could be melded into a unified fighting force with a strong sense of national identity.[59]

Nkrumah, however, did not inherit an army consistent with this vision. Throughout their empire, the British believed that some ethnic and racial groups made for superior soldiers. In Ghana, this martial race doctrine tended to privilege groups located on the edges of colonial governance, who had been subjugated most recently, and had been exposed to fewer "softening" influences such as missionary education. Military recruiters thereby focused their efforts on the poor and peripheral ethnic groups of the north. Through such practices, the mostly Muslim, Mole-Dagbani tribes of that region came to dominate the rank-and-file colonial infantry.[60] Officer commissions followed a different ethnic bias.

[56] Mazrui & Tidy 1984, 59 & 88.
[57] Ibid.
[58] As quoted in Adekson 1976, 256.
[59] Adekson 1976, 257.
[60] Ibid., 253–258.

Military necessities during World War II led Britain to commission the first native Ghanaian officers.[61] Unlike the rank-and-file, the British drew most of this emergent officer corps from the more educated far south of the territory. At the time of independence in 1957, 73% of officers hailed from the south: 34.6% were Ga, 23.1% Ewe, and 15% Fante.[62] Only four northerners had gained commissions by independence. The Akan and Asante, meanwhile, were severely underrepresented, constituting no more than 5–7% of soldiers at any rank.[63] Nkrumah thus inherited a national army that excluded Ghana's largest ethnic group and whose officer corps was dominated by southern groups while its rank-and-file was largely comprised of northerners.

In the first three years of his presidency, Nkrumah devised inclusive policies to correct these colonial recruitment patterns. Recruitment, promotion, and retention measures were designed to diversify the military in as non-threatening a manner as possible, using rapid expansion to allow dominant groups numerical increases while reducing their overall proportional representation. Between 1957–1959, Nkrumah doubled the size of the army and established both a navy and air force.[64] By 1966, the army had reached 14,600 men, more than a threefold increase since 1957.[65] This allowed him to augment the proportional representation of previously excluded groups, especially the Akan, in both the officer corps and rank-and-file without necessitating measures that would anger other groups such as strict quotas, forced retirements, blocked promotions, or the exclusion of particular ethnicities from recruitment drives. One rather clever program tackled multiple historic imbalances at once: northern over-representation in the rank-and-file was reduced through retraining programs targeted at Mole-Dagbani soldiers, promoting them into the officer corps where they were severely under-represented.[66] Through such measures, Nkrumah demonstrated a significant commitment to inclusion and diversity while reducing Ga and Ewe domination of the officer corps.

This commitment to inclusivity and ethnic neutrality was deeply challenged in the early 1960s, however, when Ewe and Ga politicians

---

[61] Clayton 1989, 258.
[62] Adekson 1976, 253.
[63] Ibid.
[64] Keegan 1983, 216–218.
[65] Adekson 1976, 259.
[66] This was not, however, a very successful effort as only two additional Mole-Dagbani officers were commissioned in the nine years following independence. Ibid., 258–259; Boahen 1988, 209.

and military and police officers were rumored to have orchestrated two separate assassination attempts against Nkrumah's life. In August 1962, a hand grenade was detonated near the president while he was publicly greeting supporters in the northern town of Kulungugu. While the incident still remains shrouded in mystery, Nkrumah believed that prominent Ga politicians had masterminded the plot. In reaction, he charged a Ga Warrant Officer with supplying the grenade and dismissed and detained three Ga cabinet ministers, who were later tried and sentenced to death for treason along with other suspected conspirators.[67]

Only 15 months later, an Ewe police sergeant recently posted to Accra from the eastern region made a second attempt on the president's life. As Nkrumah approached his car outside of Flagstaff House, the police sergeant fired five shots, killing a security aide. Having run out of bullets, he then chased the president around the courtyard while his police protection detail stood by. The assailant later claimed that the Deputy Commissioner of Police had directed him to kill the president. Convinced of a larger conspiracy and fearing further attacks, Nkrumah disarmed the police, arrested more Ga politicians, and fired eight Ga police chiefs, bypassing normal institutional procedures and replacing them with officers from different ethnic backgrounds.[68]

These assassination attempts led Nkrumah to develop deep suspicions of an "ethnic plot" against him and to radically shift policy away from promoting nationalism within the military and toward ethnic manipulation. From 1963 to 1966, he developed a complex system of institutional controls that relied on ethnic loyalty and ethnic factionalism to guard against potential coups and assassination attempts launched from within the security forces. First, Nkrumah began building coethnic units upon whose loyalty he could rely. By 1966, for example, the elite Counter-Intelligence Unit was comprised mainly of officers from

---

[67] Adekson 1976, 264; TNA DO 195/273 47, "Letter from the British High Commissioner to the West Africa Department, Commonwealth Relations Office," October 3, 1964.

[68] Ibid., 264–266; TNA DO 195/216 139, "Despatch No. 2/66: Ghana: The Overthrow of Nkrumah," March 28, 1966; TNA DO 195/272 1, "Telegram No. 9 from Accra to the Commonwealth Relations Office," January 2, 1964; TNA DO 195/272 6, "Assassination Attempt: Telegram No. 12 from Accra to the Commonwealth Relations Office," January 3, 1964; TNA DO 195/272 7, "Attempted Assassination: Telegram No. 14 from Accra to the Commonwealth Relations Office," January 2, 1964; TNA DO 195/272 23, "Assassination Attempt: Telegram No. 44 from Accra to the Commonwealth Relations Office," January 8, 1964; TNA DO 195/272 24, "Ghana," [undated]; TNA DO 195/272 30, "Assassination Attempt: Letter from the Acting British High Commissioner to the Commonwealth Relations Office," January 18, 1964.

Nkrumah's own small Nzima ethnic group and Nzima occupied important positions such as the Director of Military Intelligence.[69] Northerners
were the only other trusted group of soldiers. Ga and Ewe officers,
on the other hand, fell under political suspicion and were accused of
tribalism and excluded or rotated to benign posts far from the capital.[70]
Second, existing ethnic antagonisms were exploited to provide checks and
balances against the coordination and execution of coups. Units whose
rank-and-file soldiers were recruited from the north were placed under
the command of southern officers and vice versa. Two or more officers
from different ethnic backgrounds were also appointed to command
positions with overlapping responsibilities. Field units would thereby
come under the authority of multiple officers with different ethnic ties
and loyalties such that any suspicious actions or movements would more
likely be reported. Finally, competing security agencies were stacked with
rival ethnic groups in order to further encourage intelligence gathering
and the reporting of any "ethnic plots."[71] Through these measures,
Nkrumah recontaminated the army with the very ethnic antagonisms and
imbalances he had initially sought to remedy.

High Potential for Resistance: Ethnic Diversity in the Officer Corps and the Absence of British Protection

As previously discussed, via colonial recruitment practices and his own
initial policies, by the time Nkrumah turned to building coethnic army
units and otherwise ethnically manipulating security institutions, he
commanded an already highly diverse military. Nor could he any longer
rely on British troops to protect his government. In the immediate
post-independence period, the British had maintained a strong presence
of seconded officers within the Ghanaian military. By Nkrumah's own
executive order, however, they had been precipitously dismissed in
1961, just before the assassination attempts. Combined, these conditions
left Nkrumah's government vulnerable to a potential military coup by
simultaneously threatening officers while dismissing foreign protection.

For the first three years following decolonization, the Ghanaian military relied heavily on seconded British officers to fill the high and middle
ranks of its command hierarchy. This resulted from two considerations.
First, Nkrumah was attempting to restructure the military and to correct

---

69 Adekson 1976, 264; TNA DO 153/37 104B, "Summary No. 7/66: Current Events in
Ghana," March 4, 1966.
70 Adekson 1976, 266–267.
71 Ibid., 264–267; Hutchful 2003, 80.

the historic imbalances in ethnic representation created by colonial policy. This involved admitting large numbers of Akan and Asante soldiers into the army, given their severe historic under-representation. Yet, opening the ranks to the Akan was risky given the political rivalry between Nkrumah's party, the CPP, and the Akan-based NLM, especially considering that their election campaigning had recently degenerated into widespread violence. According to Adekson, concerns over the loyalty of Akan officers, and also potentially Mole-Dagbani officers, led Nkrumah to lean on the remaining British officers for security and protection.[72]

Second, slow Africanization of the officer corps in the run up to independence meant that Ghana lacked sufficient well-trained native officers to fill the ranks. In 1957, there were still only 29 native officers out of a total of 214.[73] British seconded officers were simply needed while new cohorts of Ghanaians were being trained at Sandhurst and Eaton Hall. Indeed, the number of British officers and NCOs serving in Ghana actually increased after decolonization: from 185 in April 1957 to 200 in January 1960.[74] The top brass also remained entirely British, including the Chief of Defense Staff, with no African officers above the rank of major.[75]

Africanization of the officer corps proceeded with purposeful caution until September 22, 1961 when, by executive order, Nkrumah abruptly dismissed the remaining seconded British officers and NCOs from the command hierarchy.[76] Up until then, the aforementioned concerns over the ability to quickly train new officers to a consistent and high caliber, the potential for future promotion blockages, and the insurance British officers provided against a possible military takeover had kept the pace of Africanization slow.[77] None of these constraints had miraculously lifted in

---

[72] Adekson 1976, 258.

[73] Clayton 1989, 258; TNA DO 35/9216 30, "Ghana – Functions of United Kingdom Officers and NCOs Seconded to the Ghana Armed Forces," April 25, 1957.

[74] TNA DO 35/9216 30, "Ghana – Functions of United Kingdom Officers and NCOs Seconded to the Ghana Armed Forces," April 25, 1957; TNA DO 35/9217, "Anglo-French Official Talks on Africa – June 1960: Ghana Defense," [undated]; January 1960.

[75] Adekson 1976, 253 & 258; Boahen 1988, 218–219; TNA CO 968/681 67, "Telegram from Sgd. H.W. Browne to Colonel W. Russell Edmonds," September 4, 1959; TNA CO 968/682 116, "Letter from Brigadier H.A. Lascelles of the War Office to Sir Patrick Dean of the Foreign Office," November 27, 1959; TNA DO 35/9216 30, "Ghana – Functions of United Kingdom Officers and NCOs Seconded to the Ghana Armed Forces," April 25, 1957; Keegan 1983, 216–218.

[76] Adekson 1976, 260.

[77] Hutchful 1979, 610; The National Archives of the UK (TNA), Records of the Ministry of Defense (DEFE) 13/105 1, "Telegram from Accra to the Commonwealth Relations Office," June 26, 1960.

1961. Nor had Nkrumah's goals suddenly changed: from the early days of independence, he had advocated for the full Ghanaianization of the office corps as quickly as possible but balanced that goal against expansion of the armed forces.[78] Rather, the most likely explanation for Nkrumah's precipitous reversal in policy can be traced to events external to Ghana. In August 1960, the Congo politically collapsed after a mass mutiny by its armed forces. The mutiny began in the Kinshasha barracks after Belgian General Emile Janssens gathered the soldiers for a meeting and wrote on the blackboard "before independence = after independence." This unveiled reference to the continued white Belgian monopoly over the officer corps induced a rage that spread like wildfire through the rank-and-file. Belgium had commissioned exactly zero African officers prior to decolonization. Fears of mass mutiny against still predominantly white officer corps' spread across the continent, leading to intense pressures for rapid Africanization.[79]

In response, Nkrumah terminated the current arrangements of seconding British officers into command positions and instead negotiated for a British joint services training team. Rather than holding authority themselves within the command hierarchy, the British would temporarily shadow Ghanaian officers as they learned on the job and would continue their training assistance across all three branches of military service, with most aid concentrated on the new navy and air force. This change was accompanied by a significant and immediate draw down in British forces: to 85 officers by May 1962.[80] Thus, by the time Nkrumah began ethnically manipulating security institutions in 1964, he had largely eroded any protection the British could have provided – they stationed no combat troops near Ghanaian territory, their remaining officers were relegated to training duties, and they had a minimal presence in the army.

The Resulting Instability: Descent into Chaos

In 1966, a successful coup attempt by Ewe officers against Nkrumah unseated what was left of the nationalizing agenda of the CCP and

---

[78] TNA DO 35/9217 73, "Anglo-French Talks on Africa – June 1960: Ghana Defense," [undated]; TNA DO 35/9227 1, "Letter from the British High Commissioner in Accra to the Commonwealth Relations Office," November 25, 1959.
[79] Aboagye 1999, 15–116; Adekson 1979, 161; Young 1965, 315–317.
[80] TNA DEFE 13/105 51, "British Joint Services Training Team in Ghana," April 16, 1962; TNA DEFE 13/105 52, "No. 181 Guidance from Foreign Office to Certain of Her Majesty's Representatives," May 3, 1962.

initiated a downward spiral of instability. In the subsequent 18 years, there would be nine additional attempted military coups as well as frequent purges, plots, and self-consuming intra-military violence. Efforts to build or dismantle systems of ethnic privilege within the military do not explain every Ghanaian coup and economic explanations must be accorded heavy influence in some cases. Nonetheless, much of the rebellion and violence did result from such efforts and their chaotic aftermath, including the deepening schism between Ewe and Akan officers.

The 1966 Coup and 1967 Counter-Coup

Nkrumah's turn toward northern and Nzima favoritism, and against the Ewe, likely inspired the 1966 coup that deposed his government. In many ways, the coup was overdetermined: economic stagnation, severed diplomatic relations with Britain that meant withdrawal from the commonwealth and the end of military assistance,[81] increasing government unpopularity due to Nkrumah's slide towards authoritarianism, as well as his interference with military corporate interests and his ethnic manipulations within the army and police, all combined to create a perfect storm of soldier dissatisfaction. Perhaps most importantly, by this time Nkrumah was increasingly intruding into day-to-day military matters. He had established both a presidential guard and an un-uniformed security service, responsible solely to himself, that interfered with the lives and work of the regular armed services.[82] In 1965, he reorganized the Ministry of Defense to grant himself "more direct and personal control over the Armed Forces" and dismissed two top officers for suspected political disloyalty.[83] Nkrumah also planned to politically indoctrinate the military, appointing officers in charge of ideological studies to every base and garrison.[84] Papers found after the coup, in the residence of one of Nkrumah's most loyal generals, further indicated that Nkrumah was in the process of dismissing senior army and police officers while expanding the comparatively privileged presidential guard.[85] Through these actions,

---

[81] TNA DO 153/35 6, "Despatch No. 1/66," January 13, 1966.

[82] Adekson 1976, 247, 252–254, & 263; Boahen 1988, 218–219; TNA DO 153/37 104B, "Summary No. 7/66: Current Events in Ghana," March 4, 1966.

[83] TNA DO 195/225 30, "The Change of Command in the Ghana Armed Forces," July 31, 1965; TNA DO 195/225 33, "Periodic Report No. 7: Ghana – August to December 1965," December 31, 1965.

[84] TNA DO 153/45 56, "Political Indoctrination for the Ghana Army," May 19, 1964.

[85] TNA DO 153/37 91, "Letter from the Defense Liaison Officer to the Commonwealth Relations Office," March 3, 1966; TNA DO 195/217 126, "Despatch No. 3: Ghana: The Rebirth of Freedom," April 8, 1966.

Nkrumah had threatened the interests and professionalism of the military as a whole.

Yet, it was Ewe officers, who had held a privileged position within the officer corps and were now being menaced with marginalization and exclusion, who orchestrated the coup. Other non-ethnically favored groups also joined in. The coup relied heavily on ethnic ties in its planning and execution. Despite the cooptation of non-coethnics in the final stages of preparation, the inner circle of plotters was comprised of three senior Ewe and Ga officers: General Emmanuel Kotoko (Ewe), Lieutenant General Joseph Arthur Ankra (Ga), and Police Inspector-General John Harlley (Ewe). In preparing for the coup, General Kotoko was also widely believed to have recruited and drawn assistance from other Ewe soldiers. Support for the coup split along ethnic lines. Despite widespread disaffection within the army over Nkrumah's interference with internal military matters and manipulations of command assignments and officer recruitment, a faction of loyalists did defend the regime and fighting broke out between military units, especially around the capital. This violence pitted Nkrumah's Nzima and other northern defenders, mostly within the presidential guard and the President's un-uniformed personal security service, against an alliance of Akan, Ga, and Ewe rebels across all major army units.[86]

Having prevailed over the loyalists, the coup plotters established a military government, the National Liberation Council (NLC), that was dominated by Ewe and Ga officers and that quickly turned toward building coethnic security institutions. Four of the seven original NLC members came from these two ethnic groups, with only one member representing each of the Asante, Fanti, and northern tribes.[87] Given the relative proportions of the Ewe and Ga in the overall population, around 13% and 8% respectively, it is hardly surprising that this token diversity

---

[86] The navy and air force had been left out of the coup plot because of their continued close links to the British training team. The British officers remained neutral throughout the coup. Adekson 1976, 267; Hettne 1980, 179; Minorities at Risk Project 2009; TNA DO 153/37 1, "Outward Telegram No. 176 from Accra," February 24, 1966; TNA DO 153/37 15, "Outward Telegram No. 191 from Accra," February 24, 1966; TNA DO 153/37 17, "Outward Telegram No. 193," February 24, 1966; TNA DO 153/37 104B, "Summary No. 7/66: Current Events in Ghana," March 4, 1966; TNA DO 195/216 139, "Despatch No. 2/66: Ghana: The Overthrow of Nkrumah," March 28, 1966.

[87] The initial members of the NLC were: Ankrah (Ga), Harley (Ewe), Kotoka (Ewe), Occram (Fante), Nunoo (Ga), Afrifa (Asante), and Yakuba (Yendi). Hettne 1980, 179; TNA 153/37 23, "Outward Telegram No. 196 from Accra," February 28, 1966.

was received skeptically.[88] After the coup, Inspector-General Harlley and General Kotoka fully controlled appointments in the police and military. By April 1967, not much more than a year after the coup, five of the top six posts in the police were held by Ewe, seven of 20 army Colonels were Ewe, and Ewe and Ga together held 65% of senior military ranks above colonel.[89] Moreover, Hutchful argues that "most of the army and police officers on the NLC tended to draw their closest allies and advisers, both civilian and military, from their own ethnic group..."[90] The Ewe officers who had seized power thus appeared to be establishing an ethnically exclusive regime backed by an Ewe- and Ga-dominated army. Most importantly, they were perceived by others within both the civil and military spheres as constructing such dominance.[91]

On April 17, 1967, an abortive counter-coup was launched against the NLC. Lieutenant Arthur, a recently commissioned officer in temporary command of an armored squadron based near the Togo border, drove his 120 man unit to the capital under cover of darkness and under the pretext of defending the government against pro-Nkrumah insurgents. Once there, they seized the airport, the residence of the junta chairman, the army headquarters at Flagstaff House, the telephone exchange, and the broadcasting station. The remainder of the army made little effort to resist while the police seemingly went into hiding. The coup only unraveled when Arthur arrived at the main infantry unit, in search of support and ammunition (which had run out), where he was instead arrested by his more senior officers.[92]

---

[88] Adekson 1976, 252. Only a couple of months after the coup, the British noted that despite diversity on the NLC, there was a widespread feeling that Ewes and Gas were receiving disproportionate appointments, both to the council itself as well as to other important positions. TNA DO 153/35 25, "Letter from the British High Commissioner in Accra to the Commonwealth Relations Office," April 22, 1966.

[89] Baynham 1985, 631. To be fair, not all of this over-representation should be attributed to NLC policies. Early British recruitment practices combined with rapid Africanization had created a preexisting ethnic hierarchy within the military that already favored Ewe and Ga officers, despite Nkrumah's diversification efforts. The initial officer recruits mainly came from the Ewe and Ga who then benefited most from the mass promotions that occurred later. Being first into the ranks, they rose most quickly to the top of the hierarchy. And while the NLC did promote some Akans to higher rank during their short rule, given the relatively small number of total promotions, this made a marginal difference (Hutchful 1979, 614).

[90] Hutchful 1979, 615.

[91] Ibid.

[92] Singh 2014, 120–129; TNA FCO 38/149 18, "The Attempted Coup," April 18, 1967; TNA FCO 38/149 37, "The Attempted Coup," April 29, 1967; TNA FCO 38/149 50,

Rumors abounded that the insurrection had been motivated by the NLC's Ewe dominance. That General Kotoka and two other Ewe officers constituted three of the four fatalities resulting from that night's drama lent confirmatory evidence to these accusations.[93] That a large proportion of the officers involved in the coup were Asante further raised tensions between Ewe and Akan soldiers.[94]

Yet, the NLC immediately issued an announcement denying that disloyal army officers had acted on an ethnic basis. They did not want either soldiers or civilians to believe that Akan and Fanti officers had conspired to overthrow a Ga and Ewe government.[95] Indeed, the motivations of the plotters could be explained through their non-ethnic corporate interests. Two rounds of mass promotions, the first under Nkrumah and the second under the NLC, had resulted in a gluttony of young officers at the top of the military hierarchy, creating a severe long-term promotion blockage. Current junior officers were thus close in age to their superiors and yet faced the prospect of interminable career stagnation. At his trial, Lieutenant Arthur publicly asserted that the grievances of junior officers stemming from the incompetence and rapid promotion of their superiors motivated the coup. The conspirators also admitted that their primary goal had been to dismiss or execute all officers above the rank of colonel.[96]

This purely corporate interest-based interpretation of the coup, however, neglects to consider how ethnicity overlaid the command hierarchy. The combined recruitment and promotion legacies of the British colonial administrators, Nkrumah, and the NLC meant that senior positions in the military were dominated by the Ewe and Ga while many junior officers were Akan. These Akan officers feared not only that strictly rationed promotion possibilities would stifle their rise through the ranks, but that their ethnic identity would exclude them from even those limited

"Despatch No. 8 from the Acting British High Commissioner in Accra to the Secretary of State for Commonwealth Affairs," July 28, 1967.

93 FCO 38/149 11, "Telegram No. 362 from Accra," April 18, 1967; FCO 38/149 50, "Despatch No. 8 from the Acting British High Commissioner in Accra to the Secretary of State for Commonwealth Affairs," July 28, 1967.

94 Officers playing important roles in the coup attempt included Lieutenant Arthur (Ga/Fante), Major Achaab, Major Asante, Lieutenant Amankwah (Asante), Lieutenant Yeboah (Asante), Lieutenant Osei-Poku (Asante), and Lieutenant Colonel Assasie. TNA FCO 38/149 19, "The Attempted Coup," April 22, 1967; TNA FCO 38/149 20, "Press Release No. 41/1967," April 24, 1967.

95 Hettne 1980, 180; Hutchful 1979, 614.

96 Hutchful 1979, 607; TNA FCO 38/150 1, "Letter from the British High Commission in Accra to the Commonwealth Office," May 5, 1967.

opportunities. Furthermore, many army officers supported the coup attempt during its execution precisely because they regarded it as a move against Ewe domination. The NLC's post-coup behavior also supports this interpretation, despite their denial that ethnic tensions motivated the plot. Over the next two years, the NLC took important measures to decrease perceptions of its Ewe domination, restructuring itself towards more ethnic balance as well as initiating a return to civilian rule. They even appointed an Akan, Lieutenant General A.A. Afrifa, as serving chairman of the junta. Such actions suggest that the NLC privately understood the discontent of non-Ewe and Ga soldiers and took their rebellious potential seriously after the coup.[97]

The 1972 Coup

In 1969, the NLC held elections, allowing the army to transfer power back to civilians and return to the barracks. Civilian rule, however, only aggravated ethnic tensions within the military. The elections were marked by ethnic factionalism and the victorious new government of Dr. Kofi Busia quickly sought to displace Ewe and Ga dominance within the military in favor of Akans. This ethnic restructuring of the armed forces threatened Ewe and Ga officers, encouraging them to rebel and provoking counterplots to preempt the reemergence of an Ewe-dominated government. The trap of instability that Ghanaian civil-military relations had fallen into was thereby perpetuated.

Voting in the 1969 elections fell along preexisting ethnic cleavages. Two new major political parties vied for power: the Akan and Asante supported Progress Party (PP) of Dr. Kofi Busia and the Ewe-backed National Alliance of Liberals (NAL). In the Akan-dominated districts, the PP won 68 of 72 possible seats while in Ewe territory the NAL won 14 of 16 seats.[98] These voting divisions also extended into the military: the majority of Akan officers favored the PP while most Ewe officers supported the NAL.[99] Due to the Akan's largest minority status as well as their ability to gain the sympathies of other ethnic groups, perhaps as a reaction against the Ewe-dominated NLC, the PP won the election by a comfortable margin.

The new government, led by an Akan political party and dominated by Akan ministers, immediately sought to build coethnic security institutions. The restructuring even commenced during the transition period.

---

97 Dowse 1975, 26–27; Hettne 1980, 180; Hutchful 1979, 607 & 614.
98 Lumsden 1980, 472; Twumasi 1975, 143.
99 Hutchful 1979, 615.

Almost as soon as the election results were in, Afrifa began replacing Ewes in key strategic army commands with Akan officers. Upon assuming the presidency, Busia continued these efforts. Ewe officers were retired or passed over for important command posts including Army Commander, Air Force Commander, Chief of Defense Staff, Commander of the First Brigade, as well as several battalion-level commands. They were also "promoted out," a practice wherein an incompetent or potentially threatening officer is removed without losing face by promoting them to an ambassadorial position abroad or another prestigious, but non-tactical, assignment. Akan officers were then moved into these emptied command positions, thereby transferring control of the military hierarchy from one ethnic group to the other. By 1972, only one senior Ewe officer was left within the military, a sharp reversal in fortunes. Even top commands in the police passed into Akan hands. Meanwhile, the Ewe were systematically excluded from civilian power as well. Not a single cabinet or ministerial post was held by an Ewe during the Busia regime. Over 560 civil servants, mostly Ewe and Ga, were also dismissed.[100] Indeed, Baynham notes in his study of the Busia regime that the "... documentation points to a concerted effort to achieve ethnic symmetry between regime and ranking cohorts of the military in a burgeoning system of clientelism..."[101] Understandably, the new government was broadly perceived as advancing Akan interests.

Coup plots proliferated. Brigadier Kattah, an Ewe officer who had helped to overthrow Nkrumah, and his godson attempted to rouse support amongst disaffected Ewe soldiers in and around the capital. Fearing renewed Ewe domination, a counter-plot was then hatched by Imoro Ayanah, a northern civilian politician who figured his region would be excluded from power after an Ewe coup. A third plot was led jointly by Akan and Ewe officers and indeed overlapped in recruits and support with the Kattah plot, making it difficult to distinguish their motives.[102]

Well aware of the Kattah plot, the government leaned heavily on its ethnic coup-proofing, assuming the loyalty of Akan officers and discounting any threat they might pose. Indeed, one of the later coup leaders, Lieutenant-Colonel Ignatius Kutu Acheampong, had clearly been promoted to command the First Brigade because of his Asante ethnic identity, neither being highly qualified nor professionally reliable. Acheampong was also placed in charge of counter-coup operations in

---

[100] Baynham 1985, 629–632; Singh 2014, 136–137.
[101] Baynham 1985, 631.
[102] Singh 2014, 137–140.

what turned out to be a terrible strategic error on the part of the Busia regime. The government even dismissed intelligence reports indicating that Acheampong was desperately in need of cash, had been holding secret meetings with opposition leaders, and might be mounting a coup himself. Instead, they scolded the intelligence agents and reached out to Acheampong, informing him of these "baseless" accusations.[103]

The coup that ultimately materialized was thus, shockingly to the Busia government, partly led by the Akan officers they had most trusted. More expectedly, the mid-ranking Ewe officers who were being marginalized and excluded by the Busia regime also participated in and supported the seizure of power.[104] Acheampong launched the bloodless and successful coup from the base of the First Brigade in Asante territory on January 11, 1972. The date for the attempt had been moved forward, largely to preempt Kattah's imminent coup, but also because the Prime Minister had flown abroad for medical treatment. The plotters encountered no resistance as they took over their typical targets, handily capturing the capital city as the government waited fruitlessly for Acheampong himself to launch a counter-coup operation. Once the capital had fallen, the potential resistance of other Akan officers and units collapsed.[105]

Many grievances were listed by the successful putschist as motivating their actions, the most compelling of which concerned internal military factionalism, budget cutbacks, and widespread economic malaise that was having a particularly pernicious effect in Asanteland.[106] First, Acheampong declared that the ethnic manipulations of the Busia regime were aggravating tribal factionalism within the military, with potentially devastating consequences: "I watched the seed of tribal conflict being slowly sown by the actions of the Busia regime and with the blood of millions of our Nigerian brothers to warn us I acted to nip the threat in the bud."[107] Here, he references the recent Biafra civil war in Nigeria, that claimed upwards of one million lives, and began when a counter-coup orchestrated by Hausa-Fulani officers led to the breakup of the federal Nigerian military and the Ibo region's secession.[108] Acheampong seems

---

[103] Ibid., 138–140; FCO 65/1114 4, "Telegram no. 26 from Accra," January 13, 1972; FCO 65/1117 177, "The Eclipse of Ghanaian Democracy: I, The Coup d'Etat (Annex)," March 20, 1972.

[104] Goldsworthy 1973, 14; Minority Rights Group 2010.

[105] Singh 2014, 140–143; TNA FCO 65/1114 18, "Telegram No. 38 from Accra," January 14, 1972.

[106] Aboagye 1999, 100–101.

[107] Acheampong as quoted in Smock & Smock 1975, 249.

[108] Adeakin 2015, 60; Luckham 1971, 51–82.

to have drawn the lesson that recruitment and promotion policies that create ethnic divides within the military can lead to devastating ethnic war. He thus justifies his actions in terms of preventing such widespread and terrible violence – by seizing power he could end the ethnically divisive policies of the prior government.

The pro-Akan policies of the Busia regime also took place in a context of general economic decline that masked any potential benefits for Akan civilians or soldiers. Rapidly falling cocoa prices led to extreme hardships for growers, severe state budget crises, and drastic austerity programs that included military budget cuts. Cocoa had always constituted Ghana's principal export commodity, accounting for 70% of export earnings by 1970.[109] Crisis hit between 1970 and 1972, when world cocoa prices fell from $790 per ton to $360 per ton, a 45.5% decline over only three years.[110] Due to a significant overlap between Akan territory and land suitable to cocoa farming, these falling prices created severe hardships for farmers that fell disproportionately on rural Akan families.[111] Cocoa earnings also accounted for over 30% of government revenues and were used extensively to service foreign debt. The plummet in prices thus had a dramatic impact on Ghana's yearly budget and the country's capacity to repay previous loans. As a result, Ghana's patronage system broke down, resulting in the mass dismissal of civil servants and the introduction of an austerity budget, including cutbacks in military funding.[112] Tightening military budgets led, in turn, to widespread disaffection amongst junior officers and rank-and-file soldiers who witnessed the rapid decline of their standard of living, even amongst the relatively privileged Akan (at least in terms of command and promotion opportunities).[113] The favoritism of the Busia regime thus failed to translate into real gains for either Akan civilians or soldiers.

The 1972 coup points to an important interaction between economic decline and ethnic politics. Austerity increased dissatisfaction with the Busia government across the board. Budget cuts directly impacted soldiers' standard of living, making even officers like Acheampong desperate for additional sources of income. The ethnic favoritism of the regime further disadvantaged non-Akan soldiers, particularly the Ewe and Ga who were actively being purged from both civil and military institutions.

109 Goldsworthy 1973, 10.
110 Bennett 1973, 666.
111 Goldsworthy 1973, 15.
112 Bennett 1973, 665; Goldsworthy 1973, 10 & 18.
113 Baynham 1985, 632.

In a bad economy with few private sector opportunities, this precipitated personal ruin for many, incentivizing Ewe to plot re-seizing the state and re-establishing their prior dominance. Which, in turn, motivated preemptive moves by other groups who feared their exclusion from power. That a coalition of Akan and Ewe officers struck first, to prevent the more extremist Ewe plot, hardly negates the importance of these dynamics. The construction of coethnic security institutions by the Busia regime directly fed a proliferation of conspiracies that eventually spelled their undoing.

Seven More Coups and the Rise of Flight Lieutenant Jerry Rawlings

Ghana quickly descended into a chaos of soldier rebellion and violence. Between 1978 and 1984, Ghana experienced three successful coups and four failed coup attempts as well as mass purges and rampant insubordination that decimated the officer corps. Coups are generally rare events, but during this period Ghana remarkably averaged one coup attempt per year. While economic troubles and internal disagreements between junta members were contributing factors, the underlying ethnic struggle between Ewe and Akan officers drove this instability. Each faction feared exclusion at the hands of the other while often seeking dominance over the government and military for themselves. Out of the ashes, having himself destroyed the command hierarchy, rose Flight Lieutenant Jerry Rawlings who was eventually able to stabilize Ghanaian civil-military relations under an Ewe-dominated regime.

Governance under Acheampong set the stage for both the 1978 coup, which is best interpreted as a junta reshuffling, and the three related coup attempts between 1979 and 1981, led by Rawlings with Ewe soldier support. Upon taking power, Acheampong and his fellow conspirators established a military junta called the National Redemption Council (NRC). At first, the NRC sought to curtail the role of ethnicity in politics and redress past ethnic manipulations by the government. A relatively ethnically balanced governing council was constructed, including strong representation of the previously excluded Ewe.[114] Government

---

[114] The ten original members of the NRC were: Acheampong (Asante), Ashley-Lassen (Ewe), Erskine (Ewe), Beausoleil (Akwapim(Akan)/Guan), Quaye (Ewe), Agbo (Ewe), Selorney (Ewe), Baah (Brong-Ahafo), Cobbinah (Ahanta/Fante), and Benni (northerner/Dagarti). Another two members were added on January 19, 1972: Adjitey (Ga) and Felli (northerner/Navrongo). TNA FCO 65/1114 62, "Letter from the West African Department to the Treasury Chambers," January 19, 1972; TNA FCO 65/1114 67, "Telegram No. 105 from Accra," January 19, 1972; TNA FCO 65/1117 178, "The

spending was also reallocated to correct the Busia regime's neglect of the Ewe homeland in the Volta region. At the extreme, the NRC banned references to tribe and ethnic origins in government documents and sought to eliminate tribe specific surnames and distinctive facial markings.[115]

Nonetheless, ethnic tensions within the NRC became apparent very shortly after the coup. A struggle for power developed between the Akan and Ewe factions, personified respectively by Brigadier Ashley-Larsen and Colonel Acheampong.[116] The result was confusion and paralysis with the former Ghanaian High Commissioner to the United Kingdom lamenting that "he had no confidence in the NRC's ability to cope with the difficulties they had brought upon themselves, and would not be surprised if there was another coup in the next fortnight. If this was led by the Ewe, there would be a violent reaction from the Akan."[117] A number of Ewe officers were even arrested only a couple of weeks into the NRC's rule in an attempt, according to the British High Commissioner's office, "to strangle at birth a possible Ewe bid for power."[118]

Indeed, when support for the new government began to ebb, the NRC once again succumbed to sectarian pressures and publicly rebuked the Ewe officers who had helped bring them to power. Facing continued economic decline, the NRC turned inward: excluding civilians, renaming itself the Supreme Military Council (SMC), increasing coercion, and singling out "Ewe tribalism" as a distinct threat to national unity in order to inflame popular passions and recuperate some popularity. Around the same time as the 1972 coup, the National Liberation Movement of Western Togoland had formed. At first, the movement merely sought greater regional autonomy for the Ewe and an end to the border restrictions that hampered trade with Togo. Although the movement was small and eyed with skepticism by the Ewe population it claimed to represent, the government reacted harshly, labeling it as subversive and denouncing it repeatedly as a "tribalist threat." As a result, the movement began to speak of secession, which led to even harsher reactions by the NRC, culminating

Eclipse of Ghanaian Democracy: II, The First Two Months of Military Rule," March 20, 1972.

115 Brown 1982, 60; Chazan 1982, 464–465.
116 TNA FCO 65/1116 145, "Note for the Record prepared by H.S.H. Stanley," February 1, 1972; TNA 65/1117 178, "The Eclipse of Ghanaian Democracy: II, The First Two Months of Military Rule," March 20, 1972.
117 TNA FCO 65/1116 146, "Note for the Record prepared by H.S.H. Stanley," February 3, 1972.
118 TNA FCO 65/1115 94, "Telegram No. 241200Z from Accra," January 1972.

in coup plot accusations and purges. By 1975, Acheampong had reduced Ewe representation on the governing council and removed Ewes from the armed forces. To add insult to injury, he then arrested and tried several Ewe ex-officers on dubious charges of coup plotting.[119]

At the same time, widespread opposition emerged to the SMC, who were viewed as both corrupt and inept. Despite the return of record high world cocoa prices, the deep recession continued. Price manipulation of the marketing boards and government corruption had led farmers to either plant subsistence crops or smuggle their cocoa to more suitable markets across national borders. Unable to extract much income from exports, the government met its budget deficits by printing money, leading to debilitating inflation rates averaging over 100% per year.[120] Further cutbacks in government employment and the exclusion of civilians from the highest echelons of the regime limited patronage opportunities. Poor distribution and profiteering further exacerbated the already extreme scarcity of commodity staples, deepening intense anti-government sentiments.[121]

With criticism and pressure emanating from all fronts, the SMC decided in mid-1977 to return Ghana to civilian rule. Acheampong scheduled a referendum to gain public approval for his particular transition plan, which eschewed political parties and electoral competition in favor of creating a "union government" of police, military, and civilian representatives. Instead of ameliorating dissent, however, the referendum provided a focal point for its expression. Opponents interpreted Acheampong's plan as a means for extending military rule indefinitely.[122] For over a year, protests and violence erupted across the country, including student riots and episodes of ethnic conflict. "Unigov," as Acheampong's plan was called, won by a narrow margin in a vote marked by low turnout, credible accusations of fraud, renewed mass strikes, and ethnic political divisions. While the Asante and a coalition of small ethnic groups backed the government's proposal, the Ewe, Ga and non-Asante Akans opposed it.[123] Demoralized by the increasing disorder and unconvinced of his commitment to return to the barracks, in a bloodless coup, the other SMC members "encouraged" Acheampong to resign in July 1978.[124]

---

[119] Brown 1982, 61–63; Chazan 1982, 465.
[120] Hansen & Collins 1980, 12.
[121] Harris 1980, 226.
[122] Lumsden 1980, 472.
[123] Chazan 1982, 465–471; Lumsden 1980, 472.
[124] Lumsden 1980, 472.

Now under the leadership of Major General F.W.K. Akuffo, the SMC attempted to regain control over the transition. Akuffo released political detainees, nullified the referendum results, lifted the ban on political activity, and began prosecuting select officials for corruption and profiteering, including the military directors of the Cocoa Marketing Board. He maintained the ban on political parties, however, undermining any credible commitment to hold elections and return power to civilian hands. Akuffo feared that reemergent political parties would once again politicize ethnic cleavages, exacerbating the social tensions that had already turned violent in several regions. Folding to months of continued protests and strikes, however, elections were eventually scheduled for June 1979 and political parties once again allowed to organize and campaign.[125]

Unimpressed with the Akuffo reforms, particularly its lackluster approach to rectifying corruption and other problems within the officer corps, Flight Lieutenant Jerry Rawlings led two coup attempts in mid-1979. In both, his express purpose was to "clean house" prior to the upcoming political transition.[126] The first venture was poorly planned and easily defeated. On May 15th, Rawlings set out on a tour of army bases, accompanied by a few fellow air force co-conspirators, to rally support for a coup. Rawlings believed that ordinary soldiers and junior officers were disaffected with the regime and would join his cause with little coaxing. The economy was still in shambles and the SMC deeply unpopular. The government had also allowed military housing to sink into dilapidation, had failed to provide quality uniforms or food, and had even stopped issuing paychecks in a timely manner. Nonetheless, Rawlings failed to rally much support and was quickly arrested after the exchange of only a few shots.[127]

The second attempt took place less than a month later, on June 4, and was organized by Ewe junior officers and NCOs from the 5th Army Infantry Battalion. During the course of the night, they freed Rawlings from prison and designated him their leader. Rawlings had risen immensely in popularity since his imprisonment. Given a public platform during his court-martial proceedings, Rawlings had defended his actions against the corruption and failures of the SMC to loud cheers in the gallery

---

[125] Hansen & Collins 1980, 12; Harris 1980, 227–228; Lumsden 1980, 473.

[126] TNA FCO 65/2178 93, "Telegram No. 202 from Accra," June 7, 1979; TNA FCO 65/2178 116, "Telegram No. 217 from Accra," June 11, 1979.

[127] Singh 2014, 156; TNA FCO 65/2178 81, "Note for File: Attempted Coup d'Etat," May 17, 1979.

and acclaim by the newspapers. Once released, Rawlings became the public face of the coup, announcing their successful seizure of power over the airwaves. Although loyalist resistance was initially fierce, especially by the Recce Regiment, it collapsed within a day, initiating a new military government under the Armed Forces Revolutionary Council (AFRC).[128]

Rawlings and the AFRC immediately embarked on their project of bloody house cleaning. Executions, trials, asset seizures, long prison sentences, and public whippings were doled out with gusto. Seven senior military officers were executed almost immediately, including three former heads of state: Afrifa, Acheampong, and Akuffo. Dozens of senior police and military officers were purged and hundreds of other officers and civilians imprisoned. All senior military commands were redistributed to previously junior officers, none of whom held a rank above colonel. NCOs and rank-and-file privates were even permitted to verbally and physically assault their superiors. With explicit approval from the AFRC, insubordination and disorder consumed the ranks. This, combined with the mass purges and arrests of officers, soon led to the complete collapse of the command hierarchy. Anarchy reined in the barracks and seemingly only the personal popularity of Rawlings himself propelled the government forward.[129]

For many, this annihilation of the existing officer corps exhibited a strong ethnic dimension. Rawlings was himself half Ewe (the other half being Scottish) and had gained significant support amongst Ewe officers and NCOs. The AFRC was also perceived to be stacked with Ewe and Ga officers and to be disproportionately promoting Ewe's into important command positions. Because the previous regime had purged senior Ewe officers and replaced them with Akans, the AFRC's decimation of the senior ranks looked suspiciously like an ethnically motivated retributive attack against their traditional rivals. This, moreover, mirrored the worst predictions of the anti-Ewe propaganda widely distributed under the SMC.[130] The incoming civilian government thus inherited a military that was both near anarchy and regarded as dominated by Ewe officers who had targeted Akans in their bloody revolution.

---

[128] *The Economist* 1979 (June 9); Harris 1980, 229; Hutchful 1997a, 254; Singh 2014, 162–171; TNA FCO 65/2178 84, "Telegram No. 194 from Accra," June 6, 1979; TNA FCO 65/2178 94, "Military Unrest – 15 May 1979," May 16, 1979.

[129] Austin 1985, 94; Baynham 1985, 634–636; Hansen & Collins 1980, 3; Harris 1980, 229; Hutchful 1997b, 538; Lumsden 1980, 471; TNA FCO 65/2178 100, "Telegram No. 208 from Accra," June 8, 1979.

[130] Chazan 1982, 475; Minority Rights Group 2010.

Rawlings and the AFRC never intended to interfere with or delay the impending transfer of governance. Throughout their mere 112 days in power, they remained focused on rectifying what they deemed the sins of past governments and the corruption of the officer corps. Thus, almost oddly, while purges, arrests, and executions were taking place on a mass scale, free and fair elections were concurrently organized. And while several ethno-regional parties arose to contest the elections, it was a resurrected national party with cross-ethnic appeal that won. Led by Dr. Hilla Limann of the small, northern Sissala ethnic group, the People's National Party (PNP) took power with 62% of the presidential vote and a narrow, one-seat parliamentary majority.[131]

The victory of the PNP unleashed both hopes and fears within the military. That the Akan-backed party had failed at the polls inspired hopes of increased access to power and patronage amongst non-Akan soldiers and civilians, who had been excluded under Busia and the SMC.[132] On the other hand, these same soldiers feared their own prosecution for the violence and disorder of the AFRC interregnum, which may have been more easily forgiven had the Ga and Ewe party won. To protect his revolution and the new officer corps, Rawlings thus negotiated several constitutional provisions, granting immunity to all participants in prior coups and explicitly prohibiting any proceedings or investigations into the AFRC's short reign. Rawlings also tried to ensure his own high position within the military, where he commanded widespread loyalty and could protect the gains of his revolution.[133]

On assuming power, Limann and the PNP decided to move against the military anyway. Perhaps they reasoned that restructuring was necessary to secure civilian rule and that their chances of success were best immediately after the election, when international and civilian support ran high and they had yet to undermine their own legitimacy. Or maybe they failed to register the danger of restructuring. Whatever the motive, Limann almost immediately reorganized the police and military intelligence services, granting them broad powers to conduct covert propaganda and intelligence operations against former AFRC

---

[131] Austin 1985, 95; Brown 1982, 64–65; Harris 1980, 231; Lumsden 1980, 476. The four other major political parties that contested the elections were the Asante supported Popular Front Party, the Ewe- and Ga-based United National Convention, the Social Democratic Front supported by a coalition of northern tribes, and the Fanti-based Action Congress.

[132] Brown 1982, 65.

[133] Baynham 1985, 635–638.

members and their supporters.[134] Government efforts to discredit Rawlings included the distribution of anti-Ewe propaganda pamphlets both within the universities and the military barracks. With such provocative titles as "The Conspiracy" and "The Ewes Again," the pamphlets accused Rawlings and the AFRC of being motivated by Ewe tribalist sentiments and of now plotting to overthrow the civilian regime.[135] Only eight weeks following the transfer of power, the government then forcibly retired Rawlings along with the rest of the AFRC members, including both the Chief of Defense Staff and the Army Commander. The openings that these forced retirements created, especially those for sensitive tactical commands, were filled with non-Ewes.[136] Limann also directly appealed to fellow northern soldiers for support and solidarity, bypassing the officer corps. Suspecting trouble, he organized a counter-coup unit comprised of northern enlisted soldiers who were charged with spying on Rawlings and blocking any attempted attack he might organize.[137]

Nonetheless, facing exclusion and prosecution while witnessing continued economic crisis and unprecedented ethnic violence, Rawlings and his supporters seized power. Around 11 a.m. on New Year's Eve, 1981, amidst fighting across Accra, Rawlings' voice came over the airwaves announcing a new revolution: "Fellow Ghanaians, as you will notice, we are not playing the national anthem. In other words, this is not a coup. I ask for nothing less than a revolution – something that will transform the social and economic order of this country."[138] The coup had begun with only 8–10 men, trained in Libya, and initially garnered little support from the army units they approached. Outside of the air force base, only very reluctant assistance could be gained from factions of the 5th Battalion and the Recce Regiment. Yet, resistance was also minimal and plagued by ammunition shortages and transportation difficulties. Indeed, Major Nan Togmah of the 1st Infantry Brigade was the only officer who actively defended the regime (he was later murdered for his efforts). Neglect, past coup-proofing measures, and resignation to Rawlings' power within the military conspired to prevent loyalists from adequately responding. Once again, civilian rule was toppled and Jerry Rawlings was installed as the chairman of the new Provisional National Defense Council (PNDC).[139]

---

[134] Ibid., 639.
[135] Ibid., 640; Brown 1982, 66.
[136] Baynham 1985, 638–639.
[137] Singh 2014, 183 & 186.
[138] Jerry Rawlings as quoted in Shillington 1992, 80.
[139] *The New York Times* 1982 (January 1); Singh 2014, 186–190; TNA FCO 65/2821 3,
   "Telegram No. 390 from Accra," December 31, 1981; TNA FCO 65/2821 4, "Telegram

Intense opposition to the new regime quickly arose from both Akan and northern Muslim soldiers. Dr. Limann had been the first head of state to come from the north of Ghana and his removal was greatly resented by northerners. Indeed, at the outset the PNDC contained no northern members, although this was soon rectified. Akan soldiers also resented the purges and assassinations conducted by Rawlings during his first tenure in power, particularly the death of General Afrifa. And, despite some representation on the ruling council, anger grew amongst Akans over perceived domination by the Ewe.[140] They were not entirely off base: while the PNDC itself made an effort to be ethnically diverse, Rawlings being well aware of the danger of perceived Ewe dominance, the newly appointed army commander as well as all of the top brass across the army, navy, air force, and border guards were all Ewe.[141] Ewe favoritism in military appointments combined with Rawlings' past actions and the spate of anti-Ewe propaganda disseminated by the Limann government, led many northern and Akan officers to deem Rawlings' seizure of power as just another Ewe plot to capture the state for themselves.

Ethnically-based resentment to Rawlings' rule soon emerged in a series of counter-coup attempts by northern officers and their rank-and-file subordinates. Three serious, but ultimately unsuccessful, coup attempts were conducted by the same core group of soldiers over the next two years. On November 23, 1982, middle-ranking northern officers tried but failed to seize the army barracks on the outskirts of Accra.[142] Although many of the rebels were killed or imprisoned, others managed to escape capture and slip across the border to Togo or Côte d'Ivoire. On June 19, 1983, these exiled soldiers snuck back into Ghana, attacking three military prisons and managing to free many of their former collaborators. Together they then attempted to overthrow the government. The majority of the army, however, remained loyal and this second attempt to wrest power away

No. 391 from Accra," December 31, 1981; TNA FCO 65/2821 9, "Letter from the West African Department to the Secretary of State," December 31, 1981; TNA FCO 65/2821 27, "Telegram No. 21 from Accra," January 4, 1982; TNA FCO 65/2821 47, "Telegram No. 55 from Accra," January 12, 1982; TNA FCO 65/2822 85, "Report on the Coup of 31 Dec 81 in Ghana (Annexes A & B)," January 25, 1982.

140 *The New York Times* 1982 (January 17); *The Economist* 1982 (November 20). About a month after the coup, the members of the PNDC were: Rawlings (Ewe), Kwabena Damuah (Ewe), Nunoo-Mensah (Akan/Ewe), Boadi (Asante), Kwei (Ga), Akata-Pore (northerner), and Atim (northerner). TNA FCO 65/2822 113, "The PNDC and the Ewes," February 25, 1982.

141 TNA FCO 65/2822 69, "Ghana: Rawlings and the Ewe Tribe," January 15, 1982.

142 *The New York Times* 1982 (November 25); Shillington 1992, 105.

from Rawlings also failed.[143] The last coup attempt occurred on March 25, 1984 when exiled former soldiers based in Togo and Côte d'Ivoire once again crept back over the border to initiate an insurrection within the army.[144] As before, they failed. All three coup attempts were thus linked to the same core of disgruntled northern officers who tried repeatedly to oust Rawlings until they had all been executed, imprisoned, or exiled.

Jerry Rawlings and the PNDC survived the turmoil of these repeated coup attempts and then managed to stabilize the armed forces and end soldier rebellions. Ghana has not experienced a single coup attempt since 1984. What evidence is available suggests that Rawlings was able to do so partly through constructing coethnic Ewe security institutions, at least in the short term. The revolutionary house cleaning of the AFRC combined with the exodus of officers immediately after Rawlings' second seizure of power – all officers above the rank of lieutenant colonel were put on indefinite leave and many other officers were arrested or killed – resulted in the destruction of the senior command hierarchy and another complete breakdown in military discipline.[145] This gave Rawlings a partial blank slate from which to rebuild the officer corps. Under the PNDC, he also continued purging and assassinating the remaining, low-ranking Akan and northern soldiers. Massive structural reorganization occurred between 1984–1987: officers were rotated rapidly between command posts, rebellious units purged or disbanded, new militias created, parallel security organizations created, and intelligence units dissolved and wholly replaced. Throughout, Rawlings relied heavily on Ewe officers to fill the ranks and implement reforms.[146]

Nevertheless, eventually, in an effort to professionalize the military, at least some diversity was reintroduced and new merit-based policies were created to end political interference in recruitment and promotion decisions.[147] Rawlings thus did not rely wholly on coethnic security institutions, especially not in the long-term. His eventual ability to transform the military into a diverse and professional organization is worthy of deeper analysis beyond the scope of this chapter.

---

[143] *BBC* 1983 (June 22); *BBC* 1983 (June 30); *BBC* 1983 (August 6); Shillington 1992, 113.

[144] At least 11 of the soldiers captured in this final coup had already been sentenced to death for their participation in the June 19th attempt (*Christian Science Monitor* 1984 (March 30); *Globe and Mail* 1984 (March 26)).

[145] TNA FCO 65/2822 85, "Report on the Coup of 31 Dec 81 in Ghana (Annex B)," January 25, 1982; TNA FCO 65/2822 90, "Ghana – Situation Six Weeks On," February 11, 1982.

[146] Hansen 1991, 40; Hutchful 1997(b), 256–258; Hutchful 2003, 86–87.

[147] Ibid.

Alternative Explanations

Ghana's spate of military coups between 1966 and the early 1980s was remarkable both for the sheer volume of attempts and for the destruction they wrought on the military hierarchy. The motivations of conspirators were complex, varied, and difficult to disentangle. Unlike in the other cases, economic explanations are compelling here. Throughout this period, Ghana faced repeated economic crises and most of the coup attempts correspond to times of deep recession, high inflation, and severe austerity measures (see Figure 4.2). Both the Busia and Limann civilian regimes, in particular, struggled to end corruption and implement much-needed reforms. Nor was the military institutionally shielded from the general economic climate: soldiers witnessed a sharp decline in their standard of living and military organizational efficiency was threatened through material shortages and neglect. The underlying state of the economy thus fueled a serious threat to the corporate interests of the military.

While granting appropriate weight to economic arguments, the case study reveals the importance of ethnic politics and the effect that constructing ethnic armies has on political stability. Ethnic exclusion by itself, however, does not compellingly explain Ghana's coups: no leader, until perhaps Rawlings, actually achieved the exclusion of ethnic rivals from the military. The instability ceased, moreover, under Rawlings' second regime, which was marked by Ewe dominance. Rather, it was the process of trying to build coethnic security institutions that mattered. Nkrumah's turn toward ethnic manipulation of the army infected Ghanaian civil-military relations with ethnic antagonisms. The resultant struggle between Ewe and Akan soldiers then rent the ranks. Repeated attempts to privilege one ethnic group and exclude others, within the context of an officer corps whose diversity was never completely diminished, underlay much of Ghana's instability.

CONCLUSION

Both Ghana and Senegal gained independence with leaders committed to an inclusive vision of the state and initially constructed ethnically diverse security institutions. Yet, Kwame Nkrumah of Ghana soon abandoned inclusivity and began ethnically manipulating the military and even constructing coethnic units. As a result of this decision, Ewe and Ga officers facing discrimination and exclusion seized power, setting Ghana on a path of repeated military coups and instability largely driven by the contestation for political dominance between the Ewe and Akan. Léopold Senghor of Senegal, on the other hand, remained committed to diversity and inclusivity. Unlike so much of sub-Saharan Africa, Senegal escaped military intervention in politics, never having experienced either a coup attempt or military governance.

The case comparison further highlights the importance of ethnic politicization in conditioning the ability of leaders to implement inclusive military recruitment and promotion policies. Early political parties in Senegal formed along an urban–rural divide and utilized the Muslim brotherhoods to mobilize voters on a non-ethnic basis. Early Ghanaian political parties, on the other hand, often reflected ethnic cleavages and mobilized voters with ethnic appeals. Preindependence election campaigning even turned violent, resulting in clashes between Nkrumah's nationalistic CCP and the Akan-based NLM. Due to this high degree of ethnic politicization, Nkrumah interpreted two later assassination attempts against his life as ethnic conspiracies and turned against the Ewe and Ga officers of the military and police. Deep ethnic politicization may thus severely constrain the ability of leaders to maintain their commitment to diversity.

5

Dismantling Ethnic Armies: African Militaries and Democratization

Democracy is a benign anarchy of diversity.

– Claude Ake[1]

Dismantling ethnically exclusionary security institutions also provokes organized and violent soldier rebellion. Historically dominant groups with disproportionate access to power and patronage opportunities within state institutions usually fail to peacefully relinquish their privilege. Whether they subscribe to beliefs about their natural or earned superiority, or merely fear revenge and domination at the hands of historically oppressed groups, they often fight to maintain the status quo. This helps us understand the timing of rebellion by advantaged groups: violence occurs in the face of change.

Democratization engenders such a moment of potentially profound change for African ethnic armies. Most states in Africa are highly diverse. The establishment of competitive elections thus creates a high probability that executive power will change hands between leaders from different ethnic groups, regardless of the depth of other democratic reforms. The new leader might be committed to inclusion and diversity, or may seek to create coethnic security institutions of their own. Both policies require dismantling the inherited ethnic army. Facing either the threat or reality of a leader who no longer shares their identity, ethnic armies will thus fear their own destruction. To protect their power and privilege, they

---

[1] As quoted in Ojo 2006, 261. Claude Ake, a Nigerian scholar and political activist, perished in a plane crash believed to have been orchestrated by the Abacha regime, of whom he was a deep critic.

resist democratization by blocking liberalization, reversing the outcomes of elections, or deposing elected leaders.

This chapter compares three cases of democratization to trace the mechanisms of this argument: Nigeria, Benin, and Senegal. All three democratization efforts began in the late 1980s and early 1990s amidst severe economic crisis and under heavy pressure from both international donors and domestic protestors. Yet, each country's soldiers reacted differently to liberalization. In Nigeria, senior northern military officers annulled the election results and canceled the democratic transition when it became apparent that Moshood Abiola of the southern Yoruba had won. In Benin, rogue northern officers similarly resisted the election of a southerner. However, they failed to gain much traction within the army as a whole and their small-scale violence never threatened the new democratic government. In Senegal, no military resistance of any form arose against democratization and the military has even become a staunch defender of constitutionalism. These differing outcomes can be explained as a function of each country's military recruitment and promotion practices: while Nigeria's military was historically dominated by northern, and especially Hausa-Fulani officers, Senegal maintained an inclusive and diverse military. Benin falls in the middle: although the officer corps was traditionally diverse, discriminatory promotion policies did lead to some northern officers gaining unfair advantages. The degree of ethnic privilege in each military thus explains its reaction to democratization.

THE LOGIC OF CASE SELECTION

The three cases – Nigeria, Benin, and Senegal – were chosen to broadly control for context and to compare the full range of outcomes. By the late 1980s, all three countries were facing severe economic crises, replete with government insolvency, and were forced to impose austerity measures. The resulting sharp decline in living standards provoked mass discontent, large demonstrations, and rioting. This, combined with international donor interests and the end of the Cold War, created immense shared pressures for democratization. All three regimes thus embarked on a program of liberalization in the early 1990s facing generally similar contexts of economic collapse, popular protests, and foreign pressure. All three also held elections in which the victorious new president came from a different ethnic group than the pre-transition leader. Yet, they experienced divergent outcomes both in how their military institutions reacted to liberalization and in the success of democratization.

Contextual differences always exist between cases and it is important to keep in mind where these divergences have theoretical relevance. It is often argued that natural resources promote both authoritarianism and instability.[2] Alone among the selected cases, Nigeria possesses vast oil wealth. Oil rents enhance the personal enrichment and patronage opportunities that come with control over state institutions and provide incentives for autocrats to cling to power. Neither Senegal nor Benin benefit from such significant mineral or oil resources and both depend on agricultural exports for state revenue, respectively groundnuts and cotton.[3] Nigeria's oil may thus have paved a harder road to democracy in and of itself. Significant differences in population size, land mass, and colonial rule also set Nigeria apart: compared to Senegal and Benin, Nigeria is a large and heavily populated country with a British, as opposed to French, institutional and colonial legacy. While no difference was found between French and British heritage in the statistics chapter, and small and sparsely populated African states have also been significantly prone to civil-military instability, these factors should still be kept in mind.

Senegal, on the other hand, benefits from two important legacies that may have facilitated successful liberalization and decreased the likelihood of military intervention. First, Senegal has no history of military coups and had been governed by a civilian, one-party state since independence. Although by no means democratic, Senegal's pre-transition government was less repressive than many autocracies and liberalizing reforms had begun much earlier, with constrained multi-partyism reintroduced in the late 1970s. Second, Senegal has never experienced much ethnic politicization, with its early political parties reflecting an urban/rural divide and later routinely organized on ideological grounds. Such low ethnic politicization could decrease the potential for violence during elections, thereby dampening motivations for military intervention. Benin and Nigeria, in contrast, had both experienced many coup attempts after independence, were governed by military dictatorships when they attempted their democratic transitions, and have a legacy of high ethnic politicization. Senegal may thus have encountered an easier path to democracy.

---

[2] Bellin 2004; Collier & Hoeffler 2005; Humphreys 2005.
[3] Galvan 2001; Gisselquist 2008, 806; Magnusson 2001, 217. At the time of its democratic transition, Benin possessed only one small, offshore oil field with diminishing output (Magnusson 2001, 217).

Despite these important differences, in the analysis that follows I seek to demonstrate that the military was a critical actor within the democratic transition whose reaction to liberalization varied according to past ethnic recruitment practices. The degree to which pre-transition leaders had engaged in ethnic stacking predicts how each of these militaries behaved during the democratization process and whether they allowed newly elected leaders to take power.

NIGERIA: THE FAILED 1993 DEMOCRATIC TRANSITION

In the late 1980s, economic crisis and growing popular unrest led General Ibrahim Babaginda to unseat Nigeria's existing military junta and embark on a phased transition to democracy. Gradual reforms led to real progress. By the end of 1992, a national assembly had been seated and elected civilian politicians controlled all state and local governments. Presidential elections were held in June 1993 and declared free and fair by both foreign and domestic observers. Then, before the full results had even been released and despite having spent millions on the transition, Babaginda annulled the results. Soon thereafter yet another coup returned Nigeria to repressive military governance. It was Africa's most notable, and tragically close, failed transition to democracy.

This abrupt change of heart was rooted in the historic ethnic patronage structure of the Nigerian military. Long dominated by the northern Hausa-Fulani, the senior officer corps had grown accustomed to holding political positions that granted them access to significant state revenues, particularly oil rents. These funds not only led to personal enrichment, but also to the construction of clientelist networks within the military that protected the wealthy "godfathers" from internal challenges. The 1993 presidential elections threatened this system of ethnic privilege and patronage. Early results indicated that the military's preferred northern candidate, Bashir Tofa, had lost resoundingly to the southern Yoruba candidate, Moshood Abiola. Fearing forced retirements, corruption prosecutions, and an end to northern dominance, the military stepped in and aborted the democratic experiment.

Babaginda's Managed Democratic Transition

By the 1980s, the Nigerian economy was in free fall. Corruption and mismanagement under both the Buhari military regime and the prior, short-lived civilian government had devastated the economy, despite exorbitant oil wealth. Ordinary Nigerians faced high inflation, rising urban unemployment, dwindling real incomes, food scarcity, and deteriorating public services. Even hospitals and schools had significantly declined in the quality of services they could provide. All of which led to widespread strikes and protests against the regime as well as to ethnic and religious communal violence.[4]

Against this backdrop, in 1985, the military junta internally convulsed. General Ibrahim Babaginda and his followers staged a successful coup and then, understanding their predicament and beset by foreign debt, embarked on an IMF and World Bank recommended austerity program. The reforms, many of which were necessary for long-term recovery, included devaluing the currency, lifting price controls, and laying off public sector employees. As a result, unemployment increased and the cost of food and commodities soared. The poor could no longer afford basic staples and the middle class lost the ability to purchase now outrageously expensive imported goods. While ordinary Nigerians suffered under these austerity measures, the politicians and military officers at the top continued to enrich themselves from oil exports. Discontent and protests proliferated.[5]

Facing intense domestic pressure for change, in 1987 Babaginda initiated a controlled democratization program. An electoral commission was established to manage and oversee elections and a new constitution was adopted under the guidance of a constitutional review committee, although it was granted few real powers to amend the document, especially in the domains of finance and security.[6] Initially, Babaginda allowed political associations and parties to form organically and apply for recognition and the right to compete in elections. Upon further consideration, however, the military government refused to approve the new parties, claiming they were mere surrogates for politicians banned from electoral competition due to allegations of past corruption.[7] Instead, Babaginda created two new political parties, one supposedly ideologically center-left and the other center-right.[8]

These two state guided parties then contested local, gubernatorial, and national assembly elections under an open-ballot system. As opposed to the standard Western secret ballot, voters would visibly line-up behind

---

4 Ehwarieme 2011, 499; Ihonvbere 1991, 607; Lewis 1994, 337.
5 Ihonvbere 1991, 612–613; Ihonvbere 1996, 196; Mahmud 1993, 87.
6 Kieh & Agbese 1993, 409; Ojo 2000, 8–9; Okoroji 1993, 124.
7 Okoroji 1993, 125.
8 Amadife 1999, 629; Ihonvbere 1996, 197.

signs or pictures denoting their candidate of choice.[9] By 1991, state and local officials had been successfully elected and, in January 1992, military governors in all 30 states handed power over to the civilians. By the end of the year, legislative elections had also been held and the new two chamber national assembly inaugurated.[10] All that remained was to transfer executive power to an elected president.

The Annulled Presidential Election

The presidential elections had proved difficult. Between 1990 and 1992, Babaginda postponed them four times, leading some to question whether the military regime was serious about the transition.[11] The 1992 presidential primaries then suffered from widespread corruption. They were canceled and all candidates barred from future political participation. Fearing further delays or that the military would halt the transition altogether, the civilian politicians adhered to the new rules. The next round of primaries ran smoothly and were deemed transparent and fair.[12] Bashir Tofa emerged as the presidential candidate for the center-right party and became the military's favorite contender. Tofa was from the northern Hausa heartland of Kano, maintained a close personal relationship with Babaginda, and had previously publicly advocated that the military remain in power for another decade.[13] Moshood Abiola won the primary for the center-left party. Although he was personally encouraged to run by Babaginda himself, Abiola had a more strained relationship with other senior officers. He was Yoruba, from the south, and had distanced himself from the military regime, using the newspapers he owned to openly criticize their social and economic policies. He had also previously voiced dissent over the appointment of several powerful military officers as state governors.[14]

On June 12, 1993, the presidential elections were finally held. They were closely observed: over 3000 domestic election monitors were joined by dozens of international and commonwealth observers and many foreign and local journalists. All concurred that the election had been peaceful, free and fair, and conducted within the rules set down by the

---

[9] Okoroji 1993, 125.
[10] Kieh & Agbese 1993, 409; Mahmud 1993, 89.
[11] Durotoye & Griffiths 1997, 140; Mahmud 1993, 87.
[12] Campbell 1994, 182–183; Durotoye & Griffiths 1997, 141.
[13] Campbell 1994, 184; Lewis 1994, 325; Okoroji 1993, 126.
[14] Campbell 1994, 185; Okoroji 1993, 128.

transition framework.[15] Although voter turnout was low, estimated at only 35%, there was little evidence of any systematic vote rigging or fraud.[16] Despite a military embargo,[17] Nigeria's stubbornly independent press leaked partial results indicating a decisive victory for Abiola. With 58% of the overall vote, Abiola had carried states in each of the major regions: not just in the south and in Yoruba territory but across the middle belt and far north as well. Indeed, both parties won support across traditional regional and ethnic divides, suggesting that the two party system had overcome Nigeria's historic problem of political parties mobilizing exclusionary ethnic constituencies. The public welcomed the results and there were no protests against Abiola's victory, not even in the north.[18]

Yet, less than a week later and before the full results could be published, Babaginda annulled the elections and blocked Abiola from assuming the presidency. After six years of difficult work and millions spent, the democratic transition was simply canceled.[19] Babaginda declared that both candidates had used their personal finances in inappropriate ways to influence the outcome. Abiola and the center-left party, in particular, were accused of enticing voters with simple commodities such as rice and soap and of bribing state police commissioners, journalists, and members of the election commission.[20] Such allegations wrung false: these had been the freest and fairest elections in Nigeria's history.[21]

The annulment provoked outrage. Protests and strikes erupted across the country, dozens of military officers resigned in protest, and both the United Kingdom and the United States applied targeted sanctions against Nigeria's military personnel and curtailed military assistance programs.[22] The Yoruba region perceived the annulment as reluctance on the part of Hausa-Fulani military officers to let go the reins of power.[23] Demonstrations and riots brought the region's economy to a standstill and troops were called in to quell the unrest, resulting in mass shootings

[15] Campbell 1994, 191; Okoroji 1993, 126.
[16] Lewis 1994, 326; Ojo 2000, 10.
[17] A group of businessmen, politicians, and military officers had obtained a court order from a suspiciously new recruit to the bench. The ruling ordered the election results to be withheld until the electoral commission could investigate allegations of vote rigging (Butts & Metz 1996, 6).
[18] Campbell 1994, 182 & 186; Lewis 1994, 326–327; Mahmud 1993, 90.
[19] Campbell 1994, 191; Mahmud 1993, 88; Ojo 2000, 16.
[20] Okoroji 1993, 127.
[21] Ihonvbere 1996, 199–200.
[22] Amadife 1999, 630; Butts & Metz 1996, 7; Campbell 1994, 192.
[23] Butts & Metz 1996, 7.

and the deaths of over a hundred demonstrators.[24] Yoruba leaders then began threatening secession. In anticipation of another civil war and the communal purges that had preceded the last one, Yoruba, Ibo, and other minorities began moving en masse back to their ethnic homelands.[25]

Facing impending chaos, Babaginda resigned, promising new elections and handing power to an interim government led by his close friend, Ernest Shonekan. Like Abiola, Shonekan was Yoruba and his appointment was seen as a belated attempt to ease tensions with the south and convince them the annulment had not been ethnically motivated. However, real power remained with the military, concentrated in the hands of General Sani Abacha, a northern Muslim Hausa from Kano who was appointed defense minister.[26]

Babaginda's resignation did little to calm the situation. Demonstrations continued and the economic crisis deepened. To address budget shortfalls, Shonekan lifted petroleum subsidies and printed money. As a result, domestic oil prices increased sevenfold, leading to general strikes that paralyzed Lagos and other cities.[27] The oil-producing regions then began protesting oil extraction that, due to the returned revenue structure, only benefited the central government.[28] Inflation also skyrocketed, reaching 100% and making the Nigerian currency hardly worth the paper it was printed on. Shortages of basic goods became endemic.[29] Claiming to save the nation from chaos, on November 18, 1993, General Abacha formally seized power.[30] He immediately suspended the constitution, abolished all electoral institutions, dissolved the political parties and national legislature, dismissed all elected state and local authorities (over 600 in total), and installed military governors.[31] Nigeria's democratic experiment had truly ended.

Patronage and the Hausa-Fulani-Dominated Officer Corps

Why did Babaginda and the military junta annul the election results and abort democratization, catapulting Nigeria into economic and political

[24] Campbell 1994, 192; Lewis 1994, 327; Okoroji 1993, 129.
[25] Butts & Metz 1996, 7; Campbell 1994, 193; Lewis 1994, 327; Ojo 2000, 12.
[26] Amadife 1999, 631; Dunmar 2002, 26; Lewis 1994, 328; Mahmud 1993, 88; Okoroji 1993, 129.
[27] Lewis 1994, 328.
[28] Butts & Metz 1996, 8.
[29] Ibid.
[30] Mahmud 1993, 88–89.
[31] Bratton & van de Walle 1997, 212; Campbell 1994, 194; Lewis 1994, 323.

turmoil? The most compelling explanation is that senior northern Hausa-Fulani officers, who had long dominated the military and held privileged political positions granting them access to oil rents and patronage resources, feared that a southern Yoruba civilian president would take away all of their wealth and power.

Ethnicity has shaped the Nigerian military since its colonial founding. British recruiters initially targeted the northern Hausa for service in the colonial army, believing them to possess superior martial skills. So much so that 75% of colonial riflemen hailed from the north and Hausa became the lingua franca of the Nigerian units.[32] As independence approached, however, the British adopted merit-based recruitment and promotion criteria, with a heavy focus on educational achievements. This enabled southerners, and particularly the Ibo, to dominate the Africanizing officer corps. Indirect colonial rule had protected the Muslim north and its Koranic schools from Christian missionary encroachment, leading to large educational disparities between the regions. Southerners thus had far greater opportunities to obtain a Western education, facilitating their rise in the ranks. At the time of decolonization, over 60% of the officer corps was southern and less than 20% northern, with the remainder coming from the highly diverse middle belt region.[33]

Post-independence events, however, rapidly ended southern control over the officer corps. Ethnic tensions resulting from high ethnic politi-cization,[34] perceptions of northern control over the civilian government, and a deteriorating security situation in the western region combined to inspire two military coups in 1966. The first, which took place on January 15, was led largely by Ibo officers and failed. Yet, the plotters assassinated enough national and regional leaders to cause a crisis of governance, forcing the remaining civilian authorities to relinquish power to Major-General Ironsi, a non-involved but still Ibo officer. The coup was thus perceived as an "ethnic plot" to seize the state, regardless of the coup

---

32 Horowitz 1985, 447–448.
33 Adeakin 2015, 57; Amadife 1999, 623; Dunmar 2002, 19; Horowitz 1985, 451. While regionally incorporated into the north at the time of independence, the middle belt has never been considered truly northern and Hausa-Fulani officers did not perceive middle belt officers as allies (Adeakin 2015, 57; Horowitz 1985, 456).
34 Early Nigerian political parties were regionally-based and corresponded to the three principle ethnic groups of those regions: the Northern People's Congress (NPC) was supported by the Hausa-Fulani of the north, the Action Group (AG) was supported by the Yoruba of the southwest, and the National Council of Nigeria and Cameroons (NCNC) was supported by the Ibo of the southeast (Feit 1968, 184–185; Horowitz 1985, 71; Mazrui & Tidy 1984, 92–95).

plotters' true motivations. This precipitated a successful counter-coup by the remaining Hausa-Fulani officers.[35] On taking power, the northerners purged the ranks and killed an unprecedented number of Ibo officers.[36] They then broke the army apart, ordering soldiers back to their home territories according to their ascriptive identity: Ibos were sent to the southeast, Yoruba to the southwest, and Hausa-Fulani to the north. These actions, combined with general fears of the now northern-dominated military government, led the Ibo region to secede and resulted in a devastating civil war.[37]

The purges combined with the civil war created a Hausa-Fulani-dominated military, especially amongst the senior ranks, that persisted until the democratic transition. It is important to note that, over the decades, southerners were still commissioned as officers and the middle belt was even overrepresented in the officer corps compared to its population share. The higher ranks of the army, however, were dominated by northerners and especially the Hausa-Fulani.[38] Babaginda himself was Hausa and it was his clique of fellow northern officers who wielded power immediately preceding the failed 1993 transition. He also stacked his council of ministers disproportionately with northerners, who additionally controlled the most valuable and strategic ministerial portfolios.[39] According to officers interviewed by Adeakin, ethnic identity and linguistic fluency in Hausa even determined career trajectories and opportunities for success within the military hierarchy.[40] Northerners certainly held a favored position within Nigeria's security institutions.

Ethnic privilege under the Babaginda regime entailed patronage possibilities unparalleled in sub-Saharan Africa. High-ranking military officers had long benefited from standard perks such as housing, cars, and cash allowances. Under Nigeria's many military dictatorships, they had also occupied political offices with accompanying rent-seeking opportunities and had become embedded in almost every sector of the

---

[35] See Luckham 1971, 17–79.
[36] Adeakin 2015, 60; Amadife 1999, 625.
[37] See Luckham 1971, 304–325.
[38] Adeakin 2015, 70; Bratton & van de Walle 1997, 216; Butts & Metz 1996, 5; Campbell 1994, 181; Manea & Rüland 2013, 65; Mustapha 1999, 285. A slight deviation from this pattern occurred under the military dictatorship of General Yakubu Gowon, who ruled from 1966 to 1975. Gowon, although a northerner, was from the minority Christian Latang group and promoted coethnics into key political and command positions (Adeakin 2015, 63).
[39] Dunmar 2002, 18 & 26; Ihonvbere 1991, 617.
[40] Adeakin 2015, 39.

economy, from shipping to manufacturing.[41] The Gulf War oil boom of the early 1990s, however, sent billions of dollars flowing into the public coffers, which were then quickly channeled into private hands. Corruption reached altogether new heights and senior officers amassed personal fortunes.[42] They also leveraged their windfall to support an extensive system of patronage within the military: "military godfathers" used their access to large sums of cash to support networks of lower ranking soldier-clients, trading material support for personal loyalty. Senior officers and their privileged clients became rich, living in mansions and driving Mercedes, while the rank-and-file and those excluded from this patronage boon suffered austerity along with ordinary Nigerians.[43] Material opportunities thus overlapped significantly with practices of ethnic inclusion and exclusion. The northern officers at the top of the military hierarchy were able to capture oil and other rents, bolstering their power and privilege through the creation of personally loyal patronage networks.

Indeed, northern dominance within the Babaginda regime – and the exclusion of everyone else from power and its associated rents – caused such deep resentment that a faction of junior officers rebelled. Led by Major Orka, the 1990 coup attempt was carried out by, and explicitly in the name of, southern and middle belt officers.[44] Although they did not hold the airwaves for long, Orka's radio broadcast railed against northerners, claiming that they "think it is their birth-right to dominate until eternity the political and economic privileges of this great country" and that their "quest for domination, oppression, and marginalisation is against the wish of God and therefore, must be resisted with all vehemence."[45] Orka then took an unprecedented step and announced that his regime would excise five northern states from the country. In his opinion, the north was too greedy and power hungry to remain in the nation.[46] Soon defeated by loyalists, the coup resulted in large-scale purges and executions, mainly of southern and middle belt officers: at least 69 officers were executed and hundreds of others forcibly retired.[47] The military was left even more solidly in northern hands.

[41] Kieh & Agbese 1993, 417; Lewis 1994, 329.
[42] Campbell 1994, 180–189; Kieh & Agbese 1993, 417; Lewis 1994, 338.
[43] Butts & Metz 1996, 5.
[44] Dunmar 2002, 27–28; Ihonvbere 1991, 602.
[45] Orka as quoted in Ihonvbere 1991, 616.
[46] Ibid.
[47] Ibid., 602 & 623.

Thus, by the time of the 1993 presidential elections, the senior officer corps was dominated by northerners (and the Hausa-Fulani in particular), benefited from extraordinary personal enrichment and patronage opportunities, and had just executed a large number of non-northern junior officers. Given this context, it makes sense that the top brass would prefer that Bashir Tofa, a fellow northerner and strong military supporter, win the presidency. They also had good reason to dread an Abiola victory. He was southern, Yoruba, and a critic of the military regime. Northerners generally feared retribution under a southern Yoruba controlled government for their years of dominance and past abuses.[48] Additionally, Abiola was rumored to have compiled a list of senior army officers whom he wished to retire upon taking power.[49] And reports circulated that the majority of rank-and-file soldiers and very junior officers, whose loyalty to the senior ranks was questionable at best after the recent coup attempt, had voted for him.[50] A week prior to the election, high-ranking officers met to discuss opinion polls showing Abiola's clear lead. According to Campbell, they concluded at that time that Abiola "was too strong and too independent to be a comfortable partner in a 'managed' transition."[51] Abiola was a threat.

Indeed, the two most common explanations proffered for the election annulment focus on these factors of patronage and ethnicity. First, some argue that senior military officers worried that their days of plenty had come to an end and that Abiola would prosecute them for past enrichment. They thus canceled the transition to protect their wealth.[52] Second, others contend that Hausa-Fulani politicians and military officers feared that the election of a southerner spelled the permanent end of northern dominance over, and perhaps even inclusion in, the government. Once granted power, the south might never let go. Thus, the military was unwilling to step aside once it became clear that Abiola would carry the election.[53]

Of course, these explanations are not mutually exclusive and, within the theoretical framework developed here, reinforce one another. The system of ethnic privilege built within the military granted northern officers access to material benefits and patronage opportunities based

---

48 Okoroji 1993, 128.
49 Okoroji 1993, 127.
50 Campbell 1994, 188.
51 Ibid., 190.
52 Butts & Metz 1996, 6; Mahmud 1993, 90.
53 Adeakin 2015, 66; Bratton & van de Walle 1997, 216; Butts & Metz 1996, 6; Campbell 1994, 190.

on their ethnic identity. Democratization created the risk that elections would bring to power a leader no longer sharing the identity of the ethnic army. This threatened the ethnic army's intertwined power and material privileges, motivating them to rebel. In the Nigerian case, Abiola's victory at the polls gave substance to this threat and the senior officers reacted by immediately annulling the elections and canceling the democratic experiment, leading to a renewed era of military dictatorship.

Epilogue: Successful Democratization

Despite descending once again into repressive military governance, Nigerians did not wait long for another chance to democratize. On June 8, 1998, Sani Abacha died in somewhat scandalous circumstances involving imported Indian prostitutes and a rumored viagra overdose.[54] Following his death, the military embarked on another managed transition and new presidential elections. This time, even though the military elite was still predominantly northern, they selected two presidential candidates who were both southern and Yoruba. This was a compensatory move to calm tensions with the Yoruba region. Not only did the last presidential election's annulment still rankle, but Moshood Abiola had mysteriously died while in state custody, stoking outrage in the south and leading to renewed fears of civil war.[55]

The military's preferred candidate was Olusegun Obasanjo, a retired general and former military leader. Even though he had been jailed by Abacha, along with 40 other military officers, for suggesting power be returned to civilians, the senior ranks considered him sympathetic and unlikely to enact major changes or prosecute the military elite for past abuses.[56] Retired army officers even helped bank roll Obasanjo's campaign.[57] Neither did the Yoruba consider Obasanjo their candidate. Yoruba leaders and politicians dismissed Obasanjo as a stooge of the northern military–political establishment and he ultimately faired poorly in the Yoruba states: capturing only 20% of the vote.[58] With Obasanjo polling ahead nationally, the elections were allowed to proceed and their results upheld.

Then Obasanjo surprised the military. Upon assuming office, instead of deferring or avoiding military reform as expected, he promptly retired

---

54 Mustapha 1999, 280.
55 Adeakin 2015, 67; Manea & Rüland 2013, 64.
56 Ibid.; Dunmar 2002, 29.
57 Mustapha 1999, 285.
58 Williams 1999, 410.

93 high-ranking officers, including 26 army generals – all of whom had previously held political positions and benefited from rent-seeking. Further undermining the northern dominance of the senior ranks, he filled the now open positions with soldiers from minority ethnic groups of the middle belt region.[59] Further reforms emphasized merit in the recruitment and selection of officers, established a principle of equal representation from each state across all ranks, and improved the welfare of soldiers without reference to ethnic background.[60] Obasanjo has thus been credited with easing ethnic antagonisms within the military.[61] Nigeria has not faced a coup attempt since, despite several turnovers in executive power. Although Nigeria still has a long road to travel toward democratic consolidation, the dismantlement of its ethnic army removes a fundamental roadblock to this goal.

BENIN: RESISTANCE TO THE SUCCESSFUL 1990 DEMOCRATIC TRANSITION

Benin is often extolled as a model of democratization in Africa. Mass protests resulting from severe economic hardship pressured a long-ruling military dictatorship to concede power. A sovereign national conference was held, representing diverse sectors of society, culminating in the adoption of a new democratic constitution. Within a year, free and fair elections had been held for local and national offices and a new civilian government had been installed. Despite the country's poverty and historic tendency towards military intervention and governance, democracy has survived and even consolidated.

Benin's democratic transition was not without its hiccups, however. A minority of northern military officers initially resisted ceding power. Some adamantly opposed negotiating with the opposition during the national conference and a handful attempted, but failed, to either assassinate the newly elected president or seize power. The same group of northern soldiers was also purportedly responsible for a series of subsequent domestic terror attacks against southerners. None of these acts posed a serious threat to the government and all were relatively minor, poorly coordinated, and lacked any real support within the military.

Historic ethnic tensions and recruitment practices within Benin's security institutions help explain both this resistance and its inability to attract

---

[59] Adeakin 2015, 39; Manea & Rüland 2013, 65.
[60] Adeakin 2015, 72–73.
[61] Ibid., 39.

broader support. Prior to the democratic transition, Mathieu Kérékou had led Benin's Marxist-Leninist leaning military regime for 12 years. Primarily conditioning loyalty on ideological grounds, he had instituted a regional quota system for military recruitment, including within the officer corps. Nonetheless, promotion practices tended to favor fellow northerners, leading to disproportionate northern representation at the higher ranks. Benin's military was thus neither ideally inclusive nor truly ethnically stacked. That ethnically-based privileges did exist explains why some northerners would resist democratization to protect their "unfair" promotions. That the military was generally inclusive and professional explains why rebellious officers found little support amongst their peers.

Pressures for Democratization and the National Conference

Economic crisis combined with paralyzing public demonstrations and French pressure led the Kérékou regime to embark on a consultative reform process, ultimately leading to elections and democratization. By the early 1980s, Benin's economy had all but collapsed. Policy misman-agement, rampant corruption, and recession in neighboring Nigeria (a key trading partner), all fed into declining welfare across society. The state could no longer regularly pay its employees, even its soldiers. To meet dwindling budgets, many civil servants were laid off and the remainder faced salary reductions. Student scholarships were also reduced and the long-standing practice of guaranteeing state employment for all national university graduates was terminated.[62] None of these measures solved the crisis: sustained negative growth rates persisted, the accumulation of large foreign debts accelerated, and the government remained bankrupt.[63] Matters worsened in 1989 when the state-owned banking sector collapsed, leading to a liquidity crisis and drying up the necessary credit for many public and private businesses to continue operating.[64] Seeking emergency relief, the government signed an agreement with the IMF and World Bank, receiving desperately needed loans in exchange for consenting to structural adjustment. The resulting strict austerity measures mandated reductions in state subsidies, privatization of state-owned businesses, and further cuts to civil service employment and student scholarships.[65]

[62] Gisselquist 2008, 795; Heilbrunn 1993, 283; Morency-Laflamme 2015, 465.
[63] Gazibo 2005, 74–75.
[64] Gisselquist 2008, 796; Heilbrunn 1993, 278; Magnusson 2001, 218.
[65] Gazibo 2005, 74; Heilbrunn 1993, 281.

Austerity measures only worsened declining living standards and employment prospects for ordinary citizens, amplifying protests and strikes and rendering Benin basically ungovernable by the end of 1989. Demonstrations had become routine throughout the decade, led largely by students and underground unions. In January, however, after the government had failed to pay salaries and student scholarships for several months, protests greatly intensified. Tens of thousands of civil servants joined in, demanding payment of their salary arrears and calling for liberalization. By July, nearly the entire civil service was on strike, bringing government services and operations to a standstill. 40,000 demonstrators in Contonou alone openly called for Kérékou's resignation. By December, whole cities were paralyzed by protests and nation-wide strikes had nearly destroyed what was left of the national economy. Concerted action by students, civil servants, and trade unions had brought the government to its knees.[66]

Although Kérékou initially responded with repression, he quickly began making concessions. At first, the army was called in and ordered to surround public buildings and arrest both protestors and strike leaders. The demonstrations only grew in volume and intensity.[67] The French government then stepped in, encouraging liberalization and advising Kérékou that a national conference would provide useful council in designing and implementing reforms. The French even offered to pay for such a conference and went so far as to withhold emergency relief funds until after it was held.[68] Facing domestic anarchy and external pressure, Kérékou quickly embarked on a series of steps to ease public dissent. He began by renouncing Marxism-Leninism, then granted amnesty to political dissidents, and finally conceded to the national conference.[69]

The conference, a model later replicated throughout Francophone Africa, brought together representatives from all sectors of society to discuss the crisis and propose reforms. Participants were drawn from the current government, the military, the political opposition, student organizations, trade unions, and churches, amongst other civil society groups. Once convened, the national conference declared its own sovereignty, a move which Kérékou reluctantly accepted. They then embarked on a rapid program of democratization, establishing an interim government

---

[66] Akindes 2015, 54; Gazibo 2005, 74; Gisselquist 2008, 796; Heilbrunn 1993, 283–286; Magnusson 2001, 218; Morency-Laflamme 2015, 463–465.

[67] Morency-Laflamme 2015, 465.

[68] Gisselquist 2008, 796 & 807.

[69] Ibid., 796–797; Magnusson 2001, 218.

and determining a schedule for multiparty elections. Within a single year, by 1991, a new democratic constitution had been adopted by popular referendum and elections had been held for local, provincial, and national assembly representatives as well as for the presidency. Although there were some reported incidents of violence, and Kérékou refused to concede until he was granted immunity for past crimes, the elections marked a watershed moment in Benin's political development: deemed free and fair, Christophe Soglo beat Kérékou by a decisive 67.5% to 32.5%, ushering in a democratic alternation of government.[70]

Northern Military Resistance to Democratization

While the military as a whole supported the democratization project and their own return to the barracks, resistance did emerge from a minority of northern officers. Three incidents, in particular, stand out. First, during the national conference, some northern officers adamantly opposed negotiating with the opposition and instead supported continued rule by the Kérékou regime. Colonel Maurice Kouandaté, a powerful northern former junta leader and key participant in past coups, even publicly declared that any attempt to remove Kérékou from power would result in his intervention and dissolution of the national conference. Yet, he was unable to gain sufficient support within the military to back up his threats with action.[71]

Second, a small clique of northern officers apparently attempted to assassinate or overthrow Soglo in 1992, after he assumed the presidency. The details are murky, but shots were fired outside the presidential palace. Captain Pascal Tawes was later arrested, along with several other northern officers, and the incident is sometimes coded as a coup attempt.[72] Whatever their ultimate intentions, the plot was poorly organized, failed to gain traction amongst other soldiers, and was quickly crushed. No other coup attempts followed.[73]

Finally, a subsequent string of domestic terrorist attacks was attributed to Captain Tawes and his small band of followers. 1994 proved a difficult year for the fledgling democratic regime in general: a 50% devaluation of the regional French West African currency (CFA) led to renewed economic

---

[70] Gisselquist 2008, 797–798; Heilbrunn 1993, 278.
[71] Morency-Laflamme 2015, 467.
[72] McGowan 2003 includes the case as a failed coup attempt while Powell & Thyne 2011 exclude it from their data.
[73] Clark 2007, 149–150; Lindberg & Clark 2007, 97.

and social turmoil, including urban strikes and student protests that turned violent.[74] Hundreds and thousands of refugees also flooded the small country from neighboring Nigeria and Togo, both of whom had aborted their democratic experiments that year.[75] Added to this insecurity were the series of terrorist attacks against southerners orchestrated by Captain Tawes. Tawes had recently escaped from prison and accumulated a small band of acolytes, some of whom were thought to be active duty soldiers. They were accused of a number of offenses against southerners living in the north, including kidnapping and killing an administrator and burning or otherwise destroying the property of other such civil servants. They may also have distributed leaflets across the north warning southerners to leave and return home. And they were blamed for setting off explosives in public spaces and government buildings across the south, including in restaurants, marketplaces, the customs headquarters, and the airport. While entailing tragic consequences for their victims and spreading fear amongst southerners, Tawes never gained a mass following and these small-scale attacks never threatened the stability of the democratic regime.[76]

Thus some resistance from northern officers did emerge against the democratization project. These few rebellious soldiers were, however, unable to gain enough support from fellow military officers, of any ethnic or regional background, to seriously threaten Benin's liberalization. Neither a serious coup attempt nor an insurgency developed. Indeed, most of the army supported the national conference, in part because the economic crisis had greatly fractionalized the army. Two failed coup attempts had occurred in 1988 and there had been increasingly open dissent on the part of rank-and-file soldiers and junior officers over pay arrears. Such military infighting and disciplinary breakdowns led many senior officers to join their subordinates in favoring a return to the barracks.[77]

Kérékou and Diversity in the Military

Benin's somewhat unorthodox combination of inclusivity and discrimination within its military institutions explains this middling outcome, in

---

[74] Magnusson 2001, 221–223.
[75] Ibid., 221.
[76] Ibid., 223.
[77] Morency-Laflamme 2015, 467.

between the absence of resistance and a full-fledged attempt to counter-mand democratization. Building ethnic armies as a loyalty mechanism and coup-proofing strategy usually entails overwhelming preference for the privileged groups – such that they dominate, at a minimum, the senior officer and important field grade ranks. On the other hand, inclusive militaries built on professional principles of merit usually eschew ethnic criteria in recruitment and promotion practices or, particularly given a past history of ethnic imbalances, have constructed systems to ensure fair representation for groups across ranks. Benin falls in between these models: under Kérékou, an ethnic quota system maintained diversity in the officer corps while promotion practices favored northerners, leading to some discrimination and preferential treatment.

Benin has a history of ethno-regional competition that shaped both early politics and military recruitment practices. French colonial administrators reinforced the existing divisions between the sparsely populated tribes of the Muslim north and the two rivalrous city-states of the south: the Fon Kingdom of Dahomey centered around Contonou and the Yoruba and Goun city of Porto Novo, allied with the Oyo Empire. As in much of West Africa, the French administered the north and south separately, with education, infrastructure, and other investments concentrated in the south. This led to the development of strong ethno-regional identities. Unsurprisingly, early political parties reflected the tripartite division between the southern Fon, the southern Yoruba and Goun, and the tribes of the north.[78]

Early military recruitment practices were also shaped by these ethnic rivalries. The late colonial military had drawn recruits primarily from the less educated north, who were still disproportionately represented amongst the rank-and-file at the time of independence.[79] Benin's first president, Hubert Maga, himself a northerner, built on these traditions and increased the recruitment of northern officers. He also packed the paramilitary gendarmerie with coethnic northern Bariba.[80] When General Christophe Soglo overthrew the government, in 1965, his regime then dismantled Maga's northern ethnic army. Instead, Soglo disproportionately recruited and promoted fellow southern Fon until they dominated the middle and upper ranks of the military, to the exclusion of northerners who now only held 14 of 90 positions in the

---

78 Decalo 1973, 451–452.
79 Akindes 2015, 40 & 47; Minority Rights Group 2010.
80 Decalo 1973, 458; Horowitz 1985, 456.

officer corps.[81] Benin's early history was thus one of constructing ethnic armies.

That changed, however, under Mathieu Kérékou's 18 years of authoritarian rule, beginning in 1972 after he violently seized power in yet another military coup. Kérékou was a committed Marxist-Leninist and, in general, his regime attempted to mobilize support along ideological lines. Ideological loyalty thus generally conditioned access to political and administrative positions rather than ethnicity.[82] Kérékou also inherited a military that, under a whirlwind rotation of prior leaders, had become riven into multiple competing ethno-clientelist factions.[83] Displacing these entrenched cliques with coethnics would have been exceedingly difficult given that smaller ethnic cleavages had already displaced larger regional identities. Kérékou also came from the small northern Somba group, which constituted no more than 5–7% of the total population.[84] Instead of supplanting the existing ethnic factions in the military, Kérékou tried to unify them and de-ethnicize the chain of command.[85] Ethnic balance within the military became a priority and, to achieve such balance, Kérékou created a regional and ethnic quota-based recruitment system that assured diversity across all ranks, even and perhaps especially in the officer corps.[86]

Northerners did, however, seem to receive preferential promotion opportunities under Kérékou and thus came to be disproportionately represented at the more senior ranks. Morency-Laflamme argues that promotions were conditioned on political loyalty, which had ethnic as well as ideological overtones. Southerners were often neglected and passed over for promotion, leading to widespread resentment.[87] That senior officers also benefited from political appointments and patronage resources deepened this discontent. Military officers served as both ministers and managers of state-owned businesses, creating prime opportunities for personal enrichment.[88] Southern disgruntlement over such discrimination at the top of the command hierarchy became evident during the economic crisis and resulting national conference. In 1988, as living standards declined and soldiers' salaries were held

---

[81] Decalo 1973, 462.
[82] Dickovick 2008, 1122; Foltz & McDonald 1995, 27.
[83] Dickovick 2008, 1124.
[84] Gisselquist 2008, 798.
[85] Dickovick 2008, 1124.
[86] Akindes 2015, 52 & 56; Morency-Laflamme 2015, 465.
[87] Morency-Laflamme 2015, 466–467.
[88] Akindes 2015, 49–51; Heilbrunn 1993, 282.

in arrears, mainly southern officers staged two failed coup attempts. During the national conference, some southern officers then negotiated directly with the opposition: in exchange for their support, they were promised top positions in the officer corps following democratization.[89] While the military remained a diverse institution, meaning Benin did not have to cope with a full-fledged ethnic army during the democratic transition,[90] it was simultaneously discriminatory. Southern officers faced marginalization while being included.

This explains why some northern officers resisted democratization, sometimes with violence, but were unable to garner support from the majority of soldiers. Ethnically-based discrimination led to unfair promotion opportunities, which entailed political appointments and material enrichment. The northern officers that had benefited most from this system wanted to maintain it. The military as a whole, however, reflected Benin's diversity and the vast majority of these soldiers welcomed democratization and their own return to the barracks, especially southern officers. Ever since, Benin's democracy has flourished: the country has has held free and fair elections every five years; witnessed four successful alternations of executive power through the ballot box (in 1991, 1996, 2006, and 2016); established a neutral constitutional court that has successfully held both the legislative and executive branches in check and resolved disputes between them; and is consistently rated as one of the freest sub-Saharan African countries, both in terms of political rights and civil liberties.[91]

SENEGAL: DEMOCRATIZATION WITHOUT MILITARY REBELLION

Senegal faced similar domestic and international pressures to liberalize in the late 1980s as Nigeria and Benin. Deep economic crisis had forced the country to seek external aid and adopt requisite structural adjustment programs, whose austerity measures only fueled already virulent domestic protest. As its neighbors democratized, especially Benin and Mali, Senegal's long-ruling Socialist Party (PS) found it increasingly difficult to refuse both donor and opposition party demands to open the political system to real competition. Unlike in Nigeria and Benin, however, democratization was not resisted by Senegal's military. Liberalization

---

[89] Morency-Laflamme 2015, 466–467.
[90] Foltz & McDonald 1995, 6.
[91] Akindes 2015, 38; Freedom House 2016a; Gisselquist 2008, 790; Magnusson 2001, 217.

was accommodated and, when executive power finally changed hands after the watershed 2000 presidential elections, the army accepted its new commander-in-chief with equanimity. Indeed, the Senegalese military has become a staunch defender of democracy: defecting from President Abdoulaye Wade's bid to unconstitutionally cling to power and supporting the opposition's victory in the 2008 elections.

While many factors have contributed to Senegal's successful democratization – not least of which include a history of political stability, greater experience with (however controlled) multiparty competition, and a robust civil society – the military could have vetoed the experiment, as militaries have done in so many other African countries. They chose not to. This decision was greatly facilitated by Senegal's long-standing commitment to inclusive and professional security institutions. Democracy posed no threat to officers who had gained their positions through competence and experience rather than through ethnic loyalty.

Pressures for Democratization and the 2000 Watershed Election

Senegal experienced the same deep economic malaise that pervaded the rest of sub-Saharan Africa in the 1980s. Failed import substitution industrialization policies, inefficiencies introduced through corruption and mismanagement of the agricultural sector, drought, and regional recession all fed into the economic crisis. To make matters worse, prices for Senegal's primary commodity, groundnuts, collapsed in the mid-1980s and failed to fully recover before declining again a few years later. The government soon found itself nearly insolvent, with mounting external debt service payments, while rural incomes crumbled and urban workers were laid off or had their wages slashed.[92] Senegal's leaders were forced to seek help from the IMF, which mandated a structural adjustment program replete with austerity measures. Structural adjustment, in turn, aggravated declining living standards. Deep cuts in agricultural subsidies led farmers to purchase lower quality seeds and forego rich fertilizers, diminishing crop yields and further harming export revenues and rural livelihoods. The removal of price controls and lowered wages also aggravated urban poverty, leading to protests and riots.[93]

After the 1988 presidential elections, discontent culminated in the worst political crisis Senegal had witnessed in decades. Despite gradual

[92] Boone 1990, 343; Weissman 1990, 1624.
[93] Diallo & Kelly 2016, 195–196; Weissman 1990, 1624 & 1628.

steps toward real political competition, including the introduction of controlled multiparty elections in the 1970s, the PS had held power since independence and Abdou Diouf the presidency for almost a decade. When they declared themselves victorious once again, the opposition challenged the election results and social protests and riots erupted across Dakar and other urban areas. In response, the government arrested opposition leaders, declared a state of emergency, and imposed a curfew that lasted for three months.[94]

Such internal strife combined with sweeping regional liberalization, especially national conferences held in the neighboring, fellow Francophone states of Benin and Mali, put extraordinary pressure on Diouf to democratize as well. Fearing the outcome of a national conference, in 1991, Diouf and the PS agreed to negotiate with the political opposition and adopted a number of substantial reforms. Most importantly, a new electoral code was instituted that included secret balloting, the right of political parties to send observers to polling places, and equal access to the media for opposition parties. Other reforms included the adoption of presidential term limits and additional measures to prevent fraud and increase the fairness and transparency of elections.[95]

While not engendering immediate change, these liberalization measures, combined with the collapse of Senegal's patronage system, eventually resulted in electoral defeat for both Diouf and the PS. Following independence, Senegal was governed as an autocratic single-party state that relied extensively on patronage to induce mass support. Agricultural subsidies and privileges in the groundnut export sector were granted to the leaders of Senegal's Sufi brotherhoods in exchange for religious edicts commanding their followers to vote for the governing party. The IMF mandated structural adjustment program, however, slashed agricultural funding and thereby severely diminished the regime's patronage resources. After the 1988 election, the Sufi religious leaders (marabouts) ceased issuing their edicts and instead adopted a position of political neutrality.[96] Lacking their support and constrained by the new electoral code, the PS' vote share steadily declined: from 71–73% in 1988, to 56–58% in 1993, to their historic loss in 2000.[97]

---

94 Villalón 1994, 164 & 173; Villalón 2015, 312.
95 Diallo & Kelly 2016, 195–196; Villalón 1994, 175; Villalón 2015, 313.
96 See discussion in Chapter 5 as well as Clark 1999; Fatton 1986; Foltz 1965.
97 Nunley 2011.

Indeed, the 2000 presidential elections are generally hailed as Senegal's watershed political moment that ushered in an era of real democratization. They marked Senegal's first instance of *alternance*, or the transfer of executive power from one political party to another. Legislative elections ended four decades of socialist dominance and, in the presidential elections, Abdoulaye Wade defeated the incumbent, Abdou Diouf. The elections were judged free and fair by international observers and Diouf quickly conceded defeat. Nor did the military resist, resulting in a smooth and peaceful democratic transition.[98]

Legacy of Military Inclusiveness

Unlike many African countries, Senegal was not burdened with an ethnically loyal army when embarking on democratization. Quite to the contrary, as recounted in Chapter 5, Senegal's military has always been inclusive. Senegal's independence leader and long-serving first president, Léopold Senghor, believed that inclusion and protection of the country's diverse ethnic and tribal communities were central to building strong institutions and a sense of nationalism. He thus recruited soldiers and officers broadly across ethnic communities. He also created a military widely regarded as professional and apolitical, with officers appointed and promoted according to professional merit rather than on the basis of ethnic or personal loyalty. Diouf upheld these traditions as have Senegal's subsequent leaders.[99]

Senegalese soldiers thus had little to fear from democratization. Promotion and recruitment policies were already compatible with democratic practices, including the regular alternation of political leaders. Nor would new leaders from different ethnic backgrounds challenge soldier's access to the ranks, unless they consciously deviated from long-standing practices that upheld diversity – an unlikely development given Senegal's history of inclusivity and low ethnic politicization. Indeed, Senegal has already experienced multiple transitions between presidents from different ethnic backgrounds. Léopold Senghor was from the Serer group and handed power to Diouf, his hand-picked successor of mixed Serer and Peulh identity. Diouf, in turn, relinquished power in 2000 to Wade who is Wolof. And Wade accepted his defeat at the polls in 2012, allowing Macky

---

[98] Dahou & Foucher 2009, 15; Freedom House 2016c, "Senegal"; Kelly 2012, 121; Villalón 2015, 312.

[99] See discussion in Chapter 5 as well as Cissé 2015; Diop & Paye 1998, 319; Keegan 1983, 514–515; Markovitz 1969, 104–111; Nelson 1974, 340.

Sall of the Fula to accede to the presidency. None of these power transfers between leaders from different ethnic backgrounds has provoked any type of resistance from the military.

Epilogue: Defenders of Democracy

Beyond merely tolerating liberalization, the Senegalese military has become a staunch defender of democracy. When Abdoulaye Wade turned back towards authoritarianism and attempted to unconstitutionally perpetuate his rule, the military abandoned him. After his 2000 presidential election victory, Wade initially improved Senegal's human rights record and oversaw the adoption of a new, more liberal constitution. His flirtation with democratic rule, however, soon faltered. Wade's 2007 reelection bid was marred by irregularities and he began exhibiting worrying authoritarian tendencies, increasingly concentrating power in the presidency. Wade packed state institutions, including the judiciary and the upper house of parliament, with political loyalists and personalized his rule by appointing kin to important ministerial portfolios. Violations of civil liberties also increased, including political intimidation, police repression of protests, and the detention of journalists and opposition leaders.[100]

These autocratic moves culminated in Wade's attempt to defy the constitution and retain power past his term limits. In May 2011, he officially announced his intended run for an unconstitutional third term in office. Packed with sympathetic judges dependent on Wade's partiality and benevolence, the Constitutional Court ruled in his favor despite the clear legal violation. He then tried to reduce the vote share needed to forego a second round of elections, down to merely 25%, enabling him to more easily defeat the fractured opposition.[101] Through quasi-legal maneuvering, Wade thus threatened to rollback Senegal's tenuous democratic gains and potentially reinstate autocratic single-party rule.

Yet, Wade's bid to defy term limits failed miserably: civil society mobilized against him, he was defeated at the polls, and the military abandoned him. After Wade's 2007 reelection, a consortium of opposition leaders and NGOs traveled the country, visiting each of Senegal's administrative departments to consult with ordinary citizens on the many social, economic, and political problems facing the country. Out of this effort a new opposition movement was formed, the United to

---

[100] Dahou & Foucher 2009, 21; Freedom House 2016c, "Senegal"; Kelly 2012, 121.
[101] Kelly 2012, 127–128.

Boost Senegal coalition, which successfully defeated Wade's party in the 2009 local elections. Additional popular movements also coalesced in opposition to Wade, including Y'en a Marre (Enough is Enough) and Bes du Ñiakk (Citizen's Movement for National Refoundation). As Wade attempted to secure his third term in office, these movements organized mass protests in Dakar and other urban areas, forcing the withdrawal of his vote threshold lowering bill. This victory, in turn, inspired the June 23 Movement, comprised of 60 NGOs and opposition parties who sought to prevent Wade from winning the presidential elections.[102] Ultimately, Wade lost badly at the polls. He only garnered 32% of votes in the first round, falling well short of the required 50%. The opposition then united in support of Macky Sall, resulting in a resounding defeat for Wade in the second round of voting: 34.2% to 65.8%.[103]

While Senegal's energized civil society played an important role in ensuring free and fair elections,[104] the military also enabled a peaceful transfer of power by forsaking Wade. Having conducted their own opinion surveys, the military informed Wade of his impending loss soon after the polls closed. They also told him that he would lack security sector support if he tried to defy the election results. Wade quickly conceded defeat. Subsequent legislative elections saw Sall's United in Hope coalition win 119 of 150 seats in the National Assembly, thoroughly removing Wade and his political party from power and leading to Senegal's second electoral change in leadership.[105]

Unlike in so many other African cases, Senegal's military has embraced democratization and even become a defender of constitutionalism and elections. While many causes underly Senegal's successful liberalization and resistance to authoritarian regression, military endorsement of democracy must be counted among them. This support, in turn, was greatly facilitated by Senegal's lack of an ethnic army.

CONCLUSION

Dismantling systems of ethnic privilege within important state institutions threatens historically privileged groups, provoking reactionary violence.

---

[102] Ibid., 126–128.

[103] Freedom House 2016c, "Senegal."

[104] For example, observers were dispatched to over 11,000 polling stations, sending text message vote counts to volunteer collation centers in Dakar. In this way, civil society activists and journalists could monitor local polling and report any attempts to alter tallies as the votes were aggregated (*The Economist* 2015).

[105] Ibid.

Advantaged groups are thus most likely to rebel when facing a negative change in their status, whether after the fact or in anticipation of such downgrading. Within the particular context of military institutions, ethnic armies rebel when new leaders come to power who no longer share their identity. Such leaders have strong motivations to reform the ethnic militaries built by their predecessors – whose loyalty cannot be relied upon. This poses a direct threat to the ethnic army, who rebel in order to protect their position of power and access to material resources.

When democratization finally came to sub-Saharan Africa, it profoundly undermined political stability precisely because it threatened the continent's many ethnic armies. Whether built through collusion with departing colonial powers, achieved through the pyrrhic homogenization of diverse armies through coups and counter-coups, or created by the victory of ethnically-based rebel groups, Africa was endowed with a legacy of ethnic armies. Given the social diversity of African states, competitive democratic elections then brought to power new leaders who no longer shared the identity of the ethnic armies they inherited. Predictably, soldiers rebelled. Not all African countries, however, faced such a legacy. Those already possessing inclusive and diverse militaries had far less to fear from their own militaries when embarking on a program of liberalization. This by no means guaranteed success, but it did remove one critical barrier to democratization.

This chapter compared three countries that attempted to democratize under similar pressures and at the same historical juncture: Nigeria, Benin, and Senegal. Yet, each case experienced a different outcome. Nigeria's elections and entire democratic experiment were annulled by the military. Benin successfully democratized with limited and contained soldier violence, while Senegal's military embraced liberalization without dissent. These outcomes vary in accordance with their past military ethnic recruitment and promotion practices. Northern Hausa-Fulani officers had long dominated Nigeria's officer corps, enriching themselves and building clientelist networks from the country's vast oil revenues. When threatened by the electoral victory of a southern Yoruba, they canceled the democratic experiment. Benin, in contrast, possessed an ethnically diverse military with quotas ensuring ethnic representation at all ranks, but also practiced discrimination in promotion practices at the highest levels of the command hierarchy. Privileged northern officers demonstrated some resistance to democratization but were unable to garner sufficient support across the military as a whole to seriously challenge liberalization. Finally, Senegal had historically maintained inclusive and diverse security institutions with no evidence of ethnic discrimination or privilege. This professional and apolitical military not only tolerated but embraced democratization.

These cases further demonstrate how important variables such as natural resource rents and ethnic politicization interact with military institutions to challenge democratization. As has been discussed, high ethnic politicization made it difficult for nationalist leaders like Kwame Nkrumah of Ghana, or federalist governments like that of early Nigeria, to construct and maintain inclusive security institutions. By shaping historical military recruitment practices, ethnic politicization created a grim hurdle for later democratization: ethnic armies. High oil or other rents only enhance the incentives for these ethnic armies to maintain their power and thus their access to enriching patronage opportunities.

Conclusion

The enduring instability of the African state arguably stems from the intertwined problems of ethnic politicization and military intervention in politics. Throughout much of Africa, the military is neither a homogenous nor neutral agent, but rather an institution shaped by ideas of ethnic loyalty and complicit in ethnic conflict. As soldiers become increasingly involved in politics, using their foothold in security institutions to further ethnic agendas, they then further militarize and politicize ethnicity. This book has sought to delve into these processes, understanding how ethnicity shaped military development and then how practices of building and dismantling ethnic armies have contributed to rampant instability.

The argument rests on the claim that constructing and dismantling systems of ethnic privilege within state institutions profoundly threatens losing groups, who will protect their current power and privilege with violence. The postcolonial African state has been characterized by widespread practices of clientelism and patronage. Where such neopatrimonialism combines with ethnic control over the state, excluded groups are burdened with high economic, political, and emotional costs that engender deep-seated grievances. Exclusion, however, also diminishes the resources for resistance. The included, in contrast, can leverage existing clientelist networks, access to state resources and war material, and other institutional resources to organize and fund rebellion. The groups with both the strongest motivation to rebel and the greatest capacity to do so are those currently included but facing future exclusion. It is thus during the processes of creating or destroying systems of ethnic privilege that we are most likely to witness violence.

Soldiers rebel when leaders attempt to construct or dismantle ethnic armies. To theorize and test these dynamics, I focused on the contexts of decolonization and democratization, respectively. While internal political actors and movements were certainly important in shaping events in both periods, they arose largely due to external factors – the decline of European empires and the end of the Cold War. These shocks then created widespread opportunities for ethnically restructuring security institutions, minimizing endogenous threats to inference. It is, however, important to note that endogenous dynamics do create similar opportunities to radically restructure civil-military relations and change institutional practices within the military. The theory should apply in these moments as well.

During decolonization, leaders often built ethnic armies, provoking coups and counter-coups. Colonial recruitment practices relied on race and ethnicity as foundations for military loyalty: European officers were imported to command while politically trustworthy martial races filled the ranks. Faced with pressing threats and deteriorating regional security, many independence era African leaders followed this model, binding soldiers to the state through the dual mechanisms of coethnic loyalty and patronage. The construction of such ethnically-based militaries threatened non-favored officers with exclusion from a vital state institution, from its often vast patronage resources, and from a significant source of power to protect their future interests. Where leaders had inherited a diverse officer corps, ethnic restructuring provoked violence from the soldiers now facing exclusion based on their ethnic identity. Initial coup attempts then often sparked further coups as ethnic factions within the military vied for control over the state, leading to a cycle of violence.

The mixed-methods empirical investigation supported this hypothesis concerning the construction of ethnic armies. The statistical analysis revealed that where leaders attempted to build ethnic armies despite existing diversity in the officer corps, losing factions violently resisted their own marginalization: countries in such circumstances experienced four times as many coup attempts following decolonization. The two paired case study comparisons lend additional support: the leaders of both Cameroon and Sierra Leone decided to build military loyalty on ethnic grounds and yet this choice only had destabilizing consequences in Sierra Leone. While in Cameroon the departing French colonizers had colluded with Ahmadou Ahidjo to create a coethnic officer corps from the beginning, in Sierra Leone the British had purposefully constructed diverse military institutions. Thus, when Prime Minister Albert Margai began to ethnically restructure the military, there existed significant numbers of non-coethnic officers to resist his designs. Similarly, although both Ghana and Senegal began by creating inclusive armies, after assassination attempts against his life, Ghana's Kwame Nkrumah abandoned such policies and turned toward ethnically manipulating security institutions. As a result, Ewe and Ga officers now facing discrimination and exclusion seized power, setting Ghana on a path of repeated political instability driven by the struggle for ethnic domination over the state between the Ewe and Akan. Constructing ethnic armies despite prior diversity in the officer corps provokes rebellion.

During democratization, dismantling ethnic armies similarly motivated soldiers to rebel. Historically privileged groups will defend their domination over state institutions and access to power and patronage resources – whether they subscribe to beliefs about their own right to privilege or merely fear revenge and exclusion. In sub-Saharan Africa, democratization poses a particular threat to political stability because of these dynamics. Where there is a legacy of ethnic armies, elections in highly diverse societies threaten to bring to power leaders who no longer share the identity of their inherited security institutions. Such leaders are highly motivated to disband the ethnic army, either diversifying the officer corps to more fairly represent the ideals of a multiethnic democracy or, perhaps, replacing it with a loyal ethnic army of their own. In either case, restructuring threatens the existing ethnic army, eliciting violent resistance.

Once again, the mixed-methods analysis supported these hypotheses concerning how democratization leads to the dismantling of ethnic armies and hence to their rebellion. In the statistical analysis, where elections or other constitutional means brought to power leaders who no longer shared the identity of the ethnic armies they inherited, coup risk increased from under 25% to 50–66%. The case study analysis, comparing similar democratization projects in Nigeria, Benin, and Senegal, affirmed these findings. The degree of military resistance to liberalization reflected past ethnic recruitment and promotion practices. In Nigeria, northern Hausa-Fulani officers had long dominated the senior ranks of Nigeria's military as well as its political institutions. When threatened by the electoral victory of a southern Yoruba, it was precisely these officers who annulled the democratic experiment. In contrast, when embarking on democratization, Benin possessed an ethnically diverse military with a quota system ensuring regional representation. Discrimination in promotion policies was, however, practiced at the highest ranks leading to limited ethnic privilege for some northern officers. These officers did resist democratization, including small-scale violent actions, but could never garner enough support across the military as a whole to seriously challenge liberalization. In contrast, Senegal's historically inclusive and diverse army embraced democracy. Dismantling ethnic armies threatens political stability as soldiers protect their privileged position.

CONTRIBUTIONS

This book makes an important contribution to our understanding of ethnic conflict and when ethnic groups are likely to rebel. Previous research has shown that the institutionalization of ethnic categories generates emotional dynamics that increase the risk of conflict and that grievances matter deeply: both political exclusion and horizontal inequalities, or large social and economic disparities between groups, motivate rebellion. In addition to these other mechanisms – whose importance is not diminished – the very processes of creating and dismantling ethnically exclusionary state institutions also engenders violent, organized political resistance.

Moreover, because currently included groups facing exclusion possess both the motivation and resources to rebel, they are especially likely to do so. This helps us to better understand the timing and relative rarity of ethnic rebellion, as well as the counterintuitive inclination of historically privileged groups to rise up. While grievances may persist over many years, it is in relatively brief intervals that entire systems of ethnic privilege are created or destroyed. Such moments of deep change provoke violence from losing groups, regardless of their existing relative political or socioeconomic position. This builds on an important scholarly finding and notable exception to the general focus on grievances: statistical work has found that "recently downgraded" groups are especially likely to revolt in order to restore their previously advantaged political position. My theoretical framework places this finding in context, further develops the causal mechanisms behind why downgraded groups rebel, and subsumes it within a broader understanding of how systems of ethnic privilege function within state institutions and how both their construction and dismantling lead to violence.

Beyond its contribution to the ethnic conflict literature, this book helps us to better understand the role of the military in African politics and the causes and dynamics of military coups. Despite a substantial case study literature indicating the importance of ethnic politics to African coups, early statistical work found no evidence of any generalizable effects. This led later work on coups to largely neglect ethnicity, even as a control variable. Two notable exceptions have resisted this trend: Roessler argues that ethnic inclusion in the security forces permits antagonistic ethnic groups a foothold within the government from which to launch coups,[1] while Houle and Bodea find that horizontal inequalities also increase the likelihood of coup attempts.[2] My argument contributes to this renewed inclusion of ethnicity in the study of military coups. Ethnic practices by the state, here discriminatory recruitment policies and patronage building within military institutions, directly influence coup propensity. I also test this argument cross-nationally, employing original measures of ethnic civil-military dynamics, transcending the limitations of past case study research and demonstrating generalizable patterns – that constructing and dismantling systems of ethnic privilege within the military provokes violence across contexts.

This book also contributes to the vast literature on democratization and, in particular, to the small but growing literature on the role of the military in democratization processes. While older works analyzed the conditions under which military regimes could be coaxed out of power, and the consequences of these pacted transitions on democratic consolidation, newer studies have focused on how military coups themselves may either facilitate or hinder democratization. My results confirm that militaries pose a substantial threat to democratization in Africa: 34% of electoral transfers of executive power have been overthrown by their own militaries. Yet, my findings also suggest that not all militaries react the same when encountering liberalization and not all coups pose an identical challenge to liberalization. Rather, the past choices of leaders to build ethnic armies conditions whether militaries will step in to support democratic processes or restore autocracy. Ethnic armies pose a dangerous threat to democratization because their privileges and access to patronage resources depend on an inherently non-inclusive and undemocratic vision of the state. Ethnic armies are unlikely to peacefully relinquish their power and their coups will reverse democratic gains. Inclusive militaries, on the other hand, are far less likely to resist liberalization. And in the rare event that they do seize power, the long-term effect on democratization may not be as deleterious, depending on the underlying reasons for the uprising.

[1] Roessler 2011.
[2] Houle and Bodea 2017.

Finally, my findings carry with them grave implications for post-conflict peace-building. By their very nature, ethnic civil wars intensify the salience of ethnicity and deepen cleavages between groups. This no doubt contributes to ethnic politicization, particularly where peace-building efforts coincide with elections. Here, former rebel groups often compete as new political parties while continuing to draw support from particular ethnic communities. I have shown that this kind of ethnic politicization consistently undermined leaders' efforts to build inclusive security institutions in the past, often resulting in eventual ethnic stacking practices. Ethnic politicization thus threatens a key component of many contemporary peace agreements: military integration, or reforms that increase ethnic group access to the armed forces by including former rebels. Where heightened ethnic politicization leads to the obstruction or reversal of military integration, it may provoke a return to war.

Of course, my work also raises important unanswered questions and directions for future research. First and foremost, my theoretical framework should be broadly applicable across state institutions but was only empirically tested on soldiers and military coups. Future work should assess how the construction and dismantling of systems of ethnic privilege within and across other state institutions (such as legislatures, civil services, judiciaries, etc.) impacts other forms of ethnic violence (riots, insurgencies, terrorism, etc.). Second, do these dynamics extend beyond Africa? Presumably, they should apply wherever ethnicity is central to politics and the state has engaged in practices of building systems of ethnic privilege. Further work should investigate my hypotheses within and across regions. Finally, I analyze the intertwined mechanisms of ethnic loyalty and ethnically-based patronage but cannot empirically distinguish between them. How important is the ethnic basis of a patronage network to inducing rebellion when that network is threatened with expulsion from state institutions? Will other types of clientelist networks also violently resist? Answering such questions is vital to further understanding the exact role that ethnicity itself plays in engendering violence.

POLICY IMPLICATIONS: INTERNATIONAL ASSISTANCE

My work suggests that, for many African countries, military reform is necessary to achieve stable democratic institutions. Numerous stubbornly authoritarian regimes are still backed by the loyalty of ethnic armies. In Chad, Idriss Déby has relied on a coethnic Zhagawa-dominated military since he took power in 1994.[3] In the same year, Paul Kagame led an ethnically exclusive Tutsi rebel group to victory in Rwanda and has refused to diversify the security sector ever since, creating legal restrictions that bar Hutu from military and police service.[4] Even Yoweri Museveni of Uganda, despite cross-ethnic coalition building during his rebel days, has stacked the Defense Forces Council and the top positions of the military hierarchy with fellow Banyankole.[5] Other offenders include Paul Biya of Cameroon, Denis Sassou-Nguessou of Congo (Brazzaville), Faure Gnassingbé of Togo, and the recently ousted Robert Mugabe of Zimbabwe.[6]

Partially liberalized countries such as Kenya and Burundi have also been struggling with ethnic tensions and legacies of ethnic privilege in their armies. Under Mwai Kibaki and Uhuru Kenyatta, Kikuyu officers have been favored within the Kenyan defense forces and Kikuyu members of the internal security apparatus have been strategically deployed during elections to facilitate pro-regime violence.[7] Burundi, meanwhile, is sliding backwards. Following its civil war, Burundi achieved full ethnic integration of the military. After a recent coup attempt, however, President Nkurunziza conflated Tutsi soldiers with the threat to his regime – even though the plotters were Hutu – rotating some to remote posts and arresting or assassinating others. Having defied his term limits, embraced authoritarianism, and begun restacking the military with coethnics, Nkurunziza has brought Burundi to the brink of renewed civil war.[8]

These armies must be restructured to allow for democratization such that soldiers are no longer recruited and promoted based on their ethnic identity and personal loyalty to the president. Only then can power be safely transferred between elected leaders without the constant danger of coups. Militaries must also be insulated from political tampering, especially ethnically motivated tampering, so that soldiers do not fear future exclusion from state security institutions. Africa thus needs the proliferation and entrenchment of merit-based military institutions, buffered by strong ministries of defense that can provide impersonal civilian

---

3 Massey & May 2006, 444.
4 Minorities at Risk 2009; Minority Rights Group 2010.
5 Carbone 2008, 46–47; Kagoro 2016, 168.
6 Gros 1995, 122; Konings 1996, 251; Minorities at Risk 2009; Minority Rights Group 2010; Snyder 1986, 134.
7 Hassan 2017; Hornsby 2013, 712–713.
8 Samii 2013; Ssuuna & Kaneza 2015.

control. Once well-established, systems of merit-based recruitment and promotion protect soldiers from negative career outcomes due to their ethnic identity, such as being demoted, passed over for promotion, or even purged or imprisoned. Soldiers then have fewer reasons to fear personal consequences from democratization and its frequent rotations of power.

External actors can assist with such reform in three key ways: by providing protection, training, and financial incentives. First, as I have shown, reform can threaten established ethnic armies and destabilize regimes over the short-term. Ethnic armies rarely passively accept their own dismantling. The on-the-ground presence of neutral foreign troops or advisors can dampen fears, ensure fairness, and even physically shield civilian governments as they grapple with reform. Second, security sector reform programs and military-to-military exchange and training programs can offer direct assistance in developing and implementing new merit-based systems. Finally, financial incentives can reward African governments for engaging in and sustaining reform.

Protective Boots on the Ground

Dismantling ethnic patronage networks within security institutions directly threatens officers with the capabilities to violently resist. Officers may fear their own inability to meet new meritocratic standards. Or they may fear supposedly democratic reforms merely provide a legitimate cover story for displacing the current ethnic army in favor of another. In either case, the existing army may resist restructuring, creating the very instability such reform ultimately seeks to prevent.

Dovetailing with the concept of foreign protection, regional and international actors could play a vital role in helping reforming governments to overcome these short-term challenges by sending advisors or troops. The initial transition from ethnic loyalty to meritocratic recruitment and promotion policies constitutes the most precarious period of restructuring. During this time, anxieties may run high as new systems quickly replace old practices and previously excluded groups have entered the military in significant but small numbers, posing a threat to the existing dominant group but still easily sidelined or purged. The presence of ground troops or military advisors can dampen fears and shield civilian governments as restructuring commences. Just as in the aftermath of civil wars, foreign personnel are neutral to existing conflicts and can pass reliable information to all sides about compliance with regulations, rumored troop movements, and other indicators of defection from, or cooperation with, the new system. They can thus reduce uncertainty and prevent accidents from spiraling out of control.[9] Foreign troops or advisors can also act as early warning systems for coup plots by monitoring military movements, thereby discouraging hardliners from violent resistance. Close monitoring removes from any planned coup the elements of stealth and surprise, which are crucial to success.

Sending significant numbers of military personnel in support of reform, however, would encounter serious obstacles. Placing troops on the ground relies on both the willingness of the host country to accept foreign military personnel and the inclination of external actors to supply them. African countries themselves have expressed deep reservations: the African Union has long emphasized finding African solutions to African problems and the common stance of the vast majority of African countries is to discourage hosting foreign troops.[10] Given limited resources, pressing security commitments in other regions, and domestic unwillingness to consider ground troop deployments in the aftermath of the wars in Iraq and Afghanistan, Western powers with the desire to promote democracy and the capacity to send troops may be unwilling to do so.

Sending advisors may be a more palatable and realistic option. British Military Advisory and Training Teams (BMATT) have assisted a number of African governments with post-conflict security sector reform, including Sierra Leone and South Africa.[11] The British also maintain a training unit in Kenya. The United States' Africa Command (AFRICOM) also possesses the ability to support short advisory and training missions through its attached brigade and even sent 50–60 uniformed military advisors to Liberia on a longer mission to aid with post-conflict reforms.[12] The United Nations and other Western countries have engaged in similar missions with, for example, Belgium and the Netherlands seconding officers to the Burundian military after its civil war.[13] African nations thus commonly host advisors and international actors seem willing to provide

---

[9] On the positive benefits of peacekeepers in post-conflict peace building, see Fortna 2008, 93–98.
[10] Brown 2013, 57 & 62.
[11] Cawthra 2003.
[12] Ibid., 35 & 77–78.
[13] Samii 2010, 21.

them. Whether small advising teams could deter or prevent determined military opposition to reform remains an open question.

Training in Support of Merit

Even if fledgling democracies engaging in military reform cannot be directly protected, training assistance is still vital to their success. For countries that have long operated by other norms, creating and maintaining systems of merit-based recruitment and promotion is neither intuitive nor easy. Reformers must tackle a wide variety of institutional and normative changes. They may need to establish or overhaul military academies and staff colleges, developing appropriate curricula and tying advancement in the ranks to continuing education. They must decide the qualities and achievements they wish to reward and then accordingly develop standards, performance indicators, pay scales, entrance and advancement tests, and promotion criteria for each rank and career track. And both civilian and military personnel must be trained to administer and continually improve these systems.

Well versed in these procedures, international organizations and Western militaries can offer critical assistance to fledgling democracies in the process of building merit-based security institutions. Moreover, such training could relatively easily be tied into existing programs. For example, International Military Education Training (IMET) programs already focus on human rights, military professionalization, civilian control of the military, and judicial reform.[14] Building merit-based systems seems a natural extension to this important work. United Nations missions to countries recovering from civil war could also integrate these types of changes into existing security sector reform programs.

BMATT teams have been heavily involved throughout Africa and their prolonged mission to Sierra Leone, which has entirely reconstituted that nation's military, serves as a particularly good example of what dedicated assistance can achieve. Sierra Leone was burdened by a long history of ethnic armies, from Mende domination under Sir Albert Margai to Limba domination under Siaka Stevens and Joseph Momoh. After Sierra Leone's devastating civil war, army restructuring under British tutelage included provisions for fair representation of all ethnic groups

---

14 Brown 2013, 36.

and merit-based recruitment and promotion policies.[15] Sierra Leone has remained politically stable since.

AFRICOM is also already extensively involved in training partner nations to enhance their own long-term ability to provide security. The Africa Contingency Operations and Training Assistance (ACOTA) program, part of the Global Peace Operations Initiative (GPOI), has partnered with 25 African countries to train over 77,000 African peacekeepers. In the last few years, the program has shifted away from direct training and toward enhancing local training infrastructures.[16] Similarly, Operation Juniper Shield has trained company-sized forces from ten African nations in the trans-Sahel to increase border security and counter the illicit flow of people, goods, and arms across the region.[17] These existing advisory teams could assist in expanding military education programs to prepare soldiers for merit-based promotion protocols and help develop performance indicators and promotion criteria while already deployed on existing missions. Indeed, security sector reform and peacekeeping missions provide a rare opportunity to fold measures that promote merit into existing efforts and even to rebuild the defense sector from the ground-up.

Financial Incentives

Finally, external actors can develop financial incentives that reward African countries for establishing merit-based recruitment and promotion systems and dissuade their dismantlement. Military aid, or broader forms of development aid, can be tied directly to maintaining meritocratic and politically neutral security institutions. Beyond aid, other types of rewards could include additional spaces in military education and exchange programs, priority assignment to regional and international peacekeeping operations, and higher pay rates for participation in them. Such financial and prestige rewards would encourage governments to begin reforms and make it costly for them to tamper with merit-based systems in the future.

Of course, financial incentives have their limitations. All countries give military aid for a variety of reasons – including for counter-terrorism, counter-narcotics, and other strategic purposes – and may not be inclined to tie much of their aid package to merit-based restructuring. Threatening

---

[15] Gbla 2006, 83.
[16] US Department of State 2015.
[17] Brown 2013, 34.

to withhold aid and other rewards may also lack credibility and thus effectiveness. Militaries in strategically important countries, like Egypt, know that the US is unlikely to significantly cut their aid and can resist pressures for change. China and Russia can also replace withheld aid with less conditionality.

Making participation in peacekeeping operations contingent on reform criteria would also pose difficulties. Current African peacekeeping missions rely heavily on contingents from autocratic and semi-autocratic countries because very few African nations are both democratic and willing to contribute troops.[18] Such supply deficiencies severely restrict the ability of international and regional organizations to place conditions on those willing to participate. Indeed, current policies of suspending development aid, as well as membership in regional organizations, in the wake of coups have shown meager results.[19] Militaries in countries such as Guinea-Bissau and Niger frequently seize power, resulting in the abeyance of aid, then schedule elections and retreat to the barracks. The international community quickly restores aid and, when elections fail to go their way or other domestic turmoil strikes, the same militaries intervene again. Suspending aid in the wake of coups, given its quick restoration after a transition back to civilian rule, thus seems to discourage militaries from governing but not from intervening in politics.

Finally, regimes may simply value ethnically loyal militaries more than the costs incurred for refusing or undoing reforms. Autocratic leaders who have long relied on the loyalty of ethnic armies to stabilize their rule, in particular, will likely refuse to initiate restructuring. Even leaders of partially liberalized or democratizing states may balk when faced with deep ethnic politicization and the prospect of ethnic rebellion. The temptation to secure loyalty through coethnicity may simply be too great.

Nonetheless, financial rewards may shift incentives enough at the margins to encourage leaders of fledgling democracies to support and maintain merit-based reform. Additionally, given sub-Saharan African's

---

[18] Ibid., 80–81.

[19] International organizations, regional organizations, and individual countries have all suspended aid and diplomatic relations after military coups. The United States is required to suspend aid under the 1961 Foreign Assistance Act, as they have done in cases like Mali, as well as to cease any security assistance to a military that has seized power (Ham 2013, 10; Mark 2012). The European Union considers cases on an individual basis but has at least partially suspended aid and cooperation in the past (Anderson 2015). And the African Union censures states, suspends their membership, and even applies sanctions after coups (Powell & Lasley 2012).

relative strategic unimportance, and the perennial cash-strapped nature of its governments, funding conditionality may be both feasible and influential.

THE DOMESTIC STRUGGLE FOR JUSTICE AND DEMOCRACY

Inclusive, merit-based military institutions are normatively desirable, supportive of multi-ethnic democracy, and necessary for lasting peace and stability. Given the highly multi-ethnic character of most African societies, we should embrace the normative ideals of diverse institutions and democratic elections that allow for power to rotate between individuals and groups of different identities. The alternative is an ethnic state that indefinitely excludes much of its population from power. Such states fail to meet important standards of justice and equity and are prone to insurgency and the devastation of civil war. Multi-ethnic democracy, and indeed long-term peace and stability, thus require dismantling ethnic armies.

Yet, restructuring security institutions involves intense danger. Dismantling ethnic patronage networks within the military and building merit-based recruitment and promotion systems in their place provokes resistance from soldiers accustomed to their ethnic privilege. Ethnic armies will not sit idly by and allow for their own demise. Their rebellion can also have devastating effects, including violence and the retrenchment of autocratic governance.

I have suggested that the international community can play a limited role in helping willing governments to reform their security institutions, particularly where peacekeepers or other monitors have already been deployed. External military personnel can serve as neutral arbiters, offer training and educational assistance in the mechanics of running a merit-based army, and detect coup plots where they are physically present. We can reward, assist, and even protect those African governments who are trying to build a better democratic future for their country. Yet, outsiders may have little sway over the long-term entrenchment of merit-based security institutions. Once foreign missions depart, they can no longer ensure that civilian leaders will not revert to ethnic recruitment practices. Nor can they prevent disenchanted or fearful officers from taking violent action.

Lasting military reform is an ordeal that must be grappled with domestically. As with most valuable endeavors, it will be difficult and full of setbacks. Transforming militaries into diverse and professional organizations is, nonetheless, an integral part of democratization. It should accompany, and will be re-enforced by, other liberal reforms that bolster the rule of law and place checks on executive power. And it is achievable. Despite initial failures, countries like Ghana have ultimately overcome their legacy of ethnic armies. Slowly but steadily, they have transformed their militaries into professional, merit-based institutions and transferred power between leaders via free and fair elections, without provoking soldier rebellion. An inclusive military is worth the struggle.

Appendix A

Preindependence Ethnic Violence and Ethnic Politicization Data

Qualitative narratives with full source information and more detailed coding guidelines are available in the Online Supplementary Materials, Appendix A. The narratives first establish the landscape of political parties during the period of analysis and whether they have an ethnic basis of support. Any reported violent incidents are then discussed and their potential ethnic basis. Brief descriptions of how the two main variables were coded and a table summarizing the data is provided below.

Preindependence Ethnic Politicization: To capture ethnic politicization, I compiled data on the vote share captured by ethnic political parties in the elections immediately preceding independence. For each country, I first identified the last national election prior to decolonization and then the political parties competing for office. Each party was coded as ethnic, non-ethnic, or multi-ethnic, following Kanchan Chandra's criteria for classification based on whether parties draw their support from a particular ethnic constituency (or constituencies) and whether they exclude other groups. Ethnic parties draw their support from specific ethnic group(s) while intentionally excluding others. Multi-ethnic parties attract the support of specific ethnic group(s) but do not intentionally exclude. And non-ethnic parties draw diverse support across all groups.[1] I then tallied the share of the total national vote captured by ethnic political parties in that final national election prior to independence. Where some political parties could not be coded, usually because they

---

[1] Chandra 2011, 162–164. This also accords with Horowitz's understanding of what constitutes an ethnic political party (1985, 293).

TABLE A.1. *Preindependence Ethnic Violence and Ethnic Politicization*

Country	Ethnic Violence	Existence of Ethnic Parties	Ethnic Parties Vote Share
Algeria	0	0	na
Angola	1	1	na
Benin	0	1	100
Botswana	0	1	5
Burkina Faso	na	1	56
Burundi	1	0	0
Cameroon	0	0	0
Cape Verde	0	0	na
Central African Republic	0	0	0
Chad	0	1	100
Comoros	na	?	?
Congo-Brazzaville	1	1	41
Côte d'Ivoire	0	1	5
DRC	0	1	29
Djibouti	1	1	na
Egypt	0	?	?
Equatorial Guinea	0	1	5
Eritrea	1	0	na
Ethiopia	0	0	na
Gabon	0	1	8
Gambia	0	1	38
Ghana	1	1	36
Guinea	1	1	6
Guinea-Bissau	1	0	na
Kenya	0	1	33
Lesotho	0	0	0
Liberia	0	1	100
Libya	0	1	13
Madagascar	0	1	38
Malawi	0	0	0
Mali	0	0	0
Mauritania	0	0	0
Mauritius	1	1	100
Morocco	0	0	na
Mozambique	0	0	na
Namibia	0	1	40
Niger	0	0	0
Nigeria	1	1	96

Country	Ethnic Violence	Existence of Ethnic Parties	Ethnic Parties Vote Share
Rwanda	1	1	95
São Tomé & Príncipe	0	0	0
Senegal	0	0	0
Seychelles	0	0	0
Sierra Leone	1	1	52
Somalia	0	1	27
South Africa	1	1	35
Sudan	0	1	100
Swaziland	0	0	0
Tanzania	0	0	0
Togo	0	1	25
Tunisia	1	0	0
Uganda	0	1	98
Zambia	0	1	1
Zimbabwe	1	1	95

drew little support and there is little written about them, I calculated the possible range of the vote captured by ethnic political parties, with the low end based on all missing parties being coded non-ethnic and the high end based on all missing parties being coded ethnic. I then take the mid-point of this range as the estimated captured vote share for ethnic political parties. In the table, "na" means that no election occurred prior to independence while a "?" means that not enough information could be found to code the country.

Preindependence Ethnic Violence: Two types of ethnic violence were coded for each African state in the period immediately preceding independence: ethnic riots and violence committed by ethnically-based political parties. The variable is coded 1 if any such incident took place between World War II and the year of decolonization for each African country, and 0 otherwise. Exceptions to this time frame of analysis include Egypt, Eritrea, Ethiopia, Liberia, Namibia, South Africa, and Zimbabwe, which did not gain independence at the same time as the vast majority of African countries. For each of these cases, the period analyzed is justified at the beginning of the qualitative narrative. Not included are secessionist movements, anti-colonial rebellions (unless it contained an inter-ethnic dimension of violence), anti-foreign immigrant violence, or violence directed by or against European settlers. Riots are considered ethnic if evidence exists that the targets of violence were selected based on their ethnic identity. Political party violence was deemed ethnic if the political party was considered organized around the interests of an ethnic group (or small set of allied groups) and evidence exists that the victims of violence were selected based on their ethnic identity.

Appendix B

Military Coup Data

Military coup data was derived by cross-referencing three large datasets of coups and irregular transfers of power: McGowan's database of sub-Saharan African military coups, the Archigos dataset of political leaders and irregular exits from office, and Powell and Thyne's global data on successful and failed coup attempts (July 2016 version). This process produced a large number of discrepancies, with some coups included in one or more datasets while being excluded from others. There were also differences over the timing of coup attempts and whether they succeeded. Moreover, not all of these sources distinguished between military coups and coups conducted by other insider political factions. Discrepancies were resolved by examining existing dataset narratives and by consulting newspaper and secondary sources. McGowan's coding procedures for military coups were followed: a faction of the current government's military forces had to be involved in an attempt to overthrow the national government; evidence must exist of actual military force, whether in the form of violence or the occupation of important government buildings or transportation or communication centers; and, to count as a success, the coup leaders (or their appointed head-of-state) had to hold power for at least one week. Appendix B of the Online Supplementary Materials provides full documentation for all resolved disputes, including final coding decisions and sources, as well as narratives and coding decisions for all coup attempts post 2006 (which only the Powell & Thyne dataset include thus necessitating cross-referencing with media and secondary sources).

TABLE B.1. *African Military Coups, 1952–2016*

Country	Year	Attempts	Successes
Algeria	1965	1	1
Algeria	1967	1	0
Algeria	1992	1	1
Angola	1977	1	0
Benin	1963	1	1
Benin	1965	2	2
Benin	1967	1	1
Benin	1969	1	1
Benin	1972	2	1
Benin	1975	1	0
Benin	1992	1	0
Burkina Faso	1966	1	1
Burkina Faso	1974	1	1
Burkina Faso	1980	1	1
Burkina Faso	1982	1	1
Burkina Faso	1983	2	1
Burkina Faso	1987	1	1
Burkina Faso	2014	1	1
Burkina Faso	2015	1	0
Burundi	1965	1	0
Burundi	1966	2	2
Burundi	1976	1	1
Burundi	1987	1	1
Burundi	1992	1	0
Burundi	1993	2	0
Burundi	1994	1	0
Burundi	1996	1	1
Burundi	2001	2	0
Burundi	2015	1	0
Cameroon	1984	1	0
Central African Republic	1966	1	1
Central African Republic	1974	1	0
Central African Republic	1976	1	0
Central African Republic	1979	1	1
Central African Republic	1981	1	1
Central African Republic	1982	1	0
Central African Republic	1996	1	0
Central African Republic	2001	1	0
Central African Republic	2003	1	1
Chad	1975	1	1

Country	Year	Attempts	Successes
Chad	1977	1	0
Chad	1989	1	0
Chad	1991	1	0
Chad	1993	1	0
Comoros	1985	1	0
Comoros	1987	1	0
Comoros	1989	1	1
Comoros	1992	1	0
Comoros	1999	1	1
Comoros	2000	1	0
Congo-Brazzaville	1963	1	1
Congo-Brazzaville	1966	1	0
Congo-Brazzaville	1968	3	1
Congo-Brazzaville	1970	1	0
Congo-Brazzaville	1972	1	0
Congo-Brazzaville	1977	1	0
Congo-Brazzaville	1992	1	0
Côte d'Ivoire	1999	1	1
Côte d'Ivoire	2000	1	0
Côte d'Ivoire	2001	1	0
Côte d'Ivoire	2002	1	0
DRC	1960	1	1
DRC	1963	1	0
DRC	1965	1	1
DRC	2004	2	0
Djibouti	1991	1	0
Egypt	1952	1	1
Egypt	1954	1	1
Egypt	2011	1	1
Egypt	2013	1	1
Equatorial Guinea	1979	1	1
Equatorial Guinea	1981	1	0
Equatorial Guinea	1983	1	0
Equatorial Guinea	1986	1	0
Ethiopia	1960	1	0
Ethiopia	1974	2	2
Ethiopia	1977	1	1
Ethiopia	1989	1	0
Gabon	1964	1	0
Gambia	1994	2	1

(continued)

Country	Year	Attempts	Successes
Ghana	1966	1	1
Ghana	1967	1	0
Ghana	1972	1	1
Ghana	1978	1	1
Ghana	1979	2	1
Ghana	1981	1	1
Ghana	1982	1	0
Ghana	1983	1	0
Ghana	1984	1	0
Guinea	1984	1	1
Guinea	1985	1	0
Guinea	1996	1	0
Guinea	2008	1	1
Guinea	2011	1	0
Guinea-Bissau	1980	1	1
Guinea-Bissau	1993	1	0
Guinea-Bissau	1998	1	0
Guinea-Bissau	1999	1	1
Guinea-Bissau	2000	1	0
Guinea-Bissau	2003	1	1
Guinea-Bissau	2008	1	0
Guinea-Bissau	2009	1	1
Guinea-Bissau	2010	1	0
Guinea-Bissau	2011	1	0
Guinea-Bissau	2012	2	1
Kenya	1982	1	0
Lesotho	1986	1	1
Lesotho	1991	2	1
Lesotho	1994	1	1
Lesotho	2014	1	0
Liberia	1980	1	1
Liberia	1985	2	0
Liberia	1994	1	0
Libya	1969	1	1
Libya	1993	1	0
Madagascar	1972	1	1
Madagascar	1974	1	0
Madagascar	1975	1	0
Madagascar	2006	1	0
Madagascar	2009	1	1

Country	Year	Attempts	Successes
Madagascar	2010	1	0
Mali	1968	1	1
Mali	1991	1	1
Mali	2012	2	1
Mauritania	1978	1	1
Mauritania	1979	1	1
Mauritania	1980	1	1
Mauritania	1981	1	0
Mauritania	1984	1	1
Mauritania	2003	1	0
Mauritania	2005	1	1
Mauritania	2008	1	1
Morocco	1971	1	0
Morocco	1972	1	0
Mozambique	1975	1	0
Niger	1974	1	1
Niger	1976	1	0
Niger	1983	1	0
Niger	1996	1	1
Niger	1999	1	1
Niger	2010	1	1
Nigeria	1966	2	2
Nigeria	1975	1	1
Nigeria	1976	1	0
Nigeria	1983	1	1
Nigeria	1985	1	1
Nigeria	1990	1	0
Nigeria	1993	1	1
Rwanda	1973	1	1
Rwanda	1994	1	1
São Tomé and Príncipe	1995	1	0
São Tomé and Príncipe	2003	1	1
Sierra Leone	1967	2	1
Sierra Leone	1968	1	1
Sierra Leone	1971	1	0
Sierra Leone	1987	1	0
Sierra Leone	1992	2	1
Sierra Leone	1995	1	0
Sierra Leone	1996	2	1
Sierra Leone	1997	1	1

(continued)

Country	Year	Attempts	Successes
Sierra Leone	2000	1	0
Sierra Leone	2003	1	0
Somalia	1961	1	0
Somalia	1969	1	1
Somalia	1978	1	0
Sudan	1958	1	1
Sudan	1959	3	0
Sudan	1966	1	0
Sudan	1969	1	1
Sudan	1971	1	0
Sudan	1975	1	0
Sudan	1976	1	0
Sudan	1977	1	0
Sudan	1978	1	0
Sudan	1983	1	0
Sudan	1985	1	1
Sudan	1989	1	1
Sudan	1990	1	0
Swaziland	1984	1	0
Togo	1963	1	1
Togo	1967	1	1
Togo	1991	5	0
Togo	2005	1	1
Uganda	1971	2	1
Uganda	1974	2	0
Uganda	1975	2	0
Uganda	1976	2	0
Uganda	1977	1	0
Uganda	1980	1	1
Uganda	1985	1	1
Uganda	1988	1	0
Zambia	1980	1	0
Zambia	1990	1	0
Zambia	1997	1	0
Zimbabwe	1982	1	0
Total		225	98

Appendix C

Ethnicity and the Military Data

This appendix contains the raw data for the originally coded variables on ethnic recruitment practices within African militaries: loyalty choice at decolonization, the diversity of the late colonial officer corps and whether it matched the ethnic identity of the new leader, later ethnic changes in leadership after electoral or other constitutional transfers of power, and whether the prior leader had ethnically stacked the military. The Online Supplementary Materials, Appendix C, contains the coding procedures and full qualitative narratives, including source documentation and final coding decisions.

TABLE C.1. *Summary Statistics for Decolonization Variables*

Variable	Min	Max	# coded 1	% coded 1	N
Ethnic loyalty	0	1	21	42.0	50
Unmatched officer corps	0	1	23	44.2	52

TABLE C.2. *Summary Statistics for Democratization Variables*

Variable	Min	Max	# coded 1	% coded 1	Mean	Std Dev	N
Ethnic change	0	1	61	59.8			102
Prior ethnic army	0	1	42	44.2			95
Coup attempt	0	1	28	27.5			102
Years until coup*	0	4			1.9		28

* Only calculated for the countries that had a coup attempt in the four years following the transfer of power.

TABLE C.3. *Ethnicity and the Military: Decolonization Data*

Country	Ethnic Loyalty	Ethnicity of Leader	Officer Corps at Independence	Unmatched Officer Corps
Algeria	yes	Arab	mixed Arab and Berber	yes
Angola	no	Mestiço	Mestiço dominated	no
Benin	yes	Bariba/Mossi	Fon dominated	yes
Botswana	no	Tswana	no African officers	no
Burkina Faso	no	Mossi	Mossi dominated	no
Burundi	no	Tutsi	mixed Hutu and Tutsi	yes
Cameroon	yes	Fulani	Fulani/Peuhl dominated	no
Cape Verde	no	Mestiço	all Mestiço	no
Central African Republic	?	M'Baka	all M'Baka	no
Chad	yes	Sara	Sara dominated	no
Comoros	?	Anjouan	?	?
Congo-Brazzaville	no	Lari	M'Boshi dominated or diverse	yes
Côte d'Ivoire	yes	Baoule	no African officers	no
DRC	no	Tetela	no African officers	no
Djibouti	yes	Issa	mixed Issa and Afar	yes
Egypt	no	Arab	diverse	yes
Equatorial Guinea	yes	Esangui Fang	no African officers	no
Eritrea	no	Biher-Tigrinya	diverse	yes
Ethiopia	no	Amhara	diverse	yes
Gabon	yes	Estuary Fang	Woleu Ntem Fang dominated	yes

Country		Ethnic group	Description	
Gambia	na	Mandinka	no African officers	no
Ghana	no	Nzima	Ewe, Ga, and Fante dominated	yes
Guinea	no	Malinké	diverse	yes
Guinea-Bissau	no	Mestiço	Balanta dominated	yes
Kenya	yes	Kikuyu	Kamba and Kalenjin dominated	yes
Lesotho	no	Basotho	no African officers or Basotho	no
Liberia	yes	Americo-Liberian	Americo-Liberian dominated	no
Libya	yes	Sanusi/Cyrenaican	Sanusi/Cyrenaican dominated	no
Madagascar	no	Tsimihety/Côtier	Merina dominated	yes
Malawi	yes	Chewa	no African officers	no
Mali	no	Malinké	Bambara dominated	yes
Mauritania	yes	Maure	Maure dominated	no
Mauritius	no	Hindu	no African officers	no
Morocco	no	Arab/Alawite	Berber dominated	yes
Mozambique	no	Shangaan	no African officers	no
Namibia	no	Ovambo	no African officers or Ovambo dominated	no
Niger	yes	Djerma	Djerma dominated	no
Nigeria	no	Gere/fulani	Igbo dominated	yes
Rwanda	yes	Hutu	all Hutu	no
São Tomé and Príncipe	no	Mestiço	no African Officers or all Mestiço	no
Senegal	no	Serer	diverse	yes
Seychelles	no	Mestiço	no African officers	no
Sierra Leone	yes	southern Mende	preponderance of northern tribes	yes

(continued)

TABLE C.3 *(continued)*

Country	Ethnic Loyalty	Ethnicity of Leader	Officer Corps at Independence	Unmatched Officer Corps
Somalia	yes	Hawiye	Darood dominant	yes
South Africa	no	diverse	Xhosa	yes
Sudan	yes	Muslim Jellaba	Muslim Jellaba dominated	no
Swaziland	no	Swazi	no African officers or all Swazi	no
Tanzania	no	Zanaki	no African officers	no
Togo	yes	Ewe	Ewe and Mina dominated	no
Tunisia	no	Arab	all Arab	no
Uganda	yes	Langi	diverse	yes
Zambia	no	Bemba	no African officers	no
Zimbabwe	yes	Shona	diverse	yes

TABLE C.4. *Ethnicity and the Military: Democratization Data*

Country	Year	Reason for Power Transfer	Ethnic Change?	Prior Ethnic Army?	Coup Attempt?	Years until Coup
Algeria	1978	Natural Death	no	yes	no	–
Algeria	1999	Elections	no	?	no	–
Angola	1979	Natural Death	yes	no	no	–
Benin	1964	Coup then Elections	yes	yes	1965	1
Benin	1991	Elections	yes	no	1992	1
Benin	1996	Elections	yes	no	no	–
Benin	2006	Elections	yes	no	no	–
Botswana	1980	Natural Death	no	no	no	–
Botswana	1998	Retirement	no	no	no	–
Botswana	2008	Resignation	no	no	no	–
Burundi	1993	Elections	yes	yes	1993	0
Burundi	2003	Peace Agreement	yes	yes	no	–
Burundi	2005	Elections	no	no	no	–
Cameroon	1982	Retirement then Elections	yes	yes	1984	2
Cape Verde	1991	Elections	no	yes	no	–
Cape Verde	2001	Elections	no	yes	no	–
Cape Verde	2011	Elections	no	yes	no	–
Central African Republic	1993	Elections	yes	yes	1996	3
Comoros	1990	Coup then Elections	yes	?	1992	2
Comoros	1996	Coup then Elections	no	?	no	–

(continued)

227

TABLE C.4 *(continued)*

Country	Year	Reason for Power Transfer	Ethnic Change?	Prior Ethnic Army?	Coup Attempt?	Years until Coup
Comoros	1998	Natural Death	yes	?	1999	1
Comoros	2006	Elections	yes	?	no	–
Comoros	2011	Elections	yes	?	no	–
Congo-Brazzaville	1992	Elections	yes	yes	no	–
Côte d'Ivoire	1993	Natural Death	no	yes	no	–
Côte d'Ivoire	2000	Coup then Elections	yes	yes	2001	1
Côte d'Ivoire	2011	Coup then Elections	yes	no	no	–
Djibouti	1999	Elections	no	yes	no	–
Egypt	1970	Natural Death	no	yes	no	–
Egypt	2012	Coup then Elections	no	yes	2013	1
Ethiopia	2012	Natural Death	yes	no	no	–
Gabon	1967	Natural Death	yes	yes	no	–
Gabon	2009	Natural Death	no	yes	no	–
Ghana	1969	Resignation then Elections	yes	yes	1972	3
Ghana	1979	Coup then Elections	yes	yes	1981	2
Ghana	2000	Elections	yes	no	no	–
Ghana	2009	Elections	yes	no	no	–
Ghana	2012	Natural Death	yes	no	no	–
Guinea	2010	Natural Death then Elections	yes	yes	2011	1
Guinea Bissau	2000	Coup then Elections	yes	no	2000	0

Country	Year	Event				
Guinea Bissau	2005	Coup then Elections	yes	yes	2008	3
Guinea Bissau	2009	Coup then Elections	yes	no	2010	1
Kenya	1978	Natural Death	yes	yes	1982	4
Kenya	2002	Elections	yes	yes	no	–
Lesotho	1993	Coup then Elections	no	yes	1994	1
Lesotho	1998	Elections	no	yes	no	–
Lesotho	2012	Elections	no	yes	2014	2
Liberia	1971	Natural Death	no	yes	no	–
Liberia	1997	Peace Treaty then Elections	yes	no	no	–
Liberia	2005	Elections	yes	no	no	–
Madagascar	1993	Elections	no	no	no	–
Madagascar	1996	Impeachment then Elections	no	no	no	–
Madagascar	2002	Elections	yes	no	2006	4
Malawi	1994	Retirement then Elections	yes	yes	no	–
Malawi	2004	Elections	yes	yes	no	–
Malawi	2012	Natural Death	yes	?	no	–
Mali	1992	Coup then Elections	no	no	no	–
Mali	2002	Elections	no	no	no	–
Mauritania	2007	Coup then Elections	no	yes	2008	1
Mauritius	1982	Elections	no	no	no	–
Mauritius	1995	Elections	no	no	no	–
Mauritius	2000	Elections	no	no	no	–
Mauritius	2003	Resignation	yes	no	no	–
Mauritius	2005	Elections	yes	no	no	–
Mozambique	1986	Natural Death	no	no	no	–

(continued)

TABLE C.4 *(continued)*

Country	Year	Reason for Power Transfer	Ethnic Change?	Prior Ethnic Army?	Coup Attempt?	Years until Coup
Mozambique	2005	Elections	yes	no	no	–
Namibia	2004	Elections	no	no	no	–
Niger	1993	Elections	yes	yes	1996	3
Niger	1999	Coup then Elections	yes	no	no	–
Niger	2011	Coup then Elections	yes	no	no	–
Nigeria	1979	Elections	yes	no	1983	4
Nigeria	1999	Natural Death then Elections	yes	yes	no	–
Nigeria	2007	Elections	yes	no	no	–
Nigeria	2010	Elections	yes	no	no	–
Rwanda	2000	Resignation	yes	no	no	–
São Tomé and Príncipe	1991	Elections	no	yes	1995	4
São Tomé and Príncipe	2001	Elections	no	yes	2003	2
São Tomé and Príncipe	2011	Elections	no	yes	no	–
Senegal	1981	Retirement	no	no	no	–
Senegal	2000	Elections	yes	no	no	–
Senegal	2012	Elections	yes	no	no	–
Seychelles	2004	Resignation	no	yes	no	–
Sierra Leone	1964	Natural Death	no	no	no	–
Sierra Leone	1967	Elections	yes	yes	1967	0
Sierra Leone	1996	Coup then Elections	yes	yes	1996	0

Sierra Leone	2007	Peace Treaty then Elections	yes	no	no	—
Somalia	1967	Elections	yes	yes	1969	2
Somalia	2012	Elections	no	yes	no	—
South Africa	1994	Elections	yes	no	no	—
South Africa	1999	Elections	no	no	no	—
South Africa	2008	Resignation	yes	no	no	—
South Africa	2009	Elections	yes	no	no	—
Sudan	1986	Coup then Elections	no	yes	1989	3
Tanzania	1985	Retirement	yes	no	no	—
Tanzania	1995	Elections	yes	no	no	—
Tanzania	2005	Elections	yes	no	no	—
Tunisia	1987	Retirement	no	yes	no	—
Tunisia	2011	Elections	no	yes	no	—
Zambia	1991	Elections	no	no	no	—
Zambia	2002	Elections	yes	no	no	—
Zambia	2008	Natural Death then Elections	yes	no	no	—
Zambia	2011	Elections	yes	no	no	—

Appendix D

Supplementary Material for Regression Analysis

This appendix contains full descriptions of all control variables used in the regression analysis. Summary statistics and tables containing the full results of all robustness checks can be found in the corresponding appendix in the Online Supplementary Materials.

African Union Member: Coded 1 if, after the Lomè Declaration of July 2000 that required coups to be condemned and sanctions imposed, the country was a non-suspended member of the African Union (AU) in the year of the power transfer. Also coded 1 if the power transfer was part of a planned return to civilian rule that led to the reinstatement of membership. Morocco was not admitted as a member of the AU until January 2017. Eritrea voluntarily broke with the AU from November 2009 to January 2011. The following countries have been suspended: Burkina Faso (September 2015), Central African Republic (March 2013–April 2016), Côte d'Ivoire (November 2010–April 2011), Egypt (July 2013–June 2014), Guinea (December 2008–December 2010), Guinea-Bissau (April 2012–present), Madagascar (March 2009–January 2014), Mali (March 2012–October 2012), Mauritania (August 2005–March 2007; August 2008–July 2009), Niger (February 2010–March 2011), and Togo (February–May 2005). See Omorogbe 2011; also *The Guardian*, March 23, 2012; *International Business Times*, January 31, 2017; *Reuters*, January 27, 2014; *Voice of Africa*, September 18, 2015. In practice, every transition after 1999 received a coding of 1.

Anti-colonial Insurgency: This variable was coded as 1 if any political movement engaged in armed resistance against colonialism, or apartheid in the case of the southern African countries, in the decade prior to independence, regardless of whether they won that struggle. Otherwise, the variable is coded o. Cases of armed resistance include the ALN in Algeria, UNITA and the MPLA in Angola, the ALNK in Cameroon, the PAIGC in Cape Verde and Guinea-Bissau, the EPLF in Eritrea, the Mau Mau uprising in Kenya, the Malagasy Emergency, the ALN in Morocco, FRELIMO in Mozambique, SWAPO in Namibia, the ANC in South Africa, the PSD in Tunisia, and ZANU and ZAPU in Zimbabwe.

Change in Expenditures per Soldier: Percent change in military expenditures per soldier in the four years following a power transfer. If a coup or other change in leadership occurred prior to four years, the window of observation was truncated and the variable calculated over the shorter time period. Data drawn from the Correlates of War National Military Capabilities dataset, version 5.0 (Singer, Bremer, & Stuckey 1972).

Change in Military Expenditures: Percent change in military expenditures in the four years following a power transfer. If a coup or other change in leadership occurred prior to four years, the window of observation was truncated and the variable calculated over the shorter time period. Data drawn from the Correlates of War National Military Capabilities dataset, version 5.0 (Singer, Bremer, & Stuckey 1972).

Change in Military Personnel: Percent change in the number of military personnel in the four years following a power transfer. If a coup or other change in leadership occurred prior to four years, the window of observation was truncated and the variable calculated over the shorter time period. Data drawn from the Correlates of War National Military Capabilities dataset, version 5.0 (Singer, Bremer, & Stuckey 1972).

Change in Civil Liberties: Coded as the difference in the Freedom House civil liberty score between the year in which the election was held and the end of the four-year window of observation after the power transfer. If a coup or other change in leadership occurred prior to four years, the window of observation was truncated and the variable calculated over the shorter time period. A negative score indicates that civil liberties have improved, for example if the score changed from 2 to 1.

Civil Liberties: The Freedom House civil liberties score for the year of the power transfer. Coded on a scale from 1 to 7 with 1 being the highest, or most free.

Civil Armed Conflict: For the decolonization data, the civil war variable is coded 1 if a civil war breaks out within five years of independence, and 0 otherwise. For the democratization data, the civil war variable is coded 1 if there is an ongoing civil war in the year of the transition or in any part of the four-year observation window following it, and 0 otherwise. Data is drawn from the UCDP/PRIO Armed Conflict Dataset version 17.1 (Gleditsch et al. 2002). UCDP has a conflict threshold of 25 battle deaths in a year. Coups were removed by line-item deleting any observation with a military faction as a participant.

Coup Caused Transfer: Coded 1 if the constitutional or electoral transfer of power immediately followed a successful coup (within two years), and 0 otherwise. See Table C.3.

Diamond Production: Drawn from Humphrey's 2005 data. Yearly production in carats per capita. The data was expanded through 2016 using population data from the World Bank and mineral data from the US Geological Survey, Mineral Information for Africa and the Middle East at https://minerals.usgs.gov/minerals/pubs/country/africa.html (last accessed July 9, 2017). All diamond data is based on official trade statistics and thus does not include black market or illicit production, which occurs frequently in conflict and post-conflict countries.

Economic Shock (≥1%): Coded 1 if, in any year during the four-year period following the leadership transition, the country experienced a negative growth rate of 1% or more, and 0 otherwise. If during the four-year period of observation there was a coup attempt or another constitutional change in leadership, the period was truncated so as not to introduce the potential for reverse causality or other threats to inference. Coup attempts themselves have been known to have disastrous effects on economic growth, especially when they descend into widespread violence. Calculated from the World Bank's World Development Indicators (2015).

Economic Shock (≥3%): Coded parallel to *Economic shock (≥1%)* but for a negative growth rate of 3% or more in the four-year period following the leadership transition. Calculated from the World Bank's World Development Indicators (2015).

Economic Shock (≥5%): Coded parallel to *Economic shock (≥1%)* but for a negative growth rate of 5% or more in the four-year period following the leadership transition. Calculated from the World Bank's World Development Indicators (2015).

Economic Shock (≥10%): Coded parallel to *Economic shock (≥1%)* but for a negative growth rate of 10% or more in the four-year period following the leadership transition. Calculated from the World Bank's World Development Indicators (2015). Only one country had a growth rate this low, Nigeria in 1985, and so the variable is not ultimately included in the regression analysis.

Ethnic Diversity: In baseline models, Roeder's 2001 ELF score is used. Alternative measures include the ethnic fractionalization scores of Alesina et al. 2003, Fearon 2003, and Posner 2004a.

Ethnic Parties: Coded in the immediate pre-decolonization elections. See Appendix A for full coding guidelines.

Ethnic Parties Vote Share: Coded in the immediate pre-decolonization elections. See Appendix A for full coding guidelines.

Ethnic Violence: Coded in the immediate pre-decolonization period. See Appendix A for full coding guidelines.

Expenditures per Soldier: Calculated by dividing military expenditures by military personnel for each year, both drawn from the Correlates of War National Military Capabilities dataset, version 5.0 (Singer, Bremer, & Stuckey 1972).

Foreign Military Protection: A country is coded as having foreign military protection if, in the immediate years following independence, a foreign government had garrisoned its own combat troops on the country's soil or maintained a military base. The French, for example, maintained base facilities in Benin, Cameroon, the Central African Republic, Chad, Congo-Brazzaville, Côte d'Ivoire, Gabon, Madagascar, Mauritania, Niger, Senegal, and Togo through at least 1968 (Crocker 1968, 22). Britain maintained military bases in Egypt (Suez) until 1954, Kenya for only a couple years after base completion in the early 1960s, and Libya until the mid-1970s (Crocker 1974, 280–282; Keegan 1983, 366–375; TNA WO 32/16259 54A, "Memo to the Minister of Defense regarding the permanent stationing of a strategic reserve force in Kenya," May

13, 1958). The US also maintained a military base in Libya until the mid-1970s (Keegan 1983, 366–375) and Cuba sent combat troops to Angola to support the government in its counterinsurgency efforts after independence (Keegan 1983, 15–17). Arguably, foreign military protection also exists if a significant proportion of the officer corps is comprised of seconded, foreign personnel. However, this was a ubiquitous condition in postcolonial Africa. The only countries that did not rely excessively on foreign officers in the first years of independence were those that fought anti-colonial insurgencies and thus had built military forces of their own. These countries are, however, captured by the *Anticolonial insurgency* variable and thus foreign military protection is constrained to the maintenance of foreign military bases.

Free and Fair: Indicates whether an election was considered free and fair (1 if yes; else 0). Drawn from Lindberg's data on African elections (2006).

French Colonialism: Coded 1 if the territory was colonized by France, and 0 otherwise. In the rare case where colonial authority switched hands, France is only coded as the colonizer if they controlled the territory immediately prior to independence.

Group Over 50% of Population: Drawn from Fearon's 2003 data on ethnic fractionalization. Indicator variable coded 1 if any ethnic group constitutes over 50% of the total population, and 0 otherwise.

Herbst Difficult Geography: Coded 1 if a country fits Herbst's categories of "difficult" or "hinterland" geography, and 0 otherwise. Difficult geography entails either noncontiguous territory or two or more dense population centers separated by wide swaths of poorly inhabited territory. Hinterland geography refers to a single dense population center around the capital with large areas of relatively uninhabited territory extending far away from the capital. Each of these conditions theoretically makes it difficult for countries to consolidate power over their entire territory, increasing the capacity of potential dissenters to mount a challenge. Data drawn from Herbst 2000.

Interstate War: For the decolonization data, the *Interstate war* variable is coded 1 if a war breaks out with a foreign power within five years of independence, and 0 otherwise. For the democratization data, the civil war variable is coded 1 if there is an ongoing interstate war in the year of the transition or in any part of the four-year observation window following it (truncated in the event of a coup attempt or additional transfer of power), and 0 otherwise. Data is drawn from both the correlates of war project, Interstate Wars version 4.0 (Sarkees & Wayman 2010), and the UCDP/PRIO Armed Conflict Dataset version 17.1 (Gleditsch et al. 2002). UCDP has the lower conflict threshold, necessitating 25 battle deaths in a year to count as an armed conflict while to count as a war in COW, the conflict "must involve sustained combat, involving organized armed forces, resulting in a minimum of 1,000 battle-related combatant fatalities within a twelve month period." Moreover, to count as a participant in that war, a state must commit at least 1000 troops or suffer at least 100 battle-related fatalities. The lower UCDP threshold is used since so few African conflicts met the higher level.

Largest Group % of Population: Drawn from Fearon's 2003 data on ethnic fractionalization. Percent share in the total population of the largest ethnic group.

Ln GDP/k: Natural log of GDP per capita from the year of independence (decolonization data) or the year of the power transfer (for democratization data). The decolonization data is calculated from Maddison's 2014 historic economic and population data, which is in 1990 International Geary-Khamis dollars. To include recent observations, the democratization data is calculated from the World Bank's World Development Indicators (2015).

Lowest CAB as % of GDP: An alternative measure to capture economic downturns was constructed using the country's lowest (i.e., worst) current account balance (CAB) as a percentage of GDP in the four-year window following the power transfer. Current account balance data was drawn from the World Bank data repository (http://data.worldbank.org/indicator/BN.CAB.XOKA.CD, accessed February 10, 2018.)

Margin of Victory: Drawn from Staffan Lindberg's African elections data (2006). The margin of victory is measured by subtracting the vote share of the second place candidate or party from that of the winner. Updated through 2016 using the African Elections Database (http://africanelections.tripod.com/, accessed May 9, 2018) and other sources.

Military Expenditures: Military expenditures in thousands of 2001 US dollars. From the Correlates of War National Military Capabilities dataset, version 5.0 (Singer, Bremer, & Stuckey 1972).

Military Personnel: Number of military personnel in thousands. Zeros were changed to 0.1 to allow for the calculations of other variables. From the Correlates of War National Military Capabilities dataset, version 5.0 (Singer, Bremer, & Stuckey 1972).

Oil Exporter at Independence: Coded 1 if oil was a significant export at the time of independence, and 0 otherwise. Data drawn from a variety of sources included the CIA World Factbook (www.cia.gov/library/publications/the-world-factbook/, accessed February 10, 2018), Freedom House Reports, Humphrey's 2005 oil production and reserves data, Minority Rights Group 2010, Keegan 1983, United Nations World Economic Survey 1965, US Department of State Bilateral Relations Fact Sheets (www.state.gov/r/pa/ei/bgn/, accessed February 10, 2018), and the US Energy Information Administration (www.eia.gov/beta/international/).

Oil or Diamonds: Coded 1 if, in the year of the power transfer, the country was an exporter of oil or diamonds, and 0 otherwise. Drawn from Humphrey's 2005 data.

Oil Production: Oil production is calculated as the daily per capita barrel production for the year of the power transfer. Drawn from Humphrey's 2005 data. The data was expanded through 2016 using population data from the World Bank and mineral data from the US Geological Survey, Mineral Information for Africa and the Middle East at https://minerals.usgs.gov/minerals/pubs/country/africa.html (last accessed July 9, 2017).

Polity: Polity score from the Polity IV dataset (Marshall, Gurr, & Jaggers 2016), on a scale from −10 to 10 with −10 being most autocratic and 10 most democratic. Coded for the year of the power transfer or, if for instability reasons that year is uncoded and the regime survives, the following year.

Popular Unrest: This measure is constructed from Banks' 2001 data on social unrest and the Social Conflict Analysis Database for Africa

(Saleyhan et al. 2012). Banks indexes assassinations, purges of government officials, guerrilla activity, protests, riots, and strikes from around 1960–1999. SCAD similarly measures various forms of social unrest, from protests to rebellions to government infighting, from 1990 to 2015. As significant data was missing using either dataset individually, because of their limited temporal ranges, they were combined. The Banks index, which picks up far fewer events than SCAD, was rescaled according to the following procedure: 0 = none, 1 = low, 2 = medium, 3–4 = high, 5+ = very high. For the SCAD data, I first removed all government infighting events as they capture the same outcome as the military coups dependent variables, and then counted the number of events per country-year. The data was then converted into the index using the following codings: 0 = none, 1–4 = low, 5–10 = medium, 11–20 = high, 21+ = very high. The index then received a 0–4 numerical coding with none equal to 0 and very high equal to 4. The variable is coded in the year of the power transfer to capture the general environment of instability facing the incoming elected leader.

Prior Coups: The count of the total number of coup attempts, both successes and failures, in the ten years prior to the constitutional or electoral transfer of power. See Appendix B.

Prior Successful Coups: The count of the total number of successful coups in the ten years prior to the constitutional or electoral transfer of power. See Appendix B.

Prior Successful Constitutional Transfer: Coded 1 if at any point in the past – no matter how long ago – constitutional mechanisms led to the transfer of executive power without a successful coup attempt occurring within the subsequent four years, and 0 otherwise. See Appendix C.

Prior Successful Electoral Transfer: Coded 1 if at any point in the past – no matter how long ago – elections led to the transfer of executive power without a successful coup attempt occurring within the subsequent four years, and 0 otherwise. See Appendix C.

Regime Continuity: Drawn from Lindberg's 2006 African elections data. Coded 1 if the pre- and post-transition leaders belong to the same political party or if the post-transition leader held an integral post in the prior administration, such as the vice-president, foreign minister, or secretary of state. Otherwise coded 0.

Regime Type: A dummy variable was constructed for non-autocratic, or presumably liberalizing and democratic regimes, from the Geddes, Wright, & Frantz (2014) data on autocratic regime types, available at http://sites.psu.edu/dictators/ (accessed May 9, 2018). The variable is coded in the year after the power transfer to capture the nature of the new regime as the GWF codings often still list the old regime type in the transfer year. An exception is when the regime collapsed or was overthrown in the same year as the transfer, in which case it is coded in that year. Alternative measures, *Electoral democracy* and *Liberalizing*, were constructed only for the electoral transitions, based on Lindberg and Clark (2008, 91 & 101–103) but coded to allow for overtime variation. An electoral democracy had free and fair elections that led to the power transfer, as coded by Lindberg 2006, and a Freedom House civil liberties score of 3 or higher (i.e., 1, 2, or 3) in the year of the transition. A liberalizing regime does not qualify as an electoral democracy, but holds elections and either has a civil liberties score of 3 or higher or has improved its score compared to two years prior to the election. Coverage was expanded using Freedom House's reports on the quality of elections and its civil liberties variable.

Years since Last Coup Attempt: The number of years prior to the constitutional transfer of power since the last coup attempt. If a country had never experienced a coup attempt, the variable was coded as the time since independence. This is consistent with how Powell 2012a measures prior coup history. Data drawn from Appendices B and C.

References

Aboagye, Festus B. (1999). *The Ghana Army: A Concise Contemporary Guide to Its Regimental History 1897–1999*. Accra: Sedco Publishing Limited.

Acemoglu, Daron, Simon Johnson, & James A. Robinson (2001). "The Colonial Origins of Comparative Development: An Empirical Investigation." *The American Economic Review*, 91(5), 1369–1401.

Acemoglu, Daron, Davide Ticchi, & Andrea Vindigni (2010). "A Theory of Military Dictatorships." *American Economic Journal: Macroeconomics*, 2(1), 1–42.

Adeakin, Ibikunle Edward (2015). "A New Form of Authoritarianism? Rethinking Military Politics in Post-1999 Nigeria." Unpublished thesis at http://researchcommons.waikato.ac.nz/bitstream/handle/10289/9284/thesis.pdf?sequence=3 accessed May 7, 2018.

Adekson, J. 'Bayo (1976). "Army in a Multi-Ethnic Society: The Case of Nkrumah's Ghana." *Armed Forces & Society*, 2(2), 251–272.

  (1979). "Ethnicity and Army Recruitment in Colonial Plural Societies." *Ethnic and Racial Studies*, 2(2), 151–165.

Akindes, Simon (2015). "Civil-Military Relations in Benin: Out of the Barracks and Back – Now What?" In Martin Rupiya, Gorden Moyo, & Henrik Laugesen, eds., *The New African Civil-Military Relations*. Pretoria: The African Public Policy and Research Institute, 38–63.

Aksoy, Deniz, David B. Carter, & Joseph Wright (2015). "Terrorism and the Fate of Dictators." *World Politics*, 67(3), 423–468.

Alesina, Alberto, Arnaud Devleeschauwer, William Easterly, Sergio Kurlat, & Romain Wacziarg (2003). "Fractionalization." *Journal of Economic Growth*, 8(2), 155–194.

Alesina, Alberto, Sule Özler, Nouriel Roubini, & Philip Swagel (1996). "Political Instability and Economic Growth." *Journal of Economic Growth*, 1(2), 189–211.

Allen, Christopher (1968). "Sierra Leone Politics Since Independence." *African Affairs*, 67(269), 305–329.

Amadife, Egbunam E. (1999). "Liberalization and Democratization in Nigeria: The International and Domestic Challenge." *Journal of Black Studies*, 29(5), 619–645.

Anderson, Benedict (1983). *Imagined Communities*. London: Verso.

Anderson, Mark (2015). "EU Restores Ties with Guinea-Bissau Five Years After Coup." *The Guardian* (March 25).

Arbatli, Cemal Eren & Ekim Arbatli (2016). "External Threats and Political Survival: Can Dispute Involvement Deter Coup Attempts?" *Conflict Management and Peace Science*, 33(2), 115–152.

Arriola, Leonard R. (2009). "Patronage and Political Stability in Africa." *Comparative Political Studies*, 42(10), 1339–1362.

Asal, Victor, Michael Findley, James A. Piazza, & James Igoe Walsh (2016). "Political Exclusion, Oil, and Ethnic Armed Conflict." *Journal of Conflict Resolution*, 60(8), 1343–1367.

Asante, Richard & E. Gyimah-Badi (2004). "Ethnic Structure, Inequality and Governance of the Public Sector in Ghana." United National Research Institute for Social Development.

Atangana, Martin (2010). *The End of French Rule in Cameroon*. Lanham, Maryland: University Press of America.

Austin, Dennis (1985). "The Ghana Armed Forces and Ghanaian Society." *Third World Quarterly*, 7(1), 90–101.

Awasom, Nicodemus Fru (2002). "Politics and Constitution-Making in Francophone Cameroon, 1959–1960." *Africa Today*, 49(4), 3–30.

Azam, Jean-Paul (2001). "The Redistributive State and Conflicts in Africa." *Journal of Peace Research*, 38(4), 429–444.

Baldwin, Kate (2011). "Mission Education and Ethnic Group Status in Africa." Paper presented at the annual meeting of the American Political Science Association, Seattle, September 1–4.

(2013). "Why Vote with the Chief? Political Connections and Public Goods Provision in Zambia." *American Journal of Political Science*, 57(4), 794–809.

Banks, Aurthur (2001). *Cross-National Time-Series Data Archive*. Binghamton, NY: Computer Systems Unlimited.

Barrows, Walter L. (1976). "Ethnic Diversity and Political Instability in Black Africa." *Comparative Political Studies*, 9(2), 139–170.

Barry, Boubacar (1988). "Neocolonialism and Dependence in Senegal." In Prosser Gifford and Wm. Roger Louis, eds., *Decolonization and African Independence: The Transfers of Power, 1960–1980*. New Haven: Yale University Press, 271–294.

Barua, Pradeep P. (1992). "Ethnic Conflict in the Military of Developing Nations: A Comparative Analysis of India and Nigeria." *Armed Forces & Society*, 19(1), 123–137.

Basedau, Matthias, Gero Erdmann, Jann Lay, & Alexander Stroh (2011). "Ethnicity and Party Preference in Sub-Saharan Africa." *Democratization*, 18(2), 462–489.

Basedau, Matthias, Jonathan Fox, Jan H. Pierskalla, Geoerge Strüver, & Johannes Vüllers (2017). "Does Discrimination Breed Grievances – and Do Grievances

Breed Violence? New Evidence from an Analysis of Religious Minorities in Developing Countries." *Conflict Management and Peace Science*, 34(3), 217–239.

Bates, Robert H. (1981). *Markets and States in Tropical Africa: The Political Basis of Agricultural Policies*. Berkeley: University of California Press.

(1983). "Modernization, Ethnic Competition, and the Rationality of Politics in Contemporary Africa." In D. Rothchild & V. A. Olunsorola, eds., *State versus Ethnic Claims: African Policy Dilemmas*. Boulder, CO: Westview Press, 152–171.

Bayart, Jean-Francois (2009). *The State in Africa: The Politics of the Belly* (2nd edition). Cambridge: Polity Press.

Baynham, Simon (1985). "Divide et Impera: Civilian Control of the Military in Ghana's Second and Third Republics." *The Journal of Modern African Studies*, 23(4), 623–642.

Bazzi, Samuel & Christopher Blattman (2014). "Economic Shocks and Conflict: Evidence from Commodity Prices." *American Economic Journal: Macroeconomics*, 6(4), 1–38.

BBC (1983). "The Attempted Coup in Ghana." (June 22).

(1983). "Resumption of Trial of Remaining Accused in Earlier Coup Attempt." (June 30).

(1983). "Death Sentences in Ghana for 19th June 1983 Coup." (August 6).

(1984). "Ahmadou Ahidjos Reaction to Trial Verdict in Cameroon." (March 1).

Bebler, Anton (1975). *Military Rule in Africa: Dahomey, Ghana, Sierra Leone, and Mali*. New York: Praeger.

Beck, Linda J. (2008). *Brokering Democracy in Africa: The Rise of Clientelist Democracy in Senegal*. New York: Palgrave Macmillan.

Belkin, Aaron & Evan Schofer (2003). "Toward a Structural Understanding of Coup Risk." *Journal of Conflict Resolution*, 47(5), 594–620.

Bell, Curtis & Jun Koga Sudduth (2017). "The Causes and Outcomes of Coup during Civil War." *Journal of Conflict Resolution*, 61(7), 1432–1455.

Bellin, Eva (2004). "The Robustness of Authoritarianism in the Middle East: Exceptionalism in Comparative Perspective." *Comparative Politics*, 36(2), 139–157.

Bennett, Valerie Plave (1973). "The Motivation for Military Intervention: The Case of Ghana." *The Western Political Quarterly*, 26(4), 659–674.

Besley, Timothy & James A. Robinson (2010). "Quis Custodiet Ipsos Custodes? Civilian Control Over the Military." *Journal of the European Economic Association*, 8(2/3), 655–663.

Biddle, Stephen & Robert Zirkle (1996). "Technology, Civil-Military Relations, and Warfare in the Developing World." *Journal of Strategic Studies*, 19(2), 171–212.

Boahen, Adu (1988). "Ghana since Independence." In P. Gifford and W. R. Louis, eds., *Decolonization and African Independence: The Transfers of Power, 1960–1980*. New Haven: Yale University Press, 199–224.

Bodea, Cristina, Ibrahim Elbadawi, & Christian Houle (2017). "Do Civil Wars, Coups and Riots Have the Same Structural Determinants?" *International Interactions*, 43(3), 537–561.

Boone, Catherine (1990). "State Power and Economic Crisis in Senegal." *Comparative Politics*, 22(3), 341–357.

(2003). *Political Topographies of the African State: Territorial Authority and Institutional Choice*. Cambridge: Cambridge University Press.

(2014). *Property and Political Order in Africa: Land Rights and the Structure of Politics*. Cambridge: Cambridge University Press.

Boone, Catherine & Lydia Nyeme (2015). "Land Institutions and Political Ethnicity in Africa." *Comparative Politics*, 48(1), 67–86.

Boylan, Brandon M. (2016). "What Drives Ethnic Terrorist Campaigns? A View at the Group Level of Analysis." *Conflict Management and Peace Science*, 33(3), 250–272.

Brass, Paul (1985). "Ethnic Groups and the State." In Paul Brass, ed., *Ethnic Groups and the State*. Totowa, New Jersey: Barnes & Noble Imports.

Bratton, Michael & Nicolas van de Walle (1997). *Democratic Experiments in Africa*. Cambridge: Cambridge University Press.

Brown, David (1982). "Who Are the Tribalists? Social Pluralism and Political Ideology in Ghana." *African Affairs*, 81(322), 37–69.

Brown, David E. (2013). *AFRICOM at 5 Years: The Maturation of a New U.S. Combatant Command*. Carlisle, PA: Strategic Studies Institute, US Army War College.

Brubaker, Rogers & David D. Laitin (1998). "Ethnic and Nationalist Violence." *Annual Review of Sociology*, 24, 423–452.

Buhaug, Halvard, Lars-Erik Cederman, & Kristian Skrede Gleditsch (2013). "Square Pegs in Round Holes: Inequalities, Grievances, and Civil War." *International Studies Quarterly*, 58(2), 1–14.

Buhaug, Halvard, Lars-Erik Cederman, & Jan Ketil Rød (2008). "Disaggregating Ethno-Nationalist Civil Wars: A Dyadic Test of Exclusion Theory." *International Organization*, 62(3), 531–551.

Bunte, Jonas B. & Vinson, Laura Thaut (2016). "Local Power-Sharing Institutions and Interreligious Violence in Nigeria." *Journal of Peace Research*, 53(1), 49–65.

Butts, Kent Hughes & Steven Metz (1996). "Armies and Democracies in the New Africa: Lessons from Nigeria and South Africa." Strategic Studies Institute Monograph at http://ssi.armywarcollege.edu/pdffiles/00197.pdf, accessed February 13, 2018.

Byrnes, Rita M. (1990). "Uganda: A Country Study." *Library of Congress Country Studies* at http://memory.loc.gov/frd/cs/cshome.html, accessed February 10, 2018.

Campbell, Ian (1994). "Nigeria's Failed Transition: The 1993 Presidential Election." *Journal of Contemporary African Studies*, 12(2), 179–199.

Carbone, Giovanni M. (2008). *No-Party Democracy: Ugandan Politics in Comparative Perspective*. Boulder: Lynne Rienner.

Cartwright, John (1972). "Party Competition in a Developing Nation: The Basis of Support for an Opposition in Sierra Leone." *Journal of Commonwealth Political Studies*, 10(1), 71–90.

Casper, Brett Allen & Scott A. Tyson (2014). "Popular Protest and Elite Coordination in a Coup d'Etat." *The Journal of Politics*, 76(2), 548–564.

Cawthra, Gavin (2003). "Security Transformation in Post-Apartheid South Africa." In Gavin Cawthra and Robin Luckham, eds., *Governing Insecurity: Democratic Control of Military and Security Establishments in Transitional Democracies*. London: Zed Books, 31–56.

Cederman, Lars-Erik, Halvard Buhaug, & Jan Ketil Rød (2009). "Ethno-Nationalist Dyads and Civil War: A GIS-Based Analysis." *Journal of Conflict Resolution*, 53(4), 496–525.

Cederman, Lars-Erik & Luc Girardin (2007). "Beyond Fractionalization: Mapping Ethnicity onto Nationalist Insurgencies." *American Political Science Review*, 101(1), 173–185.

Cederman, Lars-Erik, Kristian Skrede Gleditsch, & Halvard Buhaug (2013). *Inequality, Grievances, and Civil War*. Cambridge: Cambridge University Press.

Cederman, Lars-Erik, Kristian Skrede Gleditsch, & Julian Wucherpfennig (2017). "Predicting the Decline of Ethnic Civil War: Was Gurr Right and for the Right Reasons?" *Journal of Peace Research*, 54(2), 262–274.

Cederman, Lars-Erik, Nils B. Weidmann, & Kristian Skrede Gleditsch (2011). "Horizontal Inequalities and Ethnonationalist Civil War: A Global Comparison." *American Political Science Review*, 105(3), 478–495.

Cederman, Lars-Erik, Andreas Wimmer, & Brian Min (2010). "Why Do Ethnic Groups Rebel?: New Data and Analysis." *World Politics*, 62(1), 87–119.

Chacha, Mwita & Jonathan Powell (2017). "Economic Interdependence and Post-Coup Democratization." *Democratization*, 24(5), 819–838.

Chandra, Kanchan (2011). "What Is an Ethnic Party?" *Party Politics*, 17(2), 151–169.

(2012). *Constructivist Theories of Ethnic Politics*. Oxford: Oxford University Press.

Chandra, Kanchan & Steven Wilkinson (2008). "Measuring the Effect of 'Ethnicity.'" *Comparative Political Studies*, 41(4/5), 515–563.

Chazan, Naomi (1982). "Ethnicity and Politics in Ghana." *Political Science Quarterly*, 97(3), 461–485.

Chenoweth, Erica & Maria J. Stephan (2011). *Why Civil Resistance Works: The Strategic Logic of Nonviolent Conflict*. New York: Columbia University Press.

Chiba, Daina & Kristian Skrede Gleditsch (2017). "The Shape of Things to Come? Expanding the Inequality and Grievance Model for Civil War Forecasts with Event Data." *Journal of Peace Research*, 54(2), 275–297.

Choirat, Christine, James Honaker, Kosuke Imai, Gary King, & Olivia Lau (2017). "Zelig: Everyone's Statistical Software. Version 5.1-1.90000" at http://zeligproject.org/, accessed May 7, 2018.

Christian Science Monitor, The (1984). "Ghana Coup Attempt Appears Linked to Unrest Over Austerity Plan." (March 30).

Cissé, Lamine (2015). "Security Sector Reform in Democratic Senegal." In Alan Bryden & Fairlie Chappuis, eds., *Learning from West African Experiences in Security Sector Governance*. London: Ubiquity Press, 117–137.

Clapham, Christopher (1976). *Liberia and Sierra Leone: An Essay in Comparative Politics*. Cambridge: Cambridge University Press.

Clark, Andrew F. (1999). "Imperialism, Independence, and Islam in Senegal and Mali." *Africa Today*, 46(3/4), 149–167.

Clark, John F. (2007). "The Decline of the African Military Coup." *Journal of Democracy*, 18(3), 141–155.

Clayton, Anthony (1989). *Khaki and Blue: Military and Police in British Colonial Africa*. Ohio: Center for International Studies, Ohio University.

Cole, Festus (2013a). "Civil-Military Relations in Colonial Sierra Leone: The Sierra Leone Battalion and the Crisis of Role Perspectives, 1901–1959." *Research in Sierra Leone Studies*, 1(2), 1–31.

(2013b). "The Roots of Military Praetorianism in Sierra Leone." In Sylvia Ojukutu-Macauley & Ismail Rashid, eds., *Paradoxes of History and Memory in Post-Colonial Sierra Leone*. Lanham, Maryland: Lexington Books, 153–204.

Collier, Paul (2008). "Let Us Now Praise Coups." *The Washington Post* (June 22).

Collier, Paul & Anke Hoeffler (2004). "Greed and Grievance in Civil War." *Oxford Economic Papers*, 56(4), 563–595.

(2005). "Coup Traps: Why Does Africa Have So Many Coups d'Etat?" Working paper at users.ox.ac.uk/~econpco/research/pdfs/Coup-traps.pdf, accessed February 10, 2018.

(2007). "Military Spending and the Risks of Coups d'Etats." Working paper at users.ox.ac.uk/~econpco/research/pdfs/MilitarySpendingandRisksCoups .pdf, accessed February 10, 2018.

Côté, Isabelle & Matthew I. Mitchell (2016). "Elections and 'Sons of the Soil' Conflict Dynamics in Africa and Asia." *Democratization*, 23(4), 657–677.

Cox, Thomas S. (1976). *Civil-Military Relations in Sierra Leone: A Case Study of African Soldiers in Politics*. Cambridge, MA: Harvard University Press.

Cramer, Christopher (2003). "Does Inequality Cause Conflict?" *Journal of International Development*, 15(4), 397–412.

Crocker, Chester Arthur (1968). "France's Changing Military Interests." *Africa Report*, June 1, 16–24.

(1974). "Military Dependency: The Colonial Legacy in Africa." *The Journal of Modern African Studies*, 12(2), 265–286.

Dahou, Tarik & Vincent Foucher (2009). "Senegal since 2000: Rebuilding Hegemony in a Global Age." In Abdul Raufu Mustapha & Lindsay Whitfield, eds., *Turning Points in African Democracy*. Suffolk: James Currey, 13–49.

Daley, Patricia (2006). "Ethnicity and Political Violence in Africa: The Challenge to the Burundi State." *Political Geography*, 25(6), 657–679.

Davenport, Christian & Patrick Ball (2002). "Views to a Kill: Exploring the Implications of Source Selection in the Case of Guatemalan State Terror 1977–1995." *Journal of Conflict Resolution*, 46(3), 427–450.

Davies, Victor A.B. (2000). "Sierra Leone: Ironic Tragedy." *Journal of African Economies*, 9(3), 349–369.

De Bruin, Erica (2017). "Preventing Coups d'Etat: How Counterbalancing Works." *Journal of Conflict Resolution*, forthcoming at http://journals.sagepu b.com/doi/abs/10.1177/0022002717692652, accessed February 13, 2018.

Decalo, Samuel (1973). "Regionalism, Politics, and the Military in Dahomey." *The Journal of Developing Areas*, 7(3), 449–478.

(1989). "Modalities of Civil-Military Stability in Africa." *Journal of Modern African Studies*, 27(4), 547–578.

(1990). *Coups & Army Rule in Africa*. New Haven: Yale University Press.

(1991). "Towards Understanding the Sources of Stable Civilian Rule in Africa, 1960–1990." *Journal of Contemporary African Studies*, 10(1), 66–83.

(1998). *Civil-Military Relations in Africa*. Gainesville: Florida Academic Press, Inc.

DeLancey, Mark W. (1987). "The Construction of the Cameroon Political System: The Ahidjo Years, 1958–1982." *Journal of Contemporary African Studies*, 6(1/2), 3–24.

Denny, Elaine K. & Barbara F. Walter (2014). "Ethnicity and Civil War." *Journal of Peace Research*, 51(2), 199–212.

Derpanopoulos, George, Erica Frantz, Barbara Geddes, & Joseph Wright (2016). "Are Coups Good for Democracy?" *Research and Politics*, 3(1), 1–7.

Diallo, El Hadji Samba & Catherine Lena Kelly. 2016. "Sufi Turuq and the Politics of Democratization in Senegal." *Journal of Religious and Political Practice*, 2(2), 193–211.

Dickovick, J. Tyler (2008). "Legacies of Leftism: Ideology, Ethnicity and Democracy in Benin, Ghana and Mali." *Third World Quarterly*, 29(6), 1119–1137.

Diop, Momar Coumba & Moussa Paye (1998). "The Army and Political Power in Senegal." In Eboe Hutchful & Abdoulaye Bathily, eds., *The Military and Militarism in Africa*. Dakar: CODESRIA, 315–354.

Downes, Alexander B. (2008). *Targeting Civilians in War*. Ithaca: Cornell University Press.

Dowse, Robert (1975). "Military and Police Rule." In Dennis Austin & Robin Luckham, eds., *Politicians and Soldiers in Ghana 1966–1972*. London: Frank Cass, 16–36.

Dresch, Jean, Victor Martin, Paul Pélissier, Amar Samb, & Régine Van-Chi-Bonnardel eds. (1977). *Atlas National du Sénégal*. Dakar: Institute Fondamental d'Afrique Noire.

Dunmar, Frederick C. (2002). "The History of the Nigerian Army and the Implications for the Future of Nigeria." Unpublished Masters Thesis submitted to the US Army Command and General Staff College.

Durotoye, Yomi & Robert J. Griffiths (1997). "Civilianizing Military Rule: Conditions and Processes of Political Transmutation in Ghana and Nigeria." *African Studies Review*, 40(3), 133–160.

Earl, Jennifer, Andrew Martin, John D. McCarthy, & Sarah Soule (2004). "The Use of Newspaper Data in the Study of Collective Action." *Annual Review of Sociology*, 30, 65–80.

Echenberg, Myron (1991). *Colonial Conscripts: The Tirailleurs Sénégalais in French West Africa, 1857–1960*. Portsmouth, New Hampshire: Heinemann.

Economist, The (1979). "Ghana: Is It Just to Clean the Stables?" (June 9).

(1982). "Ghana: Rumour Power." (November 20).

(2015). "Lucky Macky: Senegal Retains Its Title as Africa's Oldest Democracy" (April 7).

Ehwarieme, William (2011). "The Military Factor in Nigeria's Democratic Stability, 1999–2009." *Armed Forces & Society*, 37(3), 494–511.

Enloe, Cynthia H. (1975). "The Military Uses of Ethnicity." *Millenium*, 4(3), 220–233.

(1980). *Ethnic Soldiers: State Security in Divided Societies*. Athens, Georgia: University of Georgia Press.

Esteban, Joan & Debraj Ray (2011). "A Model of Ethnic Conflict." *Journal of the European Economic Association*, 9(3), 496–521.

Fatton, Jr., Robert (1986). "Clientelism and Patronage in Senegal." *African Studies Review*, 29(4), 61–78.

Fearon, James D. (1995). "Rationalist Explanations for War." *International Organization*, 49(3), 379–414.

(1999). "Why Ethnic Politics and 'Pork' Tend to Go Together." Working paper at https://web.stanford.edu/group/fearon-research/cgi-bin/wordpress/wp-content/uploads/2013/10/Pork.pdf, accessed February 13, 2018.

(2003). "Ethnic and Cultural Diversity by Country." *Journal of Economic Growth*, 8(2), 195–222.

(2004). "Why Do Some Civil Wars Last So Much Longer Than Others?" *Journal of Peace Research*, 41(3), 275–301.

Fearon, James D. & David D. Laitin (2003). "Ethnicity, Insurgency, and Civil War." *American Political Science Review*, 97(1), 75–90.

(2011). "Sons of the Soil, Migrants, and Civil War." *World Development*, 39(2), 199–211.

Feaver, Peter D. (1999). "Civil-Military Relations." *Annual Review of Political Science*, 2, 211–241.

Feit, Edward (1968). "Military Coups and Political Development: Some Lessons from Ghana and Nigeria." *World Politics*, 20(2), 179–193.

Finer, Samuel E. (1976). *The Man on Horseback: The Role of the Military in Politics*. Baltimore: Harmondsworth.

Fink, Elisabeth (2007). "The Radical Road Not Taken: Mamadou Dia, Léopold Sédar Senghor, and the Constitutional Crisis of December 1962." Unpublished thesis submitted to the Department of History at Columbia University.

Foltz, William J. (1965). *From French West Africa to the Mali Federation*. New Haven: Yale University Press.

Foltz, William J. & Steve McDonald, eds., (1995). *Democratization in Africa: The Role of the Military (Report on the Second Regional Conference)*. Contonou, Benin: The African-American Institute.

Fortna, Virginia Paige (2008). *Does Peacekeeping Work?: Shaping Belligerents' Choices after Civil War*. Princeton: Princeton University Press.

Franck, Raphaël & Ilia Rainer (2012). "Does the Leader's Ethnicity Matter? Ethnic Favoritism, Education, and Health in Sub-Saharan Africa." *American Political Science Review*, 106(2), 294–325.

Francois, Patrick, Ilia Rainer, & Francesco Trebbi (2015). "How Is Power Shared In Africa?" *Econometrica*, 83(2), 465–503.

Freedom House (2016a). "Benin." In *Freedom in the World: Annual Reports, 1999–2015* at https://freedomhouse.org/country/benin, accessed February 10, 2018.

(2016b). "Individual Country Ratings and Status, FIW 1973–2016" at https://freedomhouse.org/report-types/freedom-world, accessed May 23, 2016.

(2016c). "Senegal." In *Freedom in the World: Annual Reports, 1999–2015* at https://freedomhouse.org/country/senegal, accessed February 10, 2018.

Galetovic, Alexander & Ricardo Sanhueza (2000). "Citizens, Autocrats, and Plotters: A Model and New Evidence on Coups d'Etat." *Economics and Politics*, 12(1), 183–204.

Galvan, Dennis (2001). "Political Turnover and Social Change in Senegal." *Journal of Democracy*, 12(3), 51–62.

Gazibo, Mamoudou (2005). "Foreign Aid and Democratization: Benin and Niger Compared." *African Studies Review*, 48(3), 67–87.

Gbla, Osman (2006). "Security Sector Reform Under International Tutelage in Sierra Leone." *International Peacekeeping*, 13(1), 78–93.

Geddes, Barbara, Joseph Wright, & Erica Frantz (2014). "Autocratic Breakdown and Regime Transitions: A New Dataset." *Perspectives on Politics*, 12(2), 313–331.

Girod, Desha M. (2015). "Reducing Postconflict Coup Risk: The Low Windfall Coup-Proofing Hypothesis." *Conflict Management and Peace Science*, 32(2), 153–174.

Gisselquist, Rachel M. (2008). "Democratic Transition and Democratic Survival in Benin." *Democratization*, 15(4), 789–814.

Gleditsch, Kristian Skrede, Nils Petter, Peter Wallensteen, Mikael Eriksson, Margareta Sollenberg, & Håvard Strand (2002). "Armed Conflict, 1946–2001: A New Dataset." *Journal of Peace Research*, 39(5), 615–637.

Globe and Mail, The (1984). "11 Killed After Strife in Ghana." (March 26).

Goemans, Hein E., Kristian Skrede Gleditsch, & Giacomo Chiozza (2009). *Archigos: A Data Set on Leaders, 1875–2004 (version 2.9)* at www.rochester.edu/college/faculty/hgoemans/data.htm, accessed February 10, 2018.

Goertz, Gary & James Mahoney (2006). "Negative Case Selection: The Possibility Principle." In Gary Goertz, ed., *Social Science Concepts*. Princeton: Princeton University Press, 177–210.

Goldsworthy, David (1973). "Ghana's Second Republic: A Post-Mortem." *African Affairs*, 72(286), 8–25.

(1981). "Civilian Control of the Military in Black Africa." *African Affairs*, 80(318), 49–74.

Gros, Jean-Germain (1995). "The Hard Lessons of Cameroon." *Journal of Democracy*, 6(3), 112–126.

Gubler, Joshua R. & Joel Sawat Selway (2012). "Horizontal Inequality, Crosscutting Cleavages, and Civil War." *Journal of Conflict Resolution*, 56(2), 206–232.

Gurr, Ted (1970). *Why Men Rebel*. Princeton: Princeton University Press.

Habyarimana, James, Macartan Humphreys, Daniel N. Posner, & Jeremy M. Weinstein (2009). *Coethnicity: Diversity and the Dilemmas of Collective Action*. New York: Russell Sage Foundation.

Hale, Henry E. (2008). *The Foundations of Ethnic Politics: Separatism of States and Nations in Eurasia and the World*. Cambridge: Cambridge University Press.

Ham, Carter (2013). "Statement to the Senate Armed Services Committee" (March 7) at www.africom.mil/Doc/10432, accessed February 10, 2018.

Han, Enze, Joseph O'Mahoney, & Christopher Paik (2014). "External Kin, Economic Disparity and Minority Ethnic Group Mobilization." *Conflict Management and Peace Science*, 31(1), 49–69.

Hanloff, Robert Earl (1990). "Mauritania: A Country Study." *Library of Congress Country Studies* at www.loc.gov/item/89600361/, accessed February 10, 2018.

Hansen, Emmanuel (1991). *Ghana Under Rawlings: Early Years*. Lagos: Malthouse Press.

Hansen, Emmanuel & Paul Collins (1980). "The Army, the State, and the 'Rawlings Revolution' in Ghana." *African Affairs*, 79(314), 3–23.

Harbom, Lotta & Peter Wallensteen (2010). "Armed Conflicts, 1945–2009." *Journal of Peace Research*, 47(4), 501–509.

Harkness, Kristen A. & Michael Hunzeker (2015). "Military Maladaptation: Counterinsurgency and the Politics of Failure." *Journal of Strategic Studies*, 38(6), 777–800.

Harris, D.J. (1980). "The Recent Political Upheavals in Ghana." *The World Today*, 36(6), 225–232.

Hassan, Mai (2015). "Continuity Despite Change: Kenya's New Constitution and Executive Power." *Democratization*, 22(4), 587–609.

(2017). "The Strategic Shuffle: Ethnic Geography, the Internal Security Apparatus, and Elections in Kenya." *American Journal of Political Science*, 61(2), 382–395.

Hayward, Fred M. (1984). "Political Leadership, Power, and the State: Generalizations from the Case of Sierra Leone." *African Studies Review*, 27(3), 19–39.

Heilbrunn, John R. (1993). "Social Origins of National Conferences in Benin and Togo." *The Journal of Modern African Studies*, 31(2), 277–299.

Herbst, Jeffrey (2000). *States and Power in Africa: Comparative Lessons in Authority and Control*. Princeton: Princeton University Press.

Hettne, Björn (1980). "Soldiers and Politics: The Case of Ghana." *Journal of Peace Research*, 17(2), 173–193.

Hodler, Roland & Paul A. Raschky (2014). "Regional Favoritism." *Quarterly Journal of Economics*, 129(2), 995–1033.

Hornsby, Charles (2013). *Kenya: A History Since Independence*. London: I.B. Tauris & Co Ltd.

Horowitz, Donald L. (1971). "Three Dimensions of Ethnic Politics." *World Politics*, 23(2), 232–244.

(1985). *Ethnic Groups in Conflict*. Berkeley: University of California Press.

(2001). *The Deadly Ethnic Riot*. Berkeley: University of California Press.

Houle, Christian (2009). "Inequality and Democracy: Why Inequality Harms Consolidation but Does Not Affect Democratization." *World Politics*, 61(4), 589–622.

(2015). "Ethnic Inequality and the Dismantling of Democracy: A Global Analysis." *World Politics*, 67(3), 469–505.

(2016). "Why Class Inequality Breeds Coups but not Civil Wars." *Journal of Peace Research*, 53(5), 680–695.

Houle, Christian & Cristina Bodea (2017). "Ethnic Inequality and Coups in Sub-Saharan Africa." *Journal of Peace Research*, 54(3), 382–396.

Huber, John D. & Pavithra Suryanarayan (2016). "Ethnic Inequality and the Ethnification of Political Parties: Evidence from India." *World Politics*, 68(1), 149–188.

Humphreys, Macartan (2005). "Natural Resources, Conflict, and Conflict Resolution: Uncovering the Mechanisms." *Journal of Conflict Resolution*, 49(4), 508–537.

Huntington, Samuel P. (1957). *The Soldier and the State: The Theory and Politics of Civil-Military Relations*. Cambridge, MA: The Belknap Press of Harvard University Press.

(1968). *Political Order in Changing Societies* New Haven: Yale University Press.

Hutchful, Eboe (1979). "Organizational Instability in African Military Forces: The Case of the Ghanaian Army." *International Social Science Journal*, 31(4), 606–618.

(1985). "The Development of the Army Officer Corps in Ghana, 1956–1966." *Journal of African Studies*, 12(3), 163–173.

(1997a). "Military Policy and Reform in Ghana." *The Journal of Modern African Studies*, 35(2), 251–278.

(1997b). "Reconstructing Civil-Military Relations and the Collapse of Democracy in Ghana, 1979–81." *African Affairs*, 96(385), 535–560.

(2003). "Pulling Back from the Brink." In Gavin Cawthra & Robin Luckham, eds., *Governing Insecurity: Democratic Control of the Military and Security Establishments in Transitional Democracies*. London and New York: Zed Books, 78–101.

Hyde, Susan D. & Nikolay Marinov (2012). "Which Elections Can Be Lost?" *Political Analysis*, 20(2), 191–201.

Ihonvbere, Julius O. (1991). "A Critical Evaluation of the Failed 1990 Coup in Nigeria." *The Journal of Modern African Studies*, 29(4), 601–626.

(1996). "Are Things Falling Apart? The Military and the Crisis of Democratization in Nigeria." *The Journal of Modern African Studies*, 34(2), 193–225.

Imai, Kosuke, Gary King, & Olivia Lau (2008). "Toward a Common Framework for Statistical Analysis and Development." *Journal of Computational Graphics and Statistics*, 17(4), 892–913.

Jackman, Robert W. (1978). "The Predictability of Coups d'Etat: A Model with African Data." *American Political Science Review*, 72(4), 1262–1275.

Jackman, Robert W., Rosemary H.T. O'Kane, Thomas H. Johnson, Pat McGowan, & Robert O. Slater (1986). "Explaining African Coups d'Etat." *American Political Science Review*, 80(1), 225–250.

Jazayeri, Karen Bodnaruk (2016). "Identity-based Political Inequality and Protest: The Dynamic Relationship Between Political Power and Protest in the Middle East." *Conflict Management and Peace Science*, 33(4), 400–422.

Jenkins, Craig J. & Augustine J. Kposowa (1990). "Explaining Military Coups d'Etat: Black Africa, 1957–1984. *American Sociological Review*, 55(6), 861–875.

(1992). "The Political Origins of African Military Coups: Ethnic Competition, Military Centrality, and the Struggle over the Postcolonial State." *International Studies Quarterly*, 36(3), 271–291.

Johnson, Jaclyn & Clayton L. Thyne (2018). "Squeaky Wheels and Troop Loyalty: How Domestic Protests Influence Coups d'Etat, 1951–2005." *Journal of Conflict Resolution*, 62(3), 597–625.

Johnson, Paul Lorenzo & Ches Thurber (2017). "The Security Force Ethnicity (SFE) Project: Introducing a New Dataset." *Conflict Management and Peace Science*, forthcoming at http://journals.sagepub.com/doi/abs/10.1177/0738894217709012, accessed February 13, 2018.

Johnson, Thomas H., Robert O. Slater, & Pat McGowan (1984). "Explaining African Military Coups d'Etat, 1960–1982." *American Political Science Review*, 78(3), 622–640.

Jong-A-Pin, Richard & Shu Yu (2010). "Do Coup Leaders Matter? Leadership Change and Economic Growth in Politically Unstable Countries." *KOF Working Papers* 252 at http://ssrn.com/abstract=1549669, accessed February 10, 2018.

Joseph, Richard, ed. (1978). *Gaullist Africa: Cameroon under Ahmadu Ahidjo*. Enugu, Nigeria: Fourth Dimension Publishers.

Kagoro, Jude (2016). "Competitive Authoritarianism in Uganda: The Not So Hidden Hand of the Military." *Comparative Governance and Politics*, Special Issue 6, 155–172.

Kahneman, Daniel & Amos Tversky (1979). "Prospect Theory: An Analysis of Decision Under Risk." *Econometrica*, 47(2), 263–292.

Kandeh, Jimmy D. (1992). "Politicization of Ethnic Identities in Sierra Leone." *African Studies Review*, 35(1), 81–99.

(1996). "What Does the 'Militariat' Do When it Rules? Military Regimes: The Gambia, Sierra Leone and Liberia." *Review of African Political Economy*, 23(69), 387–404.

Kasara, Kimuli (2007). "Tax Me If You Can: Ethnic Geography, Democracy, and the Taxation of Agriculture in Africa." *American Political Science Review*, 101(1), 159–172.

Keegan, John (1983). *World Armies*. Detroit, Michigan: Gale Research Company.

Keesings: World News Archive (1963). "Abortive Coup by M. Mamadou Dia." Volume 9 (January).

(1967). "Parliamentary Regime Overthrown by Military Leaders." Volume 13 (April).

(1968). "Military Junta Overthrown by 'Sergeants Coup.' " Volume 14 (May).

(1971). "President Obote Overthrown by Military Coup." Volume 17 (February).

(1971). "Attempted Military Coup Against King Hassan." Volume 17 (September).

(1984). "Attempted Coup Political Changes Budget." Volume 30 (September).

Kelly, Catherine Lena (2012). "Senegal: What Will Turnover Bring?" *Journal of Democracy*, 23(3), 121–131.

Kendhammer, Brandon (2015). "Getting Our Piece of the National Cake: Consociational Power Sharing and Neopatrimonialism in Nigeria." *Nationalism and Ethnic Politics*, 21(2), 143–165.

Kieh, George Clay, Jr. & Pita Ogaba Agbese (1993). "From Politics Back to the Barracks in Nigeria: A Theoretical Exploration." *Journal of Peace Research*, 30(4), 409–426.

Kim, Nam Kyu (2016). "Revisiting Economic Shocks and Coups." *Journal of Conflict Resolution*, 60(1), 3–31.

Konings, Piet (1996). "The Post-Colonial State and Economic and Political Reforms in Cameroon." In Alex E. Fernández Jilberto & André Mommen, eds., *Liberalization in the Developing World: Institutional and Economic Changes in Latin America, Africa, and Asia*. London and New York: Routledge, 244–265.

Kposowa, Augustine J. (2006). "Erosion of the Rule of Law as a Contributing Factor in Civil Conflict: The Case of Sierra Leone." *Police Practice and Research*, 7(1), 35–48.

Kposowa, Augustine J. & J. Craig Jenkins (1993). "The Structural Sources of Military Coups in Postcolonial Africa, 1957–1984." *American Journal of Sociology*, 99(1), 126–163.

Kpundeh, Sahr John (1994). "Limiting Administrative Corruption in Sierra Leone." *The Journal of Modern African Studies*, 32(1), 139–157.

Kramon, Eric & Daniel Posner (2013). "Who Benefits from Distributive Politics? How the Outcome One Studies Affects the Answer One Gets." *Perspectives on Politics*, 11(2), 461–474.

  (2016). "Ethnic Favoritism in Education in Kenya." *Quarterly Journal of Political Science*, 11(1), 1–58.

Kuhn, Patrick M. & Nils B. Weidmann (2015). "Unequal We Fight: Between and Within-Group Inequality and Ethnic Civil War." *Political Science Research and Methods*, 3(3), 543–568.

Kuperman, Alan J. (2001). *The Limits of Humanitarian Intervention*. Washington, D.C.: Brookings Institution Press.

Lacina, Bethany (2014). "How Governments Shape the Risk of Civil Violence: India's Federal Reorganization, 1950–56." *American Journal of Political Science*, 58(3), 720–738.

  (2015). "Periphery versus Periphery: The Stakes of Separatist War." *Journal of Politics*, 77(3), 692–706.

Lefèvre, Patrick & Jean-Noël Lefèvre (2006). *Les Militaire Belge et le Rwanda, 1916–2006*. Belgium: Édition Racine.

Lemarchand, René (1972). "Political Clientelism and Ethnicity in Tropical Africa: Competing Solidarities in Nation-Building." *The American Political Science Review*, 66(1), 68–90.

Leon, Gabriel (2014). "Loyalty for Sale? Military Spending and Coups d'Etat." *Public Choice*, 159(3), 363–383.

Lewis, James I. (1998). "The MRP and the Genesis of the French Union, 1944–1948." *French History*, 12(3), 276–314.

Lewis, Janet I. (2017). "How Does Ethnic Rebellion Start?" *Comparative Political Studies*, 50(10), 1420–1450.

Lewis, Peter M. (1994). "Endgame in Nigeria? The Politics of a Failed Democratic Transition." *African Affairs*, 93(372), 323–340.

Lieberman, Evan S. & Prerna Singh (2012a). "Conceptualizing and Measuring Ethnic Politics: An Institutional Complement to Demographic, Behavioral, and Cognitive Approaches." *Studies in Comparative International Development*, 47(3), 255–286.

(2012b). "The Institutional Origins of Ethnic Violence." *Comparative Politics*, 45(1), 1–24.

(2017). "Census Enumeration and Group Conflict: A Global Analysis of the Consequences of Counting." *World Politics*, 69(1), 1–53.

Lindberg, Staffan I. (2006). *Democracy and Elections in Africa*. Baltimore: Johns Hopkins University Press.

Lindberg, Staffan I. & John F. Clark (2008). "Does Democratization Reduce the Risk of Military Interventions in Politics in Africa?" *Democratization*, 15(1), 86–105.

Little, Andrew T. (2017). "Coordination, Learning, and Coups." *Journal of Conflict Resolution*, 61(1), 204–234.

Loimeier, Roman (1996). "The Secular State and Islam in Senegal." In David Westerlund, ed., *Questioning the Secular State: The Worldwide Resurgence of Religion in Politics*. New York: St. Martin's Press, 183–197.

Londregan, John B., Henry Bienen, & Nicolas van de Walle (1995). "Ethnicity and Leadership Succession in Africa." *International Studies Quarterly*, 39(1): 1–25.

Londregan, John B. & Keith T. Poole (1990). "Poverty, the Coup Trap, and the Seizure of Executive Power." *World Politics*, 42(2), 151–183.

Luckham, Robin (1971). *The Nigerian Military: A Sociological Analysis of Authority and Revolt, 1960–67*. Cambridge: Cambridge University Press.

(1982). "French Militarism in Africa." *Review of African Political Economy*, 9(24), 55–84.

Lumsden, D. Paul (1980). "Towards Ghana's Third Republic." *Canadian Journal of African Studies*, 13(3), 471–477.

Lunde, Tormod K. (1991). "Modernization and Political Instability: Coups d'Etat in Africa, 1955–85." *Acta Sociologica*, 34(1), 13–32.

Lynch, Gabrielle & Gordon Crawford (2011). "Democratization in Africa 1990–2010: An Assessment." *Democratization*, 18(2), 275–310.

Maddison Project, The (2013). *Statistics on World Population, GDP, and Per Capita GDP, 1–2008 AD* at www.ggdc.net/maddison/maddison-project/home.htm, accessed February 10, 2018.

Magnusson, Bruce A. (2001). "Democratization and Domestic Insecurity: Navigating the Transition in Benin." *Comparative Politics*, 33(2), 211–230.

Mahmud, Sakah (1993). "The Failed Transition to Civilian Rule in Nigeria: Its Implications for Democracy and Human Rights." *Africa Today*, 40(4), 87–95.

Mamdani, Mahmood (1996). *Citizen and Subject: Contemporary Africa and the Legacy of Late Colonialism*. Princeton: Princeton University Press.

Manea, Maria-Gabriela & Jürgen Rüland (2013). "Taking Stock of Military Reform in Nigeria." In Jürgen Rüland, Maria-Gabriela Manea, & Hans Born, eds., *The Politics of Military Reform: Experiences from Indonesia and Nigeria*. Berlin: Springer-Verlag, 57–76.

Marcum, Anthony S. & Jonathan N. Brown (2016). "Overthrowing the 'Loyalty Norm': The Prevalence and Success of Coups in Small-Coalition Systems, 1950–1999." *Journal of Conflict Resolution*, 60(2), 256–282.

Marinov, Nikolay & Hein Goemans (2014). "Coups and Democracy." *British Journal of Political Science* 44(4), 799–825.

Mark, Monika (2012). "U.S. Suspends Mali's Military Aid after Coup." *The Guardian* (March 26).

Markovitz, Irving Leonard (1969). *Léopold Sédar Senghor and the Politics of Negritude*. New York: Atheneum.

   (1970). "Traditional Social Structure, the Islamic Brotherhoods, and Political Development in Senegal." *The Journal of Modern African Studies*, 8(1), 73–96.

Marshall, Monty G., Ted Robert Gurr, & Keith Jaggers (2016). "Polity IV Project: Political Regime Characteristics and Transitions, 1800–2015." Center for Systemic Peace at www.systemicpeace.org/inscrdata.html, accessed May 23, 2016.

Massey, Simon & Roy May (2006). "Commentary: The Crisis in Chad." *African Affairs*, 105(420), 443–449.

Mazrui, Ali A. & Michael Tidy (1984). *Nationalism and New States in Africa*. London: Heinemann.

Mbaku, John Mukum (2003). "Decolonization, Reunification, and Federation in Cameroon." In John Mukum Mbaku & Joseph Takougang, eds., *The Leadership Challenge in Africa: Cameroon under Paul Biya*. Trenton, New Jersey: Africa World Press, 31–66.

McCoy, Jr., William H. (1994). *Senegal and Liberia: Case Studies in IMET Training and Its Role in Internal Defense and Development*. Santa Monica, CA: Rand Corporation.

McGowan, Patrick J. (2003). "African Military Coups d'État, 1956–2001: Frequency, Trends, and Distribution." *Journal of Modern African Studies*, 41(3), 339–370.

   (2005). "Coups and Conflict in West Africa, 1955–2004: Part I, Theoretical Perspectives." *Armed Forces & Society*, 32(1), 5–23.

   (2006). "Coups and Conflict in West Africa, 1955–2004: Part II, Empirical Findings." *Armed Forces & Society*, 32(2), 234–253.

McGowan, Patrick J. & Thomas H. Johnson (1984). "African Military Coups d'Etat and Underdevelopment: A Quantitative Historical Analysis." *The Journal of Modern African Studies*, 22(4), 633–666.

Meditz, Sandra W. & Tim Merrill (1993). "Zaire: A Country Study." *Library of Congress Country Studies* at www.loc.gov/item/94025092/, accessed February 10, 2018.

Metz, Helen Chapin (1982). "Sudan: A Country Study." *Library of Congress Country Studies* at www.loc.gov/item/2014043450/, accessed February 10, 2018.

   (1993). "Algeria: A Country Study." *Library of Congress Country Studies* at www.loc.gov/item/94043019/, accessed February 10, 2018.

Minorities at Risk Project (2009). "Minorities at Risk Dataset." College Park, MD: Center for International Development and Conflict Management at www.mar.umd.edu/, accessed February 13, 2018.

Minority Rights Group (2010). "Country Overviews." World Directory of Minorities and Indigenous Peoples at www.minorityrights.org/directory, accessed February 10, 2018.

Miodownik, Dan & Ravi Bhavnani (2011). "Ethnic Minority Rule and Civil War Onset." *Conflict Management and Peace Science*, 28(5), 438–458.

Morency-Laflamme, Julien (2015). "A Missing Link? Elite Factionalism and Democratization in Africa." *Canadian Journal of African Studies*, 49(3), 459–477.

Morgenthau, Ruth Schachter (1964). *Political Parties in French-Speaking Africa*. Oxford: Clarendon Press.

Morrison, Minion K.C. (2004). "Political Parties in Ghana through Four Republics: A Path to Democratic Consolidation." *Comparative Politics*, 36(4), 421–442.

Morse, Yonatan L. (2012). "The Era of Electoral Authoritarianism." *World Politics*, 64(1), 161–198.

Mukonoweshuro, Eliphas G. (1990). "The Politics of Squalor and Dependency: Chronic Political Instability and Economic Collapse in the Comoro Islands." *African Affairs*, 89(357), 555–577.

Murshed, S. Mansoob & Scott Gates (2005). "Spatial-Horizontal Inequality and the Maoist Insurgency in Nepal." *Review of Development Economics*, 9(1), 121–134.

Mustapha, Abdul Raufu (1999). "The Nigerian Transition: Third Time Lucky or More of the Same?" *Review of African Political Economy*, 26(80), 277–291.

N'Diaye, Boubacar (2001). *The Challenge of Institutionalizing Civilian Control: Botswana, Ivory Coast, and Kenya in Comparative Perspective*. Oxford: Lexington Books.

Nelson, Harold, ed. (1974). *Area Handbook for Senegal* (2nd edition). Washington, D.C.: American University.

Newbury, Catharine (1998). "Ethnicity and the Politics of History in Rwanda." *Africa Today*, 45(1), 7–24.

New York Times, The (1982). "Ex-Officer Ousts Ghana's Government Again." (January 1).

(1982). "Many Ghanaians Interpret Coup as Tribal Plot." (January 17).

(1982). "Ghana Says It Crushed A Coup." (November 25).

Nunley, Alfred C (2011). *African Elections Database* at http://africanelections .tripod.com/index.html, accessed February 10, 2018.

O'Donnell, Guillermo & Philippe C. Schmitter (1986). *Transitions from Authoritarian Rule: Tentative Conclusions about Uncertain Democracies*. Baltimore: Johns Hopkins University Press.

Ojo, Emmanuel O. (2000). "The Military and Democratic Transition in Nigeria: An In Depth Analysis of General Babangida's Transition Program (1985–1993)." *Journal of Political and Military Sociology*, 28(1), 1–20.

(2006). "Taming the Monster: Demilitarization and Democratization in Nigeria." *Armed Forces & Society*, 32(2), 254–272.

O'Kane, Rosemary H.T. (1981). "A Probabilistic Approach to the Causes of Coups d'Etat." *British Journal of Political Science*, 11(3), 287–308.

Okoroji, Joseph C. (1993). "The Nigerian Presidential Elections." *Review of African Political Economy*, 20(58), 123–131.

Olson, Mancur (1974). *The Logic of Collective Action: Public Goods and the Theory of Groups.* Cambridge, MA: Harvard University Press.

Omorogbe, Eki Yemisi (2011). "A Club of Incumbents? The African Union and Coups d'État." *Vanderbuilt Journal of Transnational Law*, 44(1), 123–154.

(1982). *The Rise and Decline of Nations: Economic Growth, Stagflation, and Social Rigidities.* New Haven: Yale University Press.

Østby, Gudrun (2008). "Polarization, Horizontal Inequalities and Violent Civil Conflict." *Journal of Peace Research*, 45(2), 143–162.

Østby, Gudrun, Ragnhild Nordås, & Jan Rød (2009). "Regional Inequalities and Civil Conflict in Sub-Saharan Africa." *International Studies Quarterly*, 53(2), 301–324.

Parsons, Timothy H. (1999). *The African Rank-and-File: Social Implications of Colonial Military Service in the Kings African Rifles, 1902–1964.* Portsmouth, New Hampshire: Heinemann.

Piazza, James A. (2011). "Poverty, Minority Economic Discrimination, and Domestic Terrorism." *Journal of Peace Research*, 48(3), 339–353.

Pilster, Ulrich & Tobias Böhmelt (2011). "Coup-Proofing and Military Effectiveness in Interstate Wars, 1967–99." *Conflict Management and Peace Science*, 28(4), 331–350.

Piplani, Varun & Caitlin Talmadge (2016). "When War Helps Civil-Military Relations: Prolonged Interstate Conflict and the Reduced Risk of Coups." *Journal of Conflict Resolution*, 60(8), 1368–1394.

Posner, Daniel N. (2004a). "Measuring Ethnic Fractionalization in Africa." *American Journal of Political Science*, 48(4), 849–863.

(2004b). "The Political Salience of Cultural Difference: Why Chewas and Tumbukas Are Allies in Zambia and Adversaries in Malawi." *American Political Science Review*, 98(4), 529–545.

(2005). *Institutions and Ethnic Politics in Africa.* Cambridge: Cambridge University Press.

Powell, Jonathan M. (2012a). "Determinants of the Attempting and Outcome of Coups d'État." *Journal of Conflict Resolution*, 56(6), 1017–1040.

(2012b). "Regime Vulnerability and the Diversionary Threat of Force." *Journal of Conflict Resolution*, 58(1), 169–196.

Powell, Jonathan M., Chris Faulkner, William Dean, & Kyle Romano (2018). "Give Them Toys? Military Allocations and Regime Stability in Transitional Democracies." Democratization, forthcoming at https://doi.org/10.1080/13510347.2018.1450389, accessed May 9, 2018.

Powell, Jonathan M. & Trace C. Lasley (2012). "Constitutional Norms and the Decline of the Coup d'État: An Empirical Assessment." Paper presented at the annual meeting of the Southern Political Science Association, New Orleans, Louisiana, January 12.

Powell, Jonathan M. & Clayton L. Thyne (2011). "Global Instances of Coups from 1950–2010: A New Dataset." *Journal of Peace Research*, 48(2), 249–259.

Powell, Robert (2002). "Bargaining Theory and International Conflict." *Annual Review of Political Science*, 5, 1–30.

(2006). "War as a Commitment Problem." *International Organization*, 60(1), 169–203.

Przeworski, Adam, Michael Alvarez, José Antonio Cheibub, & Fernando Limongi (1996). "What Makes Democracy Endure?" *Journal of Democracy*, 7(1), 39–55.

Quinlivan, James T. (1999). "Coup-Proofing: Its Practice and Consequences in the Middle East." *International Security*, 24(2), 131–165.

Rabushka, Alvin & Kenneth A. Shepsle (1972). *Politics in Plural Societies*. Columbus, Ohio: Charles Merrill.

Ray, Subhasish (2012). "The Nonmartial Origins of the 'Martial Races'": Ethnicity and Military Service in Ex-British Colonies." *Armed Forces & Society*, 39(3), 560–575.

(2016). "Sooner or Later: The Timing of Ethnic Conflict Onsets after Independence." *Journal of Peace Research*, 53(6), 800–814.

Riedl, Rachel Beatty (2014). *Authoritarian Origins of Democratic Party Systems in Africa*. Cambridge: Cambridge University Press.

Robinson, Amanda Lee (2014). "National Versus Ethnic Identification in Africa: Modernization, Colonial Legacy, and the Origins of Territorial Nationalism." *World Politics*, 66(4), 709–746.

Roeder, Philip G. (2001). "Ethnolinguistic Fractionalization (ELF) Indices, 1961 and 1985" at http://weber.ucsd.edu/~proeder/elf.htm, accessed December 1, 2010.

Roessler, Philip (2011). "The Enemy Within: Personal Rule, Coups, and Civil War in Africa." *World Politics*, 62(2), 300–346.

(2016). *Ethnic Politics and State Power in Africa: The Logic of the Coup-Civil War Trap*. Cambridge: Cambridge University Press.

Ross, Michael L. (2004). "What Do We Know About Natural Resources and Civil War?" *Journal of Peace Research*, 41(3), 337–356.

Rustad, Siri Camilla Aas, Halvard Buhaug, Åshild Falch, & Scott Gates (2011). "All Conflict is Local." *Conflict Management and Peace Science*, 28(1), 15–40.

Salehyan, Idean, Cullen S. Hendrix, Jesse Hamner, Christina Case, Christopher Linebarger, Emily Stull, & Jennifer Williams (2012). "Social Conflict in Africa: A New Database." *International Interactions*, 38(4), 503–511.

Sambanis, Nicholas (2004). "What is Civil War? Conceptual and Empirical Complexities of an Operational Definition." *Journal of Conflict Resolution*, 48(6), 814–858.

Samii, Cyrus (2010). "Military Integration in Burundi, 2000–2006." Working paper at http://cyrussamii.com/wp-content/uploads/2015/04/samii_burundi_ssr100608.pdf, accessed February 13, 2018.

(2013). "Perils or Promise of Ethnic Integration? Evidence from a Hard Case in Burundi." *American Political Science Review*, 107(3), 558–573.

Sarkees, Meredith Reid & Frank Wayman (2010). "Resort to War: 1816–2007." Washington D.C.: CQ Press at http://www.correlatesofwar.org/data-sets/COW-war, accessed May 9, 2018.

Savage, Jesse Dillon & Jonathan D. Caverley (2017). "When Human Capital Threatens the Capitol: Foreign Aid in the Form of Military Training and Coups." *Journal of Peace Research*, 54(4), 542–557.

Scott, Samuel F. (1971). "The French Revolution and the Professionalization of the French Officers Corps." In Morris Janowitz & Jacques Van Doorn, eds., *On Military Ideology*. Rotterdam, Netherlands: Rotterdam University Press, 5–56.

Shannon, Megan, Clayton Thyne, Sarah Hayden, & Amanda Dugan (2015). "The International Community's Reaction to Coups." *Foreign Policy Analysis* 11(4), 363–376.

Shillington, Kevin (1992). *Ghana and the Rawlings Factor*. New York: St. Martin's Press.

Singer, J. David, Stuart Bremer, & John Stuckey (1972). "Capability Distribution, Uncertainty, and Major Power War, 1820–1965." In Bruce Russett, ed., *Peace, War, and Numbers*. Beverly Hills: Sage, 19–48.

Singh, Naunihal (2011). "The Barrel of a Gun: The Connection between Military Effectiveness, Civil-Military Relations, and Civil Wars." Paper presented at the annual meeting of the American Political Science Association, Seattle, September 1–4.

(2014). *Seizing Power: The Strategic Logic of Military Coups*. Baltimore: Johns Hopkins University Press.

Skocpol, Theda (1979). *States and Social Revolutions: A Comparative Analysis of France, Russia and China*. Cambridge: Cambridge University Press.

Smith, Tony (1978). "A Comparative Study of French and British Decolonization." *Comparative Studies in Society and History*, 20(1), 70–102.

Smock, David R. & Audrey C. Smock (1975). *The Politics of Pluralism: A Comparative Study of Lebanon and Ghana*. New York: Elsevier.

Snyder, Charles P. (1986). "African Ground Forces." In Bruce E. Arlinghaus & Pauline H. Baker, eds., *African Armies: Evolution and Capabilities*. Boulder, Colorado: Westview Press.

Spruyt, Hendrick (1996). *The Sovereign State and Its Competitors: An Analysis of Systems Change*. Princeton: Princeton University Press.

Ssuuna, Ignatius & Eloge Willy Kaneza (2015). "Burundi Army Defections Show Dangerous Ethnic Divisions." *Associated Press* (December 30).

Stark, Frank M. (1980). "Persuasion and Power in Cameroon." *Canadian Journal of African Studies*, 14(2), 273–293.

Stewart, Frances (1999). "Crisis Prevention: Tackling Horizontal Inequalities." Paper presented at the World Bank Conference on Evaluation and Poverty Reduction, June 15–19.

Sudduth, Jun Koga (2017a). "Coup Risk, Coup-Proofing and Leader Survival." *Journal of Peace Research*, 54(1), 3–15.

(2017b). "Strategic Logic of Elite Purges in Dictatorships." *Comparative Political Studies*, 50(13), 1768–1801.

Sutter, Daniel (1999). "Legitimacy and Military Intervention in a Democracy: Civilian Government as a Public Good." *American Journal of Economics and Sociology*, 58(1), 129–143.

(2000). "A Game-Theoretic Model of the Coup d'Etat." *Economics and Politics*, 12(2), 205–223.

Svolik, Milan W. (2008). "Authoritarian Reversals and Democratic Consolidation." *American Political Science Review*, 102(2), 153–168.

(2012). "Contracting on Violence: The Moral Hazard in Authoritarian Repression and Military Intervention in Politics." *Journal of Conflict Resolution*, 57(5), 765–794.

Takougang, Joseph (1993). "The Post-Ahidjo Era in Cameroon: Continuity and Change." *Journal of Third World Studies*, 10(2), 268–302.

(1996). "The 1992 Multiparty Elections in Cameroon: Prospects for Democracy and Democratization." *Journal of Asian and African Studies*, 31(1–2), 52–65.

(2003a). "The Demise of Biya's New Deal in Cameroon, 1982–1992." In John Mukum Mbaku & Joseph Takougang, eds., *The Leadership Challenge in Africa: Cameroon under Paul Biya*. Africa World Press, 95–122.

(2003b). "The Nature of Politics in Cameroon." In John Mukum Mbaku & Joseph Takougang, eds., *The Leadership Challenge in Africa: Cameroon under Paul Biya*. Africa World Press, 67–92.

Theobald, Robin (1982). "Patrimonialism." *World Politics*, 34(4), 548–559.

Thompson, William R. (1976). "Organizational Cohesion and Military Coup Outcomes." *Comparative Political Studies*, 9(3), 255–276.

(1980). "Corporate Coup-Maker Grievances and Types of Regime Targets." *Comparative Political Studies*, 12(4), 485–496.

Thyne, Clayton (2017). "The Impact of Coups d'Etat on Civil War Duration." *Conflict Management and Peace Science*, 34(3), 287–307.

Thyne, Clayton & Jonathan M. Powell (2016). "Coup d'Etat or Coup d'Autocracy? How Coups Impact Democratization, 1950–2008." *Foreign Policy Analysis*, 12(2), 192–193.

Tusalem, Rollin F. (2014). "Bringing the Military Back In: The Politicisation of the Military and Its Effect on Democratic Consolidation." *International Political Science Review*, 35(4), 409–429.

Twumasi, Yaw (1975). "The 1969 Election." In Dennis Austin & Robin Luckham, eds., *Politicians and Soldiers in Ghana 1966–1972*. London: Frank Cass, 140–163.

US Department of State (2015). "Global Peace Operations Initiative (GPOI)" at www.state.gov/t/pm/gpi/gpoi/index.htm, accessed February 13, 2018.

Valentino, Benjamin A. (2004). *Final Solutions: Mass Killing and Genocide in the Twentieth Century*. Ithaca: Cornell University Press.

van de Walle, Nicolas (1994). "Neopatrimonialism and Democracy in Africa, with an Illustration from Cameroon." In Jennifer A. Widner, ed., *Economic Change and Political Liberalization in Sub-Saharan Africa*. Baltimore: The Johns Hopkins University Press, 129–157.

Varshney, Ashutosh (2003). "Nationalism, Ethnic Conflict, and Rationality." *Perspective on Politics*, 1(1), 85–99.

Villalón, Leonardo A. (1994). "Democratizing a (Quasi) Democracy: The Senegalese Elections of 1993." *African Affairs*, 93(371), 163–193.

(1999). "Generational Change, Political Stagnation, and the Evolving Dynamics of Religion and Politics in Senegal." *Africa Today*, 46(3/4), 129–147.

(2015). "Cautious Democrats: Religious Actors and Democratization Processes in Senegal." *Politics and Religion*, 8(2), 305–333.

Vinter, Phil (2012). "Military Overthrows Government in Mali a Month before Elections but President has Gone Missing." *The Daily Mail* (March 22).

Wang, T.Y. (1998). "Arms Transfers and Coups d'Etat: A Study on Sub-Saharan Africa." *Journal of Peace Research*, 35(6), 659–675.

Wantchékon, Léonard (2003). "Clientelism and Voting Behavior: Evidence from a Field Experiment in Benin." *World Politics*, 55(3), 399–422.

Wantchékon, Léonard & Omar García-Ponce (2014). "Critical Junctures: Independence Movements and Democracy in Africa." Working paper at http://scholar.princeton.edu/sites/default/files/lwantche/files/insurgency_140730.pdf, accessed July 29, 2017.

Weber, Max (1978). *Economy and Society (Volume 2)*. Berkeley: University of California Press.

Weidmann, Nils B. (2016). "A Closer Look at Reporting Bias in Conflict Event Data." *American Journal of Political Science*, 60(1), 206–218.

Weissman, Stephen R. (1990). "Structural Adjustment in Africa: Insights from the Experiences of Ghana and Senegal." *World Development*, 18(12), 1621–1634.

Welch, Claude E. (1967). "Soldier and State in Africa." *The Journal of Modern African Studies*, 5(3), 305–322.

Wig, Tore (2016). "Peace from the Past: Pre-Colonial Political Institutions and Civil Wars in Africa." *Journal of Peace Research*, 53(4), 509–524.

Wig, Tore & Espen Geelmuyden Rød (2016). "Cues to Coup Plotters: Elections as Coup Triggers in Dictatorships." *Journal of Conflict Resolution*, 60(5), 787–812.

Wilkinson, Steven I. (2015). *Army and Nation: The Military and Indian Democracy since Independence*. Cambridge, MA: Harvard University Press.

Williams, Adebayo (1999). "Briefing: Nigeria: A Restoration Drama." *African Affairs*, 98(392), 407–413.

Wimmer, Andreas, Lars-Erik Cederman, & Brian Min (2009). "Ethnic Politics and Armed Conflict: A Configurational Analysis of a New Global Data Set." *American Sociological Review*, 74(2), 316–337.

Woolley, John T. (2000). "Using Media-Based Data in Studies of Politics." *American Journal of Political Science*, 44(1), 156–173.

World Bank (2015). "World Development Indicators" at http://data.worldbank.org/data-catalog/world-development-indicators, accessed June 15, 2015.

Wucherpfennig, Julian, Philipp Hunziker, & Lars-Erik Cederman (2016). "Who Inherits the State? Colonial Rule and Postcolonial Conflict." *American Journal of Political Science*, 60(4), 882–898.

Wucherpfennig, Julian, Nils B. Weidmann, Luc Girardin, Lars-Erik Cederman, & Andreas Wimmer (2011). "Politically Relevant Ethnic Groups across Space and Time: Introducing the GeoEPR Dataset." *Conflict Management and Peace Science*, 28(5), 423–437.

Young, Crawford (1965). *Politics in the Congo: Decolonization and Independence*. Princeton: Princeton University Press.

(1994). *The African Colonial State in Comparative Perspective*. New Haven: Yale University Press.

Young, Robert J.C. (2001). *Postcolonialism: An Historical Introduction*. Oxford: Blackwell Publishers Ltd.

Zack-Williams, A. & Stephen Riley (1993). "Sierra Leone: The Coup and Its Consequences." *Review of African Political Economy*, 20(56), 91–98.

Index